The
Recipe
Doctor

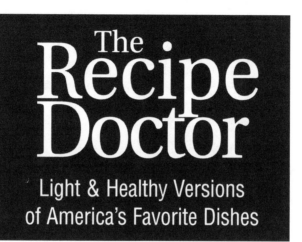

The Recipe Doctor

Light & Healthy Versions of America's Favorite Dishes

Elaine Magee, R.D.

Adams Media Corporation
Holbrook, Massachusetts

Published by
Adams Media Corporation
260 Center Street, Holbrook, MA 02343. U.S.A.
www.adamsmedia.com

ISBN: 1-58062-342-5

Printed in Canada.

J I H G F E D C B A

Library of Congress Cataloging-in-Publication Data
Magee, Elaine.
The recipe doctor / by Elaine Magee.
p.   cm.
ISBN 1-58062-342-5
1. Low-fat diet--Recipes--Miscellanea. I. Title
RM237.7 .M334   2000
641.5'638--dc21   99-056128

This publication is designed to provide accurate and authoritative information with regard to the subject matter covered. It is sold with the understanding that the publisher is not engaged in rendering legal, accounting, or other professional advice. If legal advice or other expert assistance is required, the services of a competent professional person should be sought.

— From a *Declaration of Principles* jointly adopted by a Committee of the American Bar Association and a Committee of Publishers and Associations

Cover photo by Stockfood/Watt

This book is available at quantity discounts for bulk purchases.
For information, call 1-800-872-5627.

Table of Contents

ACKNOWLEDGMENTS

This book would not have been possible without *The Recipe Doctor* column and the column would not have existed without the faith of one fine food editor, Deborah Byrd (*Contra Costa Times*). I am also deeply grateful to Karen Kirk of Knight Ridder/Tribune who went to bat for *The Recipe Doctor* column and launched it nationally, believing that this column was refreshingly different and spoke to the people. Both Deborah and Karen believed in me and gave the column a chance at a time when light columns abounded and chances were hard to come by. Thank you so much.

ABOUT *THE RECIPE DOCTOR*

People want to have their cake and eat it, too—it's the American way. More and more people are becoming health conscious, but they still want to eat the delicious foods they crave. They don't want strange recipes for strange-tasting food that takes hours to prepare and dirties all the dishes in the kitchen. I understand.

I believe food is one of the great pleasures of life and I know what it's like to work and cook for a family of four. I don't peel, sift, whisk, or pull out the double boiler unless I absolutely have to. That's what the Recipe Doctor series is all about—real recipes for real people.

I hereby declare war on bad tasting "health" food. I have seen (and tasted) the enemy and the enemy is fat-free muffins, cakes, and cookies just as much as it is the 10-ounce T-bone, 3-egg omelet, or the cream-and-butter-laden white sauces of this world.

My mission is to lighten up dishes and/or improve their nutritional attributes <u>without</u> sacrificing flavor, enjoyment, or your free time.

I vow to reduce the fat only as far as I can and still have the results taste terrific. I also cut corners in recipes where I can. (I don't want to spend hours in the kitchen and I'm figuring you don't either.) You will see some recipes calling for cake mixes or dressing or sauce packets, which I know offends some purists out there. But you'll find many "from scratch" recipes, too.

I should come clean, though, about some of my cooking biases. I am philosophically opposed to fat-free margarine, mayonnaise, and cheese. I don't believe in increasing the sugar or salt in a recipe to "get away with" using a lot less fat. And I don't believe there is a satisfactory substitute for chocolate or butter. So you will see some recipes calling for them (when they are truly the best fat for the recipe), but I do use less.

I do believe there is an ideal fat replacement and an ideal (smaller) amount of fat for almost every recipe, below which you do not want to go. Cases in point—fat-free muffins, very-low-fat cookies, oil-free salad dressings, fat-free or low-fat mayonnaise, or anything made with carob. For example, if you cut the fat more than half in a cookie recipe, it isn't a cookie anymore—it's a muffin.

Although lightening up recipes for total fat, saturated fat, cholesterol, and calories was my focus when I started The Recipe Doctor column, I have shifted to more heart protective monounsaturated fats (olive and canola oil) when possible. I even call for canola margarine sometimes because there are now a couple of brands (also low in saturated fat and trans fatty acids) available with liquid canola oil as the first ingredient. I also add nutrient-rich fruits and vegetables, whole wheat flour, and beans to recipes whenever possible to help boost fiber, vitamins, and phytochemicals.

Here's the scoop on eggs and egg substitutes (not that eggs are "bad"). I often reduce the number of egg yolks just because I can with no visible ramifications. And keeping cholesterol moderate still seems to be a good idea. I often make up the difference with egg substitute (¼ cup egg substitute = 1 whole egg or 2 egg yolks). Sometimes I opt for egg whites though, because of their ability to hold air when whipped.

When it comes to fats, basically we want to keep trans fatty acids, saturated fat, and omega-6 fatty acids low, leaving monounsaturated fats (olive oil and canola oil), omega-3 fatty acids (canola oil contains some omega-3s) as our fats of choice—fats that may be beneficial for our health in reasonable, moderate amounts.

▶ *omega-3s*—help wage war against both heart disease and cancer and they have been linked to lowering both blood pressure and serum triglyceride levels, and preventing blood clots. Omega-3s may even help increase levels of HDL (good) cholesterol.

▶ *trans fatty acids*—are considered dangerous in large amounts because they raise our LDL (bad) cholesterol blood levels while lowering our precious HDL (good) cholesterol levels.

▶ High amounts of saturated fat tend to raise LDL cholesterol levels in the blood and are associated with heart disease (saturated fat does not seem to reduce the HDL cholesterol levels like trans fatty acids do). Studies are starting to suggest a line between diets high in saturated fat and a risk of several types of cancer.

ABOUT THIS BOOK

This book is a collection of recipes from my column, The Recipe Doctor. The columns arise from real letters sent to me from real people. The names have been omitted, however, to protect their privacy. The column started in the *Contra Costa Times* Food Section in the East Bay San Francisco area. After two years the column branched out to papers across the country via the Knight Ridder/Tribune wire service.

If you like this cookbook, I hope you will spread the word of *The Recipe Doctor* and tell your friends and family about it. You can also send me recipes to "doctor up" at:

PO Box 2389
Pleasant Hill, CA 94523-0089

To find out more about my other cookbooks, nutrition books, and kids' cookbooks, visit my Web site at:

www.recipedoctor.com.

RECIPE DOCTOR TRICKS OF THE TRADE

- When you cook or bake with less fat you need to *add more of other ingredients* that help replace the qualities of the lost fat while adding flavors that complement the other ingredients in the original recipe.
- *Start with the best-tasting, freshest ingredients* you can find. Fresh garlic tastes better than garlic powder; fresh basil and parsley have more flavor than dried.
- *Choose the best-tasting light products on the market.* (You can find out which those are in my book *Taste vs. Fat.* For example choose the creamiest light cream cheese and sharpest reduced-fat cheese; Philadelphia light cream cheese, Cracker Barrel light sharp cheddar, Naturally Yours fat-free sour cream, and Louis Rich turkey bacon all taste terrific in recipes.
- *Good nonstick cookware* can help you cut the fat because it doesn't require as much fat to prevent sticking.
- I try and use basic bakeware and cookware but the cooking and baking times for the recipes will vary based on the equipment in your particular kitchen. For example, I use a gas stove and oven when testing the recipes. That's why I give a range for the cooking or baking time; each oven, whether gas or electric, is a little different so you will at least want to check the dish after the shorter cooking time.
- *Nonstick canola cooking sprays* help lubricate bakeware, cookware, and food with a minimal amount of fat by allowing you to spray tiny particles of fat onto the dish, pan, or food surface.
- Sometimes you can *opt to use a cooking method that eliminates the need for cooking fat* (broiling, roasting, poaching, steaming).
- When it is necessary to maintain the character of the food, *do use a cooking method that involves fat—just use less of it* (oven frying, sautéing, pan frying, browning).

▸ *No additional fat is needed when using cake mixes,* since most mixes already contain 4 grams of fat per serving of mix. Replace the oil called for with fruit juice, liqueur, flavored yogurt, or light sour cream, depending on the cake.

▸ *In cookie recipes you can often cut the fat by a third or half.* Fat-free cream cheese is one of the most successful fat substitutes in cookie recipes.

▸ You can use the better-tasting *diet margarines for frosting recipes* because the added water won't be a problem if the frosting stays chilled.

▸ *Use whole milk as a substitute for half and half or fat-free half and half*—it gives the recipe a richness and creaminess that you just can't get with nonfat or low-fat milk.

▸ When you change the fat content of a batter or dough, you also change the way heat is conducted through the food. I found the best results (even heat distribution and less burning) when using the *Cushionaire bakeware line* (the double thickness bakeware).

▸ There is something about the construction of *corn syrup that makes it hold on to its moisture in a baked item longer.* It actually seems to release its moisture slowly, over time, into the food. You can reduce the amount of granulated sugar called for in baking recipes and then replace some of the fat with corn syrup.

▸ *Whipped egg whites can add a light texture to baked items.* Egg whites whip best at room temperature. They must be separated from the yolk (egg yolks prevent the whites from holding air). Use a glass, copper, or stainless steel bowl for whipping egg whites (plastic tends to hold onto grease even after cleaning, and aluminum can react chemically with eggs and turn them grayish.) Don't overbeat your egg whites, as they will collapse and separate. Stabilizing ingredients (such as salt, lemon juice, and cream of tartar) help keep the whites smooth and aerated but will also slow the whipping process, so add them just after the eggs become frothy.

Chapter One

APPETIZERS

THE BEST DARN PESTO TORTA

POTATO SKINS (LIKE TGI FRIDAY'S)

FOOTHILL HOUSE ARTICHOKE SPREAD

OLIVE CHEESE BALLS

CREAMY ARTICHOKE HEART
ITALIAN BREAD SPREAD

7-LAYER MEXICAN BEAN DIP

SPINACH-BACON SPIRALS
(APPETIZER MINI-WRAPS)

Q

Dear Recipe Doctor,

I absolutely love this pesto torta recipe. It always goes over real well at parties. I can't believe how much butter is added though; can you whip this into shape?

A

At first glance this pesto torta is quite an undertaking. You need cheesecloth, you need to toast pine nuts, you reconstitute sun-dried tomatoes, you use your electric mixer and your food processor, and on and on. But whatever this recipe entails—it is well worth it! It is as colorful with its alternating layers of green, white, and red as it is delicious.

I can only imagine how delicious the original pesto torta is, comprised mainly of a mixture of half butter and half cream cheese. That's right! The original recipe calls for a pound of cream cheese and a pound of butter.

The first thing I did was switch to *light* Philadelphia cream cheese. Now, about the butter—I used 1 cup of a pretty good tasting diet margarine (with half the fat) and added another 8 ounces of light cream cheese into the fold.

I followed along with the original recipe until I came to the pesto part. The original recipe calls for ½ cup of olive oil. I brought this down to 2 tablespoons and added ⅓ cup of double strength chicken, beef, or vegetable broth. I left the toasted pine nuts alone, but I did reduce the Parmesan cheese ever so slightly. Oh, and as usual, I doubled the garlic.

THE BEST DARN PESTO TORTA

The recipe is for a 6-inch springform pan but I used a 6-inch tapered, scalloped pan. This turned out even more beautiful because you could see the different layers and colors more easily. The only problem (and it was a happy problem) was I had enough cream cheese and pesto mixture left over to make two mini tortas using custard cups. If your pan or mold is wider than 6 inches, just make fewer layers. This torta has become a family favorite. We have nicknamed it "Christmas Torta" because of its color scheme and because we have served it on Christmas Eve for the past few years—it's a real crowd pleaser!

Original recipe contains 419 calories, 43 grams fat, 23 grams saturated fat, and 98 milligrams cholesterol per serving.

Makes a 6-inch springform torta (about 16 appetizer servings)

    2 ounces sun-dried tomatoes (dry-packed)
    3 8-ounce packages light cream cheese, at room
        temperature
    1 cup + 2 tablespoons diet margarine
        (pick a good-tasting one such as I Can't Believe It's
        Not Butter Light, or Brummel & Brown Spread), at
        room temperature, divided
    2 cups fresh basil leaves, tightly packed
    ½ cup fresh parsley (Italian parsley may be substituted)
    ⅓ cup pine nuts, lightly toasted (browned) and cooled
    4 cloves garlic
    2 tablespoons olive oil
    ⅓ cup double strength chicken, beef, or vegetable broth
    ⅔ cup freshly grated Parmesan cheese

1. Soak the dried tomatoes in warm water for 20 to 30 minutes. Drain them and dry them on paper towels. Cut them into small pieces. (Some supermarkets sell chopped sun-dried tomatoes in bottles packed in oil. If you use this kind, just rinse and drain well.)

2. With an electric mixer, beat the cream cheese and 1 cup margarine together until smooth and creamy; set aside.

3. In a food processor, process the basil, parsley, pine nuts, and garlic. Add the olive oil and broth and process for 20 seconds. Scrape down the sides of bowl. Add the Parmesan and the remaining 2 tablespoons margarine and pulse the machine a few times until blended.

4. Cut an 18-inch square of cheesecloth. Moisten it with water, wring it dry, and smoothly line the springform pan with it, draping the extra over the rim of the pan.

5. Spread ⅙ of the cream cheese mixture in the bottom of the lined pan with a spatula. Spread with ¼ of the pesto (make sure pesto makes it all the way to the sides of the pan). Top the pesto with another sixth of the cream cheese. Scatter half the dried tomato pieces over this and spread with another layer of cream cheese mixture. Keep going with the layers until the pan is filled; the top layer will be the cheese mixture. (My last layer ended up being the pesto because my pan wasn't quite deep enough and I didn't have enough room for another cream cheese layer—and it turned out wonderful).

6. Tuck the ends of the cheesecloth up around the torta and gently press them down to compact the mixture slightly. Chill overnight.

7. An hour before you plan to serve the torta, unwrap the cheesecloth so it is no longer covering the top of the mold and invert the torta onto a serving dish. Gently remove the mold and then the cheesecloth. Serve with low-fat crackers or fresh French or sourdough bread slices.

Note: You can freeze the torta in its pan, tightly sealed in a plastic bag, for up to 2 months. Just thaw in refrigerator overnight.

PER SERVING: 167 calories, 8 g protein, 5 g carbohydrate, 13 g fat, 4.5 g saturated fat, 18.5 mg cholesterol, 1 g fiber, 400 mg sodium. Calories from fat: 71 percent (Obviously if you eat the torta with low-fat crackers and naturally fat-free sourdough or French bread, the percentage of calories from fat will decrease. People who are particularly watching their fat intake could spread the torta a little thin, bringing down the calories from fat even further.)

Q *Dear Recipe Doctor,*

One of my favorite appetizers to order in restaurants is potato skins. Dipping it in the ranch dressing is the best part. I know they are probably deep-fried and everything but I would really like to be able to make them at home. Any advice?

A What a coincidence, this is one of my favorite appetizers, too. I actually developed a light version a couple of years ago when I had a major hankering for them and happened to have a bag of potatoes at my disposal. Everybody thought they were very similar to the restaurant version.

Of course I took great care to make them look like the restaurant version. I fried up some Louis Rich turkey bacon and crumbled it up for my fancy bacon topping for the potato skins. I chopped up green onions and had them available for the hard core potato skin eaters. And last but not least, I made a tasty, low-fat ranch dip that is so easy to whip together.

The hardest part was trying to figure out how to make them lightly browned and crispy on the outside without deep-frying them. I tried rubbing or brushing the skins lightly with canola oil then baking them near the heat in the oven at a high temperature. This seemed to do the trick for the potatoes, but what about all the dressings?

I topped my crispy potato with a combination of grated reduced-fat sharp cheddar and reduced-fat Monterey Jack cheese. Then I sprinkled the top with turkey bacon pieces, green onions, and pepper. Then I just broiled the skins briefly to bubble the cheese. Dip them in some ranch dip and call it appetizer heaven. The ranch dip is made by stirring a tablespoon of Hidden Valley Ranch powder with 1 cup of fat-free or light sour cream and a token teaspoon or two of real mayonnaise (this helps smooth the flavor). Now that I can make these at home, I do seem to be ordering them in restaurants a whole lot less often. Frankly, I enjoy them more at home because I know I've trimmed away almost all the extra fat.

☞ POTATO SKINS (LIKE TGI FRIDAY'S) ☜

Original recipe might contain around 270 calories, 15 grams fat, 6 grams saturated fat, and 20 milligrams cholesterol per serving.

Makes 8 potato skins (about 4 servings)

4 strips Louis Rich turkey bacon
4 medium-large russet potatoes, scrubbed, baked or micro-cooked, then cooled slightly
canola oil
$\frac{1}{2}$ cup grated reduced-fat cheese, packed (I used $\frac{1}{4}$ cup reduced-fat sharp cheddar and $\frac{1}{4}$ cup of Monterey Jack)
2 green onions, trimmed and finely chopped
freshly ground pepper (optional)

RANCH DIP:
1 tablespoon Hidden Valley Ranch Dip powder
1 cup fat-free or light sour cream
1 teaspoon mayonnaise

1. Preheat oven to 450 degrees. Line a thick cookie sheet with foil. Pan-fry bacon over medium-low heat in a nonstick pan until just crispy. Set aside to cool, then crumble into little pieces.
2. Cut potatoes in half lengthwise. Scoop out most of the inside potato part, but leave about $\frac{1}{4}$ inch of potato. (Save the potato part you scooped out for mashed potatoes tomorrow.)
3. Brush the inside and skin side of potato halves lightly with canola oil and set them on prepared pan skin side down. Bake in preheated oven for about 10 minutes to lightly brown.

4. Add both types of cheese, bacon bits, and green onions to small bowl and toss to blend. Sprinkle the potatoes evenly with grated cheese mixture. Top with freshly ground pepper if desired.
5. Bake in oven until cheese is bubbly.
6. Mix ranch dip ingredients in small bowl until smooth. Set potato skins on serving dish and serve with ranch dip or light sour cream.

> PER SERVING: (not including dip) 205 calories, 8.5 g protein, 26.5 g carbohydrate, 7.5 g fat, 2.5 g saturated fat, 20 mg cholesterol, 2.5 g fiber, 270 mg sodium. Calories from fat: 32 percent.

Q *Dear Recipe Doctor,*

I've had this spread recipe for years and I really enjoy making it. It's from the Foothill House bed and breakfast in Calistoga, California. Can you show me how to reduce the fat and calories?

A This is one of those dynamite appetizer dishes that you can throw together with a moment's notice, pop it in the oven for 20 minutes, and it's bubbly and delicious.

I usually don't like anything "hot," so I definitely avoid anything "hot hot." I used mild Ortega chilies and I added a little less seasoning salt to turn down the heat. You, of course, could turn it back up just by using canned "hot" chilies and a teaspoon of seasoning salt.

It calls for ⅔ cup of real mayonnaise—which is where most of the fat grams are coming from. You could always just add low-fat or light mayonnaise instead. But that would be too easy. Lately I believe in using real mayonnaise—just a whole lot less of it. I added 3 tablespoons of the real thing and about 7 tablespoons of Best Foods low-fat mayonnaise or fat-free or light sour cream. I find that adding just a little real mayonnaise does wonders for maintaining the taste and texture of the dish.

I added the same amount of Parmesan cheese and used water-packed artichoke hearts (although if you use the oil-packed kind, just drain them and rinse them off well). I also added a few tablespoons of diced red onion—just because it seemed like a good thing to do. Garlic lovers could also add a clove or two of garlic to the mixture.

Any leftover spread can be blended with cooked pasta noodles for a quick and tasty meatless lunch or dinner the next day.

Original recipe contains 336 calories, 17 grams fat, and 18 milligrams cholesterol (including bread).

Makes about 2 cups spread (8 servings)

13–14-ounce bottle or can artichoke hearts
   (about 1¾ cups coarsely chopped)
⅔ cup grated Parmesan cheese
3 tablespoons real mayonnaise
7 tablespoons (almost ½ cup) low-fat mayonnaise or fat-free
   or light sour cream
3 tablespoons diced green chilies (mild, medium, or hot)
¾ teaspoon seasoning salt
3 tablespoons finely diced red onion
1 loaf sourdough or French bread (1 pound)

1. Preheat oven to 325 degrees.
2. Drain and coarsely chop artichoke hearts. Combine all ingredients in medium bowl and mix until well blended. Spoon into 1-quart casserole dish (or a standard sized loaf pan).
3. Bake for about 20 minutes or until lightly browned and bubbly.
4. Serve with sliced sourdough or French bread.

PER SERVING OF SPREAD: 272 calories, 10 g protein, 37 g carbohydrate, 9 g fat, 2.5 g saturated fat, 13 mg cholesterol, 4 g fiber, 720 mg sodium. Calories from fat: 30 percent.

Dear Recipe Doctor,

I hope you get a chance to doctor this up before Christmas! I make these olive cheese balls around the holidays because they're one of my husband's favorite treats. This recipe comes straight from the Betty Crocker cookbook. I'm finding it more and more difficult to make this every year, due to all the cheese and cubes of butter. Please help.

Around Christmastime my mother would always make a batch of cheese balls. True, they were cheesy and greasy—but boy were they good. A couple years ago I tried making them myself, but with Cracker Barrel reduced-fat sharp cheddar and a lot less butter. My family was skeptical. They were still delicious and cheesy, but without all the grease. I figure this is a good thing.

Imagine how my mouth watered when I read the recipe for olive cheese balls this reader sent me. I love cheese balls and I love green olives. Put them together and what have you got? An appetizer made in heaven.

The first thing I did was switch to a reduced-fat sharp cheddar cheese; there are at least a couple brands available in most supermarkets. Then I cut the butter by more than half and added fat-free cream cheese and a couple tablespoons of milk in its place. The first time I tried this less fat version of the recipe, I used large garlic-stuffed green olives. The second time I used pimento-stuffed olives. They were both party pleasers. Just a word to the wise though—make a few without the olives for the less adventurous kids in your kitchen.

~ OLIVE CHEESE BALLS ~

The original recipe contains 100 calories, 8 grams fat, and 20 milligrams cholesterol per serving.

Makes 24 balls

>   1¼ cups flour
>   ¼ cup fat-free cream cheese
>   2 cups shredded reduced-fat sharp cheddar cheese
>   (approximately 8 ounces)
>   4 tablespoons butter or margarine, melted
>   1 to 2 tablespoons milk
>   24–42 pimento- or garlic-stuffed green olives
>   (depending on size), drained
>   canola cooking spray

1. Place flour in medium bowl. Blend cream cheese into flour with a pastry blender. Stir in the shredded cheese. Drizzle butter and a tablespoon or two of milk over the top and stir to blend.
2. Work the mixture together with your hands to bring into a dough. Knead a few times. Add a teaspoon or two more milk if needed.
3. Mold a level tablespoon of dough around each larger sized olive or about ½ tablespoon dough for smaller olives. Shape into balls and place 2 inches apart on a cookie sheet that has been coated with cooking spray.
4. Cover and refrigerate at least 1 hour. Preheat oven to 400 degrees. Bake until set (about 15 minutes). Makes 24 cheese balls if using large olives and about 42 if using small olives.

PER SERVING: 69 calories, 4 g protein, 5.5 g carbohydrate, 3.5 g fat, 1.5 g saturated fat, 10 mg cholesterol, .3 g fiber, 147 mg sodium. Calories from fat: 45 percent.

Dear Recipe Doctor,

I have been making this recipe for years. People even ask me to bring this to parties. I'm wondering if there is anything I can do to make it a bit more healthful.

I know this recipe well. Just spread it over a Boboli (or packaged Italian bread shell) and pop it in the oven. In fifteen minutes, it's bubbly, delicious, and ready to serve.

Fat calories are coming at you in this recipe from several directions. It comes from the oil-soaked artichoke hearts, the mayonnaise, the cheddar and Parmesan cheeses, and the Boboli bread shell itself. You can always add low-fat or light mayonnaise instead of regular and shave off quite a few fat calories, as well as milligrams of cholesterol. But I believe in using real mayonnaise—just a whole lot less of it. So in this recipe, I added 2 tablespoons of the real thing and about ¼ cup of Best Foods low-fat mayonnaise or fat-free or light sour cream. Adding just a little real mayonnaise does wonders for maintaining the taste and texture of the dish.

I used a reduced-fat sharp cheddar but left the Parmesan cheese alone. The Parmesan cheese is too important to the taste and texture of the spread. I used water-packed artichoke hearts (although if you use the oil-packed kind, just drain them and rinse them off well). I threw in some chopped green onions for extra flavor. Garlic lovers could also add a clove or two of garlic to the mixture. I also noticed that the Safeway Select Verdi Italian bread shells had a little less fat than the Boboli brand.

I included some of this appetizer in a care package for a neighbor who had just had a baby. She must have loved it because she took time out of her newly hectic schedule to come by and ask me for the recipe.

Any leftover spread can be blended with cooked pasta for a quick and tasty meatless lunch or dinner the next day.

CREAMY ARTICHOKE HEART ITALIAN BREAD SPREAD

Original recipe contains 350 calories, 25 grams fat, 8 grams saturated fat, and 26 milligrams cholesterol per serving.

Makes 6 side servings or 12 appetizer servings

> 14-ounce can artichoke hearts (water packed),
>   coarsely chopped
> 1/3 cup grated Parmesan cheese
> 4 green onions, finely chopped
> 1/2 cup grated reduced-fat sharp cheddar cheese
> 2 tablespoons real mayonnaise
> 1/4 cup low-fat mayonnaise (light or fat-free
>   sour cream can also be used)
> 3 individual size packaged Italian bread shells
>   (Safeway Select Verdi or Boboli [each package
>   of 2 individual bread shells is 8 ounces])

1. Preheat oven to 450 degrees.
2. Blend first six ingredients in medium bowl. Spread on Italian bread shells.
3. Place bread shells on cookie sheet. Bake 10 minutes or until topping is slightly bubbly.

Note: to reduce fat further you can use 6 tablespoons (1/4 cup + 2 tablespoons) low-fat mayonnaise and omit the real mayonnaise.

PER SIDE SERVING: 278 calories, 12 g protein, 34 g carbohydrate, 11 g fat, 4 g saturated fat, 15 mg cholesterol, 4 g fiber, 637 mg sodium. Calories from fat: 35 percent.

Dear Recipe Doctor,

I've been to many a party where a multilayered bean dip has been served. I know it's loaded with fat and calories because it includes layers of sour cream, cheese, guacamole, and refried beans. Is there any way you can give me a lighter version of this tasty dip?

I've seen small parties of people blast through an entire platter of 7-layer bean dip in fifteen minutes flat. And why not! It's a delicious blend of so many of our favorite Mexican cuisine ingredients (refried beans, guacamole, sour cream, cheese, chilies, black olives, tomatoes, and onions), it's colorful, and we get to dip another one of our favorite foods in it—tortilla chips. Yep, at the get-togethers I've attended, people tended to congregate around the 7-Layer Mexican Bean Dip. So I'm way ahead of the reader. When I saw how popular this dip was, I tried my hand at a lighter version.

I started with fat-free vegetarian refried beans and spiced them up with chili powder, jalapeño sauce, and pepper. I used my favorite brand of fat-free sour cream (Naturally Yours), but if you have a favorite light sour cream, use it. There's not much I can do to lighten up the avocado—they are naturally high in fat, albeit the preferred monounsaturated fat. But I used low-fat mayonnaise to make the guacamole, which helps curb fat calories a little. And you can use reduced-fat sharp cheddar or Monterey Jack cheeses for the cheese layer.

One of the biggest sources of fat calories, though, is the food you choose to dip in the dip. There are some tasty reduced-fat tortilla chips now available in supermarkets with about 4 grams of fat per 1 ounce serving. You can also use soft flour tortillas or toasted pita bread triangles. Otherwise, an ounce of regular tortilla chips will run you about 7 grams of fat. The big bonus is that this dip, as do most bean recipes, contributes a healthy portion of fiber to your daily total.

← 7-LAYER MEXICAN BEAN DIP →

Original recipe contains 355 calories, 25 grams fat, 10 grams saturated fat, 38 milligrams cholesterol

Makes 6 hearty appetite servings

> 16-ounce can vegetarian refried beans or low-fat refried black beans
> ½ to 1 teaspoon chili powder
> black pepper to taste
> pepper sauce (green or red, mild or hot) to taste (i.e., Tabasco)
> ¾ cup fat-free or light sour cream
> 1 avocado, mashed
> 1 tablespoon low-fat mayonnaise or light sour cream
> 1½ teaspoons lemon juice
> 1 cup grated reduced-fat sharp cheddar cheese
> 1 cup finely chopped tomatoes
> 5 green onions, chopped
> 2 ounces chopped black olives

Suggested dippers: low-fat or reduced-fat tortilla chips, soft flour tortillas or pita bread cut into triangles, vegetables such as celery or carrot sticks

1. Heat beans in small saucepan over low heat until warm and softened. Stir in chili powder, black pepper, and pepper sauce to taste. Spread into 8 x 8-inch baking pan or casserole dish (or similar) and let cool.
2. Spread sour cream over the beans.
3. In small bowl or small food processor, blend avocado with mayonnaise and lemon juice. Spread guacamole evenly over sour cream.
4. Top with grated cheese. Sprinkle chopped tomatoes evenly over the top.
5. Sprinkle tomatoes with green onions and then olives.
6. Refrigerate until needed.

PER LARGE SERVING: 213 calories, 11 g protein, 21 g carbohydrate, 9.5 g fat, 3 g saturated fat, 6 g fiber, 11 mg cholesterol, 503 mg sodium. Calories from fat: 40 percent.

Q

Dear Recipe Doctor,

I love those mini-wrap appetizers where you use a flour tortilla. Do you have a recipe for one?

A

I ran across a recipe for a spinach-bacon spiral appetizer that was awfully "wrap-like." I took it to a 4th of July party and people really liked it. It has a nice balance of flavors—savory and salty from the bacon, rich and creamy from the cream cheese, and bitter from the spinach. If you really want to get fancy you can even buy different flavored and colored tortilla wraps in some supermarkets.

I happen to like using Louis Rich turkey bacon. If you cook it gently over medium-low heat in a nice nonstick pan flipping it frequently, it comes out nice and crisp. So this is what I used instead of pork bacon. I used light Philadelphia cream cheese instead of regular, but I cut down the real mayonnaise from 4 to 2 tablespoons. (You can use canola mayonnaise if you have it.) I then added 2 tablespoons of my favorite fat-free sour cream. The rest of the filling remained pretty much the same except the salt. Perhaps it is because my version had half the fat of the original, but the teaspoon of salt in the original recipe seemed too high. So I reduced it to ³/₄ teaspoon and called it perfect.

Not only will I make this often as a quick, colorful appetizer, I might just make a wrap or two for a change-of-pace lunch.

SPINACH-BACON SPIRALS
(APPETIZER MINI-WRAPS)

Original recipe contains 115 calories, 8 grams fat, 3 grams saturated fat, and 13 milligrams cholesterol per serving.

Makes 15 appetizer servings (two pieces each)

> 10-ounce package frozen chopped spinach, thawed, squeezed dry
> 4 ounces light cream cheese
> 2 tablespoons real or canola mayonnaise
> 2 tablespoons fat-free or light sour cream
> 1/2 to 3/4 teaspoon salt
> 1/2 teaspoon pepper
> 1/2 cup chopped green onions
> 6 strips Louis Rich turkey bacon, cooked until crisp and crumbled
> 3, 9-inch or 10-inch flour tortillas

1. Combine first six ingredients in mixing bowl and blend with a mixer on low speed until thoroughly blended.
2. Add green onions and bacon bits and beat on low until mixed in.
3. Lay a large square of plastic wrap on cutting board. Lay a tortilla on top. Spread 1/3 of filling evenly on the tortilla using a scraper. Roll up tortilla tightly, enclosing filling. Wrap the plastic tightly around it. Repeat with remaining tortillas and filling. Chill rolls until filling is firm, at least 1 hour or up to 4 hours.
4. Remove plastic and cut rolls crosswise on slight diagonal into 3/4-inch-thick slices. Serve cold or if you prefer them heated, preheat oven to 400 degrees. Arrange slices on a large baking sheet and bake until heated through, about 7 minutes.

PER SERVING: 83 calories, 3.5 g protein, 8.5 g carbohydrate, 4 g fat, 1 g saturated fat, 8 mg cholesterol, 1 g fiber, 290 mg sodium. Calories from fat: 44 percent

Chapter Two

SIDE DISHES

CREAM OF ARTICHOKE SOUP

SAVORY CORN CASSEROLE

SPINACH SQUARES (PRIJESNAC)

A MACARONI SALAD FOR PURISTS

POTATOES AND CARROTS AU GRATIN

SWEET POTATO CASSEROLE

BUFFALO POTATOES

Q

Dear Recipe Doctor,

Enclosed is a recipe for cream of artichoke soup. I really enjoy this soup but wonder if it's possible to cut some of the fat.

A

I'm quite sure you enjoyed this soup—what with 10 tablespoons of butter and a cup of whipping cream. Even *I* was shocked to total up the grams of fat and saturated fat per serving in the original recipe—52 grams fat, 32 grams saturated fat, and 160 milligrams of cholesterol. Mind you, this is just the first course.

So, I gladly tackled this creamy soup one spring afternoon, and I really enjoyed my light version. But if you are used to the 10 tablespoons of butter and a cup of whipping cream, I'm wondering how close I really came. I replaced the 2 tablespoons of butter, used to sauté the vegetables, with olive oil. Instead of the ½ cup of butter, used later in the recipe, I added a cup of whole milk (which sort of covered the whipping cream at the same time). I like killing two birds in the kitchen with one stone.

I also added a bit more carrot, celery, and mushrooms for flavor and it didn't hurt the fiber and vitamin total either.

CREAM OF ARTICHOKE SOUP

Original recipe contains 590 calories, 52 grams fat, 32 grams saturated fat, and 160 milligrams cholesterol per serving.

Makes 4 servings

2 tablespoons olive oil

¾ cup chopped carrot

¾ cup chopped celery

½ to ¾ cup chopped onion

1 cup chopped mushrooms

¼ cup Wondra quick-mixing flour

1 cup whole milk, divided

14½-ounce can chicken broth

3 cups quartered artichoke hearts, drained and rinsed well (about 13 ounces)

1 bay leaf

¾ teaspoon salt

½ teaspoon freshly ground pepper or to taste

pinch or two of ground red pepper or to taste

¼ teaspoon dried thyme, crumbled, or ¾ teaspoon minced fresh thyme

¼ teaspoon dried oregano, crumbled, or ¾ teaspoon minced fresh oregano

¼ teaspoon ground sage

pinch of paprika

1. Heat olive oil in large heavy skillet or saucepan over medium heat. Add carrot, celery, onion, and mushrooms. Sauté vegetables until they are soft and lightly browned (about 8 minutes). Set aside.
2. Place flour in small saucepan or bowl. Slowly stir in ½ cup of milk. Add milk mixture to the vegetables and immediately stir in chicken broth in a slow, steady stream, stirring constantly. Add artichoke hearts, bay leaf, salt, pepper, red pepper, thyme, oregano, sage, and paprika and stir well.
3. Cover pan and simmer about 30 minutes, stirring occasionally. DO NOT BOIL.
4. Stir in remaining milk and let simmer an additional minute. Again, do not boil. Remove bay leaf. Adjust seasoning to your taste. Serve immediately.

PER SERVING: 230 calories, 9 g protein, 29 g carbohydrate, 9.5 g fat, 2.5 g saturated fat, 8 mg cholesterol, 9.5 g fiber, 880 mg sodium. Calories from fat: 37 percent.

Dear Recipe Doctor,

In response to my request for corn recipes, a friend passed this recipe along, saying it was wonderful. Well, I imagine anything with this much fat should taste wonderful. I don't even want to try it unless it can be lightened up. Any suggestions?

This is one of those dishes that tastes better than it sounds—corn casserole. I suppose this recipe title describes the dish well and probably appeals to total corn lovers. But I could think of tons of side dishes people would rather make than something called corn casserole.

Actually, this savory corn dish has a perfect balance of flavors and has "comfort food" written all over it. There's also something I need to warn you about; this corn casserole has a *very* appetizing smell—the kind of smell that makes you start picking at it with a fork before it even has a chance to cool down. The kind of smell that invites even the most unassuming neighbors or guests to comment on it the minute they walk in the door—"What is that wonderful smell?"

That's not even the best part—it's easy to make, too! I used 1 tablespoon of butter instead of 8 and I used reduced-fat sharp cheddar cheese instead of regular. Instead of 2 beaten eggs, I blended 1 egg with 2 egg whites. I also used a reduced-fat cream of mushroom soup, low-fat milk, and reduced-fat Hi Ho's or Ritz crackers. The final touch was using 2 tablespoons of real mayonnaise blended with 6 tablespoons nonfat sour cream, instead of ½ cup of mayonnaise.

I don't know what the original tastes like, but this light version is delicious. If you want to serve half of it today and half of it later, place the mixture in two loaf pans instead of a 9 x 9-inch baking dish. When it cools down, just freeze one of the loaf pans for a rainy day.

⪼ SAVORY CORN CASSEROLE ⪻

Original recipe contains 300 calories, 23 grams fat (8 grams of which is saturated), and 34 milligrams cholesterol per serving.

Makes 8 side servings

> 1 tablespoon butter
> 1/2 cup reduced-fat sharp cheddar cheese
> 1/4 to 1/3 cup chopped green onions
> 2 tablespoons mayonnaise
> 6 tablespoons (1/4 cup + 2 tablespoons) fat-free sour cream
> 1/2 cup low-fat milk
> 1 egg plus 2 egg whites
> 1/2 cup (heaping) condensed cream of mushroom soup
> 16-ounce package frozen corn
> 24 reduced-fat Hi Ho or Ritz crackers, crumbled
> a pinch or two of paprika (optional)

1. Preheat oven to 350 degrees. Coat a 9 x 9-inch baking pan with canola cooking spray.
2. Melt butter in a medium microwave-safe bowl in the microwave. Mix in all other ingredients except crackers, and spread in prepared pan.
3. Cover mixture with cracker crumbs. Sprinkle a pinch or two of paprika over the top if desired. Bake until casserole is bubbly and lightly browned around the sides (about 30 minutes).

PER SERVING: 132 calories, 5 g protein, 16.5 g carbohydrates, 6 g fat, 2 g saturated fat, 12 mg cholesterol, 1.5 g fiber, 165 mg sodium. Calories from fat: 40%.

Dear Recipe Doctor,

Could you help me with this recipe my mother-in-law gave me years ago? We love it and so does everyone who has had it, but it is full of fats and we are trying to cut back. This is a very easy dish to make and also freezes well once cooked. Thanks for your help!

You certainly don't expect a side dish, especially one containing something as nutritious as spinach, to total 375 calories, 28 grams of fat (17 of which are saturated fat), and 123 milligrams cholesterol per serving! But that's exactly what this spinach recipe adds up to.

But this is my kind of recipe. You can whip it up in a couple of minutes, it doesn't call for a long list of ingredients, and it features a leafy green vegetable. There's just the little matter of fat and cholesterol. Most of the fat and cholesterol are coming from the cube of melted butter and the pound of regular fat Monterey Jack cheese.

To lighten this up, I replaced one of the eggs with egg substitute, switched to low-fat milk (although whole milk wouldn't change the nutrition totals too much), and switched to reduced-fat cheese (by Kraft) and used half as much. For good measure, I still added the melted butter, just 2 tablespoons, though, and added ⅓ cup of fat-free or light sour cream to make up the difference.

This was delicious as a side serving for dinner or warmed up for breakfast (guess what I had the next day for breakfast). I passed a few squares of this to a few of my neighbors and they all came back for the recipe.

⮞ SPINACH SQUARES (PRIJESNAC) ⮜

This makes a great make-ahead appetizer, too. Cut refrigerated, cooked Prijesnac into about 81 squares, warm in microwave, and serve each square with a toothpick.

Original recipe contains 375 calories, 28 grams fat, 17 grams saturated fat, and 123 milligrams cholesterol per serving.

Makes 9 side servings

> 1 egg
> ¼ cup egg substitute
> ½ cup low-fat milk
> 1 cup flour
> 1 teaspoon salt
> 1 teaspoon baking powder
> 2 tablespoons butter, melted
> ⅓ cup fat-free or light sour cream
> 8 ounces reduced-fat Monterey Jack cheese, cut into ½-inch cubes
> 2 10-ounce packages frozen chopped spinach, thawed
>   and drained (gently squeeze excess water with hands)

1. Preheat oven to 325 degrees. Coat a 9 x 9-inch baking dish with canola cooking spray.
2. Beat egg, egg substitute, milk, flour, salt, baking powder, melted butter, and sour cream in mixing bowl on medium-low speed until smooth batter has formed.
3. Stir in cheese cubes and spinach. Pour into prepared pan, spread evenly with spatula, and bake about 35 minutes. Test center to make sure it isn't runny. Let sit about 10 minutes before serving.

PER SERVING: 188 calories, 12.5 g protein, 17 g carbohydrate, 8 g fat, 4.5 g saturated fat, 45 mg cholesterol, 1.5 g fiber, 525 mg sodium. Calories from fat: 38 percent.

Dear Recipe Doctor,

I love this macaroni salad at Rapallo's Delicatessen in Pleasant Hill, California—it's the best I've ever tasted. Can you make a light version?

When I walked into Rapallo's and told the lady behind the counter that one of my readers thought their macaroni salad was the best they had ever tasted, she couldn't stop laughing. She said, "Maybe it's because we don't put anything in it." She was happy to share the ingredients with me (I was on my own for amounts and directions). And I have to say, she was right—this is a no-frills recipe for macaroni salad purists.

You won't find anything fancy in this salad. No pickles, no pimentos, skip the celery and olives, and hold the mustard. It comes down to four ingredients—macaroni, green onions, mayonnaise, and hard-boiled eggs. The seasonings are just salt, pepper, and parsley. I made a mayonnaise mixture using 2 tablespoons of real mayo and ¼ cup of fat-free sour cream (light can also be used). I also hard-boiled 3 eggs, as called for, but tossed two of the yolks out—one yolk added just the right amount of yellow color to the salad. I cut the calories from 202 to 145 and the fat grams from 11 grams to 3.8 grams. The cholesterol went down from 85 milligrams to 28.

But how did it taste? "Simply" delicious. This is the kind of salad that tastes even better the next day, so if you are making it for a party or barbecue, make it the night before you need it.

⮞ A MACARONI SALAD FOR PURISTS ⮜

Original recipe contains 202 calories, 11 grams fat, 2 grams saturated fat, and 85 milligrams cholesterol.

Makes 8 side servings

> 3 hard-boiled eggs
> 2 cups dry macaroni
> 3 green onions, white and part of green, finely chopped
> 2 teaspoons parsley flakes, or 2 tablespoons fresh, finely
>   chopped parsley
> 1/4 teaspoon salt
> freshly ground pepper to taste
> 2 tablespoons real mayonnaise
> 1/4 cup fat-free sour cream (light can also be used)

1. Start boiling your eggs if you haven't already done so. Then boil the macaroni noodles following directions on box (boil about 8 to 10 minutes). Drain noodles well and rinse with cold water and let cool.
2. Place noodles in serving bowl along with green onions, parsley, salt, and pepper to taste. In small bowl blend mayonnaise with sour cream; add mayonnaise mixture to the noodles in serving bowl.
3. Peel shells off eggs and remove 2 of the cooked yolks (discard or save for another use). Chop remaining eggs and stir into macaroni mixture. Add more salt and pepper if needed to taste. Let sit in refrigerator overnight (if you've got time).

PER SERVING: 145 calories, 5.5 g protein, 21.5 g carbohydrate, 3.8 g fat, .7 g saturated fat, 28 mg cholesterol, 1 g fiber, 128 mg sodium. Calories from fat: 24 percent.

Dear Recipe Doctor,

I saw this recipe (potatoes and carrots au gratin) in a holiday magazine a year ago. I want to make it, but it calls for quite a bit of margarine. Can you lighten it up for us?

Sounded good to me, too—a mixture of potatoes, carrots, and leeks covered in a creamy cheese sauce all under a toasty crumb topping. You were right, though, the original recipe racked up 10.5 grams fat, 6.5 grams saturated fat, and 32 milligrams cholesterol (40 percent calories from fat) per small side serving. Which doesn't sound so bad except that this is a vegetable dish! I like to reserve most of my saturated fat and cholesterol for my entree.

The first thing I did was make the cheese sauce with 1 tablespoon of butter instead of 2. I used whole milk instead of evaporated whole milk. I didn't do this necessarily because of the fat but because there is something about that "canned milk" flavor typical of evaporated milk that just doesn't appeal to me. Whole milk worked just fine. I used a little less Gruyère cheese. (Part-skim varieties of Gruyère and Swiss are available, too.) I switched to Wondra quick-mixing flour because it is a lot more forgiving than regular flour (you don't need butter to help blend it into the milk to make a smooth sauce).

I skipped the butter in the topping. I just blended some stuffing and Parmesan cheese lightly in a food processor, sprinkled it over the top, and glistened the top by spraying lightly with canola cooking spray. The result? Definitely yummy—and with a lot less fat. This brought it down to 3.5 grams of fat, 2 grams saturated fat, and 11 milligrams cholesterol per serving.

POTATOES AND CARROTS AU GRATIN

Original recipe contains 234 calories, 10.5 grams fat, 6.5 grams saturated fat, and 32 milligrams cholesterol per serving (at 12 servings per recipe).

Makes 8 to 12 servings

> 6 medium baking potatoes (about 2 pounds), peeled and thinly sliced
> 3 medium carrots, peeled and thinly sliced
> 2 bay leaves (optional)
> 2 leeks, cut into 1/2-inch slices (about 1 cup)
> 1 tablespoon margarine or butter
> 1 1/2 cups whole milk
> 2 tablespoons Wondra quick-mixing flour
> 1/2 teaspoon salt
> 1/2 teaspoon ground nutmeg
> 1/4 teaspoon white or black pepper
> 1/2 cup shredded Gruyère or reduced-fat Swiss cheese, packed
> 2/3 cup herb seasoned cubed stuffing
>   (such as Pepperidge Farm)
> 1/3 cup finely shredded Parmesan cheese

1. Spray bottom and sides of 9 x 13-inch baking pan with canola cooking spray. Preheat oven to 350 degrees.
2. Place potatoes, carrots, and bay leaves in a 3-quart saucepan. Add water to cover. Bring to boiling. Reduce heat, cover, and cook for 5 minutes. Add leeks and cook, covered, for 3 minutes longer or until vegetables are just tender. Drain well;

discard bay leaves. Spoon mixture evenly into prepared baking pan.

3. For sauce, melt margarine or butter in small nonstick saucepan. Add 2 tablespoons of the milk, then stir in flour, salt, nutmeg, and pepper. Stir in the remaining milk. Cook and stir until thickened and bubbly (about 3 minutes). Cook and stir for 1 minute more. Remove from heat. Stir in the Gruyère cheese; stir until smooth. Spoon cheese sauce evenly over vegetables.

4. For crumb topping, combine stuffing and Parmesan in small food processor and pulse briefly to lightly chop and blend. Sprinkle topping over potato mixture in pan. Spray cooking spray over the crumb topping. Bake uncovered about 20 minutes or until cheese sauce is bubbly around edges of dish.

PER SERVING (12 per recipe): 154 calories, 5.5 g protein, 25 g carbohydrate, 3.5 g fat, 2 g saturated fat, 11 mg cholesterol, 2 g fiber, 236 mg sodium. Calories from fat: 22 percent.

Q

Dear Recipe Doctor,

I was planning our Thanksgiving menu and thought about this old family favorite—sweet potato casserole. It has lots of butter and eggs. Can you lighten it for us? Much appreciated.

A

Save the fat grams and calories for the pumpkin pie—you won't miss them in this dish. The original recipe calls for a total of 8 tablespoons of butter and 2 eggs for 6 to 8 servings.

I did something rash and cut most of the butter from the sweet potato mixture and replaced it with reduced-calorie pancake syrup (you could use real maple syrup if you prefer). I cut out the 2 tablespoons of sugar called for in the original recipe since I was already adding in sweet syrup. I substituted egg substitute for one of the eggs called for and I used low-fat milk just because that's what I happen to have in my refrigerator. If you have whole milk, go ahead and use it because only ½ cup is used and the fat/cholesterol savings from switching to low-fat milk, per serving, will be admittedly small.

A crunchy topping is made with pecans, coconut, brown sugar, and flour, all bound together with—what else?—more melted butter. I used 1 tablespoon and reduced the flour by a tablespoon to achieve the right topping texture. It turns out great every time and no one ever notices that most of the butter is missing.

➳ SWEET POTATO CASSEROLE ➳

Original recipe contains 301 calories, 18 grams fat, 9 grams
saturated fat, and 86 milligrams cholesterol.

Makes 8 servings

4 cups hot mashed sweet potatoes
1 tablespoon butter or margarine
3 tablespoons light pancake syrup (real maple syrup can
    be substituted)
1 egg, beaten
¼ cup egg substitute
½ cup low-fat or whole milk
⅓ cup chopped pecans
⅓ cup flaked coconut (sweetened)
⅓ cup packed brown sugar
1 tablespoon flour
1 tablespoon melted butter or margarine

1. Preheat oven to 325 degrees. Coat a 1½- to 2-quart casserole
    dish with canola cooking spray.
2. With electric mixer, blend sweet potatoes, 1 tablespoon butter,
    and pancake syrup together. Beat in egg, egg substitute, and
    milk. Pour mixture into prepared casserole dish.
3. Combine pecans, coconut, brown sugar, and flour. Stir in a
    tablespoon of melted butter. Sprinkle mixture over sweet pota-
    toes. Bake in preheated oven for 1 hour.

PER SERVING: 204 calories, 4 g protein, 32.5 g carbohydrate, 7 g fat, 2.5 g saturated
fat, 32 mg cholesterol, 2.5 g fiber, 90 mg sodium. Calories from fat: 30 percent.

Q *Dear Recipe Doctor,*

My husband and I make this Buffalo potatoes recipe all the time—it is one of our favorites. Can you lighten it up for us?

A This is one of those mix-and-bake types of recipes everybody loves. Just mix a few ingredients together and throw it in the oven. And it calls for an envelope of garlic and herb soup mix—even better.

I tried lightening this recipe up twice. The first time was good, but the second time was simply delicious. The original recipe called for ⅓ cup of melted butter. The first time I lightened it up, I tried 2 tablespoons of canola oil. The second time, I tried 1 tablespoon of butter and 1 tablespoon of canola oil.

In this recipe the melted butter is the main part of the sauce that coats the potatoes (the soup mix powder and Tabasco are stirred into the butter). When I reduce the butter, I have a lot less liquid to mix the soup mix with and a lot less sauce to coat the potato wedges. So I replaced the butter with a tablespoon of honey and 2 tablespoons of beer or wine (although apple juice or broth can be substituted). If you heat the mixture briefly over medium-low heat, it all blends together nicely. Because I added only a little honey and beer, the flavor they add is nice and subtle.

I coated my baking pan with canola cooking spray so the potatoes and the seasoning sauce would not stick to the pan—it worked beautifully. The original recipe calls for 3 to 4 teaspoons Tabasco. If you are sensitive to hot spices or if these potatoes need to please younger palates, you might want to use 1½ to 2 teaspoons instead. Sure, it will take a little of the "Buffalo" out of the Buffalo potatoes, but trust me, there will still be plenty of flavor to go around.

⌒ BUFFALO POTATOES ⌒

Original recipe contains 332 calories, 33 milligrams cholesterol, and 12.5 grams fat (7.5 grams are saturated).

Makes 5 servings

1 tablespoon butter
1 tablespoon canola oil
1 tablespoon honey
2 tablespoons light or nonalcoholic beer or wine
   (apple juice or broth can be substituted)
1½–3 teaspoons Tabasco sauce (depending on preference)
1 package Lipton Recipe Secrets savory herb with garlic
5 russet potatoes, washed (not peeled)

1. Preheat oven to 400 degrees. Coat the bottom of a 9 x 13-inch baking pan with canola cooking spray.
2. Combine butter, canola oil, honey, beer, Tabasco, and soup mix in small saucepan. Cook, stirring often, over medium-low heat until butter is melted and ingredients are nicely blended. Set aside to cool.
3. Cut potatoes into wedges by cutting potatoes in half width-wise, then cutting each half into 8 wedges.
4. Place potato wedges in large bowl. Pour cooled garlic and herb sauce over potato wedges and stir to coat very well. Spread potatoes evenly in prepared pan. Pour any remaining sauce over the potatoes in pan.
5. Bake for 15 minutes. Scrape any sauce from bottom of pan with spatula and toss with potatoes. Bake 15 to 25 minutes longer or until potatoes are nicely browned and tender.

PER SERVING: 303 calories, 6 g protein, 59 g carbohydrate, 5 g fat, 5 g fiber, 6 mg cholesterol, 445 mg sodium. Calories from fat: 15 percent.

Chapter Three

☞ ENTREES ☜

CHICKEN & TURKEY

OVEN-FRIED LEMON MARINATED CHICKEN

CHICKEN FLORENTINE

MOM'S MEDITERRANEAN PASTA SALAD

BENGAL CHICKEN SALAD

CURRY CHICKEN SALAD

CHINESE CHICKEN TACOS

QUICK MINI CHICKEN TAMALES

HONEY-GLAZED CHICKEN

STRATA

SONOMA CHICKEN

QUICK CHICKEN POT PIE

PENNE IN CREAM SAUCE WITH SAUSAGE

SAUSAGE PIE

CHICKEN ENCHILADAS DIABLO

SLOW-COOKER CHICKEN FRICASSEE

CHICKEN-MANGO-AVOCADO SALAD

Q *Dear Recipe Doctor,*

I have had this recipe for marinated lemon chicken for years now. My wife and I have really cut down on our fat recently due to health problems. Can you salvage this one for us? Many thanks.

A You don't have to ask me to lighten up lemon chicken twice—it's one of my favorite entrees! I particularly like the way this recipe marinates the chicken in the lemon juice-fortified marinade, then bakes the chicken (marinade and all) for a thickened tasty serving sauce.

The first thing we do is switch to skinless, boneless chicken breasts from the quartered whole chicken called for. Actually if you want the bone in your breast, go ahead, it's just that if you use the boneless breasts, every inch of edible chicken is going to be nicely coated and baked in the delicious lemon sauce.

The original recipe calls for ¼ cup of salad oil. I cut it down to 1 tablespoon of canola oil and added a few tablespoons of chicken broth. I thought about adding something sweet instead of broth, but that would change the sauce from rather tart to rather sweet. I really liked it this way, but if you like your lemon chicken nice and sweet, add 3 tablespoons corn syrup or honey instead of the broth.

The sauce has plenty of flavor with ½ cup of lemon juice and 2 tablespoons of grated lemon peel, but I did double the garlic and used dark soy sauce for the 1 tablespoon called for—just to help boost the flavor. Regular soy sauce would work well, too. This was wonderful served with steamed rice because there is plenty of lemon sauce to go around.

⊱ OVEN-FRIED LEMON MARINATED CHICKEN ⊰

Original recipe contains 484 calories, 32 grams fat, 6 grams saturated fat, and 120 milligrams cholesterol per serving.

Makes 4 servings

> 1 tablespoon dark soy sauce (or regular soy sauce)
> 1 teaspoon salt, divided
> ¾ teaspoon pepper, divided
> 2 cloves garlic, crushed or minced
> 1 tablespoon canola oil
> 3 tablespoons double strength chicken broth
> ½ cup lemon juice
> 2 tablespoons grated lemon peel
> 4 skinless and boneless chicken breasts
> ½ cup all-purpose flour (plus more if needed)
> 1 to 2 teaspoons paprika
> fresh parsley and lemon slices for garnish (optional)

1. Combine soy sauce, ½ teaspoon salt, ½ teaspoon pepper, garlic, oil, broth, lemon juice, and lemon peel in a large zip-type bag. Mix with spoon; add chicken breasts. Refrigerate 1 hour or more.
2. Preheat oven to 350 degrees. Remove chicken from marinade and save marinade.
3. Combine flour, paprika, and remaining salt and pepper in medium bowl or another plastic bag. Add chicken to flour mixture and coat each breast completely. Arrange chicken in a 9 x 9-inch pan that has been coated with canola cooking spray. Spray tops of chicken with cooking spray.

4. Drizzle ¼ cup of marinade over chicken and bake 20 minutes, uncovered. Pour remaining marinade over chicken and bake 20 to 30 minutes until done. Garnish with lemon slices and fresh parsley if desired.

PER SERVING: 241 calories, 29 g protein, 15.5 g carbohydrate, 6.5 g fat, 1 g saturated fat, 73 mg cholesterol, 1 g fiber, 720 mg sodium. Calories from fat: 25 percent.

Dear Recipe Doctor,

A friend of mine from San Diego cooked this dish for me years ago. It made for a wonderful dinner. Can you make it even healthier?

I'm always looking for great chicken recipes to try, because we have chicken for dinner at least once a week. And after a while even chicken lovers can tire of oven-fried and barbecued chicken. Best of all, after I made a few ingredient adjustments, this recipe was pretty quick to put together. No boiling or chopping spinach. No grating Swiss cheese. No breading and frying the chicken. Just pound, season, spread, and roll. It bakes in the oven for 25 minutes while you relax (or get the rest of dinner ready).

The original recipe called for 4 tablespoons of butter; I cut it down to 1 tablespoon. I used light cream cheese instead of regular and actually increased the amount to make the filling nice and creamy. I also added fresh lemon juice to round out the flavors coming from spinach, cream cheese, Swiss and Parmesan cheese, garlic, and oregano.

The original recipe already called for skinned chicken breasts, so I didn't need to do anything there. I switched to thin slices of reduced-fat Swiss cheese (or light Jarlsberg) instead of grated regular Swiss cheese. I also used frozen, thawed chopped spinach instead of fresh, which you would have to cook, drain, and chop yourself.

The Chicken Florentine was a beautiful and delicious dinner served over steamed rice with in-season vegetables. I even enjoyed the leftovers the next day as lunch.

⇒ CHICKEN FLORENTINE ⇐

This works out to be an easy dinner. Once your chicken rolls are in the oven, start your steamed rice cooking over the stove and cook some vegetables in your microwave. After 20 minutes they will all be done. Original recipe contains 890 calories, 42 grams fat, and 175 milligrams cholesterol per serving.

Makes 4 servings

> ¹/₃ cup light cream cheese
> 1 tablespoon butter or canola margarine, melted
> ¹/₂ teaspoon oregano (optional)
> juice from ¹/₂ lemon
> about 1 cup frozen chopped spinach, thawed and gently
>   squeezed of excess water (one small box)
> 4 boneless and skinless chicken breasts
> garlic powder, salt, and pepper to taste (or use garlic salt
>   and pepper)
> 4 thin slices reduced-fat Swiss or light Jarlsberg cheese
>   (about 4 ounces)
> ¹/₄ cup shredded Parmesan cheese
> hot steamed rice (³/₄ cup per person)

1. Preheat oven to 400 degrees. Coat a 9-inch square or round baking dish with canola cooking spray.
2. Combine cream cheese, butter, oregano, and lemon in mixing bowl and beat with mixer on low until blended. Add spinach and beat on low until blended; set aside.
3. Pound each chicken breast in between two sheets of waxed paper with the flat side of a meat mallet until thin.

4. Season the top of each chicken breast with a sprinkle of salt, pepper, and garlic powder. Lay one slice of cheese on top of each breast, then spread 1/4 cup of spinach mixture down the center of the breast. Wrap the rest of the breast around (to form a chicken roll) and lay each breast, seam side down, in prepared baking dish.

5. Sprinkle the top of each breast with about 1 tablespoon of Parmesan cheese. Pour 1/4 cup of water into the pan (to keep the breasts moist). Bake until lightly browned (and chicken is cooked throughout) about 25 minutes. Serve over steamed rice.

PER SERVING (including rice): 505 calories, 45.5 g protein, 48.5 g carbohydrate, 13 g fat, 7 g saturated fat, 103 mg cholesterol, 2.5 g fiber, 484 mg sodium. Calories from fat: 24 percent.

Q   *Dear Recipe Doctor,*

My mom makes this yummy Mediterranean pasta salad, but it is literally dripping in olive oil. And she doesn't really have a recipe either. She just throws it all together using lots of garlic olive oil. I wrote down some notes though and I hope you can come up with a lighter version.

A   As I read this reader's notes I could almost taste this beautiful salad with contrasting shapes, textures, and colors—crisp sugar snap peas with green flecks of oregano and basil, deep red julienne-cut sun-dried tomatoes, thin penne pasta, and browned gourmet turkey or chicken sausage links, coarsely chopped. Plus, say the words "garlic" and "pasta" and I'm there.

Obviously the biggest issue here is the cups of olive oil. Olive oil is a monounsaturated fat, which is certainly preferable, healthwise, to saturated fat. But a cup of oil is still a cup of oil—adding 1,920 calories and 224 grams of fat. So the trick is choosing better fats when possible (like olive oil and canola oil) but still using moderate amounts. When you use less olive oil you need to add something else to coat the noodles and blend the ingredients together. I made a dressing with 3 tablespoons olive oil, garlic, marinara sauce, milk, and nonfat sour cream. Don't ask me why, it just sounded good.

Most of us won't find garlic olive oil in our local supermarket, so I blended your run-of-the-mill extra virgin type with some bottled minced garlic. If you buy the julienne-cut sun-dried tomatoes, packed in oil, you just need to drain them, then toss them in. You can save yourself a small fortune and buy frozen sugar snap peas. Just throw them into the boiling water during the last 1 to 2 minutes of cooking the noodles. The original recipe called for those gourmet turkey or chicken sausage links. I used a gourmet brand of smoked turkey and chicken sausage with sun-dried tomatoes.

Original recipe contains 400 calories, 24 grams fat, and 60 milligrams cholesterol per serving.

Makes 8 servings

13 ounces (4 cups) dry thin penne pasta
12 ounces frozen sugar snap peas (if using fresh, trim
    ends and stems)
3 links gourmet turkey or chicken sausage (or use 8 ounces
    Hillshire Farm turkey polska kielbasa)
$\frac{1}{3}$–$\frac{1}{2}$ cup julienne-cut sun-dried tomatoes (if in oil, drain;
    if dry, soak in warm water, then drain)
3 tablespoons extra virgin olive oil
2–3 teaspoons minced or chopped garlic
$\frac{1}{4}$ cup whole milk (low-fat can also be used)
2 tablespoons marinara sauce
2 tablespoons nonfat sour cream
1 teaspoon dried basil leaves
1 teaspoon dried oregano leaves
salt and freshly ground pepper (optional)

1. Bring 5 quarts of water and $\frac{1}{2}$ teaspoon salt to boil in large saucepan. Pour in pasta. Stir occasionally, and cook for 12 minutes. Pour in sugar snap peas and continue to boil 1 to 2 minutes (noodles should just be tender). Drain. Place in large serving bowl.

2. While noodles are boiling, brown thinly sliced or coarsely chopped sausage in large nonstick frying pan coated with canola cooking spray. Once cool, add to pasta in serving bowl. Stir in sun-dried tomatoes.

3. Place next seven ingredients in small food processor (or use a medium bowl and wire whisk). Purée briefly just to blend. Pour over noodle mixture and stir to blend. Season with freshly ground pepper and salt if desired. Refrigerate until needed.

PER SERVING (using gourmet smoked turkey and chicken sausage with sun-dried tomatoes): 317 calories, 14 g protein, 40 g carbohydrate, 10.5 g fat, 2.6 g saturated fat, 28 mg cholesterol, 3 g fiber, 327 mg sodium. Calories from fat: 30 percent.

Dear Recipe Doctor,

I loved this chicken salad so much that I could have eaten the whole bowl. My friend made it for me the other day. Mayonnaise, however, is a major ingredient.

This chicken salad is a very interesting mix of flavors and textures. I personally loved it. I probably could have eaten the whole bowl, too. And the best part is, I know the lower-fat recipe tasted just as great as the original! How do I know? I ran a sample to this reader and she said it tasted exactly the same as the original.

The salad ingredients remained mostly the same. I took the skin off the chicken breasts though and used fewer hard-boiled egg yolks.

The tricky part came with the dressing. The dressing calls for gobs of mayonnaise. I cut it down from 6 tablespoons to 2 and increased the sour cream from 2 tablespoons of regular sour cream to ⅓ cup of fat-free sour cream. The recipe also calls for 2 tablespoons of coconut milk. You can use 2 tablespoons of milk and ¼ teaspoon coconut extract instead if you would like.

⋐ BENGAL CHICKEN SALAD ⋑

Original recipe contains 603 calories, 32 grams fat, and 246 milligrams cholesterol per serving.

Makes 4 servings

DRESSING:
2 tablespoons mayonnaise
2 tablespoons coconut milk (canned) or 2 tablespoons milk plus ¼ teaspoon coconut extract
⅓ cup fat-free sour cream
2–3 teaspoons curry powder

SALAD:
½ large onion, cut into chunks
4 celery stalk tops
3 boneless and skinless chicken breast halves
salt and pepper to taste
1 tablespoon lemon juice
½ cup minced onion
2 cups finely sliced celery
8-ounce can sliced water chestnuts
¼ cup currants (softened in warm water and drained) or regular raisins
¾ cup chopped mango chutney (drained if liquid)
¼ cup pine nuts or slivered almonds
4 hard-boiled eggs, chopped (discard egg yolks from 2 eggs)
parsley for garnish
1 small–medium head lettuce, washed, well drained, and leaves removed

1. Mix mayonnaise, coconut milk, and sour cream in a bowl using a whip or mixer. Gradually add curry and whip until smooth. Refrigerate until needed.
2. Place onion chunks and celery tops in a large pan. Add chicken breasts and water to cover. Bring to a simmer and cook about 8 minutes. Cover pan, remove from burner, and allow to cool. When chicken is cool enough to handle, remove chicken and cut into bite-sized pieces. Add salt and pepper to taste and sprinkle with lemon juice. Refrigerate until needed.
3. When ready to serve salad, in large serving bowl toss seasoned chicken with minced onion, sliced celery, water chestnuts, currants, mango chutney, pine nuts, and dressing. Garnish salad with hardboiled egg pieces and parsley sprigs. Serve on individual beds of lettuce leaves.

PER SERVING: 480 calories, 38 g protein, 48 g carbohydrate, 15 g fat, 3.3 g saturated fat, 6.5 g fiber, 125 mg cholesterol, 412 mg sodium. Calories from fat: 28 percent.

Q   *Dear Recipe Doctor,*

I make this layered curry chicken salad for potlucks and during the weekends so my family can help themselves whenever they are hungry. The dressing is delicious, though it includes 2 cups of real mayonnaise! Can you take a look at the recipe for us?

A   Okay, I love layered salads! They are so attractive, and this one seemed fairly simple to put together, too. But 2 cups of mayonnaise is definitely a problem, considering 1 measly tablespoon contains 10 grams of fat—so 1 cup contributes 160 grams of fat. But I have come to appreciate the value of real mayonnaise.

I learned from researching my book *Taste Vs. Fat*, that most people find even light mayonnaise unacceptable. What I do now is blend real mayonnaise (or canola mayonnaise) with the top-rated light or fat-free sour cream. This seems to go over much better with just about everybody. It has a similar taste and texture to real mayonnaise but feels lighter when you are eating it.

I made a few other changes in this recipe, as well. I adjusted it to make 4 servings instead of 8 to 10. But I also used canned black beans (high in fiber and phytochemicals) instead of sugar snap peas (which are expensive) and doubled the water chestnuts and green onions. In the dressing, I used ¼ cup real mayonnaise and ¾ cup fat-free sour cream to make 1 cup of dressing, then increased the sugar slightly and doubled the ginger to balance out the tartness of the sour cream and add a little extra flavor. I also added a couple tablespoons of milk to thin it out.

I refrigerated it just as the recipe stated—the next day I had a thoroughly enjoyable, ready-made lunch. I can see why this is one of this reader's family favorites!

⌐ CURRY CHICKEN SALAD ⌐

Original recipe contains 662 calories, 52 grams fat, and 106 milligrams cholesterol per serving.

Makes 4 main dish servings

5 cups shredded lettuce
2 cups bean sprouts
8-ounce can sliced water chestnuts, drained and rinsed
4 green onions, thinly sliced
1½ cups low-sodium canned black beans, drained and rinsed
4 cooked boneless and skinless chicken breasts, cut into
    thin strips*

DRESSING:
¼ cup real mayonnaise
¾ cup Naturally Yours fat-free sour cream
    (in cowhide container)
2 tablespoons 1% low-fat milk
1 teaspoon curry powder
2 teaspoons sugar
1 teaspoon finely chopped fresh ginger (or ½ teaspoon
    ground ginger)
½ teaspoon salt
freshly ground pepper to taste

GARNISH:
¼ cup toasted slivered almonds (lightly brown in nonstick
    frying pan over medium heat)
1¼ cups quartered or halved cherry tomatoes

1. In deep 4-quart dish (or two loaf pans), layer lettuce, sprouts, water chestnuts, green onions, black beans, and chicken.
2. Combine all of the dressing ingredients. Spread the dressing evenly over the salad to cover. Cover with plastic wrap and refrigerate overnight.
3. To serve, top with slivered almonds and cherry tomatoes.

*If you don't have leftover cooked chicken breasts on hand, cook 4 thawed chicken breasts in a large saucepan along with 6 cups water or chicken broth and 1 teaspoon poultry seasoning. Bring water to boil, then cover pan and reduce heat to warm (or lowest setting). Simmer until chicken is cooked throughout (about 30 minutes). Let chicken breasts cool before slicing.

PER SERVING: 482 calories, 40 g protein, 38 g carbohydrate, 19.5 g fat, 2 g saturated fat, 10 g fiber, 81 mg cholesterol, 760 mg sodium. Calories from fat: 35 percent.

Q *Dear Recipe Doctor,*

I forget what they are officially called, but my husband and I call them "Chinese tacos," because they look like tacos but they use a lettuce leaf as the shell. Anyway, we like to order this dish at Chinese restaurants and they usually use a high-fat ground pork in the filling and deep-fried rice noodles on top. Can you possibly make up a lower-fat version? We're addicted to your column.

A I wouldn't have known what this reader was talking about a year ago, but last summer I went to a Chinese restaurant that served these "Chinese tacos" as appetizers. They had a wonderful contrast in textures—the soft savory filling with diced vegetables and crunchy noodles wrapped in a crisp lettuce leaf. But mostly I remember thinking I wanted to reinvent them at home because they were fun to eat and they tasted great. But I didn't know quite where to start.

After getting this letter I started flipping through some of my Chinese cookbooks and I finally found a recipe—it was called "Talking Noodles" from *A Taste of Chinatown*, by Joie Warner.

This recipe can actually be quick to make if you use store-bought Chinese sauces and use packaged chow mein noodles (which don't really add too much fat when used as a garnish) instead of freshly fried rice noodles. You can also blend the chicken and marinade in the food processor in the morning, let it sit in the refrigerator all day, then finish the recipe when you get home from work.

I used chicken breasts instead of ground pork, and I cut down on a couple of steps in the original recipe by marinating the chicken in the cooking sauce. Instead of 2 tablespoons cooking oil, I was able to stir-fry the filling in only 2 teaspoons. And instead of deep frying the rice noodles to make the crunchy taco topping, I used packaged chow mein noodles.

It turned out tasting very close to the restaurant dish I enjoyed last summer. And best of all, it is lower in fat and quick to make.

☞ CHINESE CHICKEN TACOS ☜

Original recipe contains 200 calories, 13 grams fat, and 28 milligrams cholesterol per serving.

Makes 8 tacos

- 2 teaspoons light soy sauce
- 4 teaspoons dry sherry
- 1 teaspoon sesame oil
- 1 teaspoon cornstarch
- 2 large (or 3 small) boneless and skinless chicken breasts
- 2 teaspoons canola oil
- 4 large cloves garlic, chopped
- 1 tablespoon finely chopped fresh ginger
- 3 whole green onions, chopped
- ½ cup finely chopped carrot (about 1 carrot)
- ½ cup finely chopped celery (about 1 small stalk)
- 2 tablespoons bottled hoisin sauce
- 2 tablespoons bottled plum sauce (you'll find both of these sauces in the Oriental food section of your supermarket)
- 8 large leaves iceberg lettuce
- ½–¾ cup crunchy chow mein noodles

1. Mix soy sauce, sherry, sesame oil, and cornstarch in 2-cup measure.
2. Place chicken breasts in food processor. Drizzle the marinade over the top and process mixture until chicken looks like ground pork. Spoon mixture back into the 2-cup measure, cover, and refrigerate for at least 30 minutes.

3.   Heat nonstick wok or large nonstick skillet on medium heat. Add canola oil and spread in pan with pancake turner. Add garlic and ginger and cook a few seconds. Add chicken mixture, breaking lumps into small pieces until cooked through. Add chopped vegetables; toss for 1 minute or until tender-crisp. Stir in hoisin and plum sauces; toss to mix.

4.   Spoon ⅛ of mixture into center of each lettuce leaf and sprinkle a tablespoon or so of chow mein noodles over the chicken mixture. Eat this with your hands! Enjoy.

PER SERVING: 103 calories, 8.5 g protein, 9.5 g carbohydrates, 3.5 g fat, .2 g saturated fat, 18 mg cholesterol, 1 g fiber, 152 mg sodium. Calories from fat: 30 percent.

Q

Dear Recipe Doctor,

My husband's family is from Mexico and he loves chicken tamales. But the recipe I have calls for lard, and lots of it. Do you have any suggestions?

A

Tamales are a festive food, often served at celebrations such as Christmas, weddings, or Cinco de Mayo. But in California people enjoy them year-round. I actually like to make up a batch in the middle of summer and freeze them. Then on hot summer nights I can just pull a few out of the freezer, unwrap them, and in 3 minutes (with the help of my trusty microwave) I have a nice meal without heating up my kitchen.

Traditionally, tamales are wrapped in soaked corn husks. But in order to make this recipe quick and easy, the tamales are wrapped in squares of foil. So after they are steamed and cooled, you can put them directly into the freezer just as they are.

Instead of lard, I made the masa paste using canola oil, chicken broth, and nonfat sour cream. The rest of the tamale ingredients are pretty harmless in terms of fat and cholesterol. I tend to use skinless chicken breast for the filling, but skinless thigh meat would work well, too. The other filling ingredients vary depending on the particular tamale recipe. I like mixing the shredded chicken with a tasty red salsa, some black olives, and onion, but feel free to add or delete filling ingredients as you see fit.

I know making a batch of tamales sounds rather ominous, not to mention time-consuming. But over the years I've lightened this recipe up in terms of fat grams as well as prep time. It's really very simple. So simple, my children help me make them. So far, everyone who has tasted these tamales has wanted the recipe. That's a pretty good sign, don't you think?

⇒ QUICK MINI CHICKEN TAMALES ⇐

Original recipe contains 202 calories, 12.5 grams fat, and 26 milligrams cholesterol per serving.

Makes about 24 tamales

> 2 cups masa harina (corn tortilla flour)
> 1¼ cups chicken broth
> ½ teaspoon salt (optional)
> 3 tablespoons canola oil
> ¼ cup nonfat or light sour cream
> 2 cups roasted or grilled finely shredded chicken
>   breast (skinless)
> 2¼-ounce can sliced or chopped olives
> 1 medium onion, finely chopped
> ½ cup green or red salsa

1. Cut 24 pieces of foil using this method: Carefully tear foil after pulling it out of the box about 6 inches. Cut this in half to make two squares from the rectangle. Do this 11 more times to make 24 squares.
2. Combine masa, chicken broth, salt, oil, and sour cream in mixing bowl. Beat briefly with mixer to make a thick paste; set aside.
3. In a medium bowl, toss the chicken, olives, onion, and salsa together.
4. Spread 1 heaping tablespoon of the paste into the shape of a 3-inch square in the center of a piece of foil. Now spoon a heaping tablespoon of the filling down the center of the masa square. Bring the opposite edges of foil together so masa edges

meet; wrap the foil (at the side) around the tamale to make a cylinder, then twist or fold under the foil at the ends. Repeat to make about 23 more tamales.

5. Place a rack in a 12- to 14-quart pan and pour in boiling water to a depth of an inch (water should not reach tamales; if rack is too low, rest it on two small cans). A metal vegetable steamer can also be used. Stack tamales in steamer, arranging loosely so steam can circulate. Bring to a boil; cover and adjust heat to keep water at a steady boil. Continue to cook, adding boiling water to maintain water level, until masa is nicely firm and does not stick to foil; open one tamale from the center of pan to test after an hour of steaming.

PER 2 TAMALES: 161 calories, 10 g protein, 17.5 g carbohydrate, 5.5 g fat, .5 g saturated fat, 20 mg cholesterol, 2.2 g fiber, 190 mg sodium. Calories from fat: 32 percent.

Dear Recipe Doctor,

I'm always looking for good chicken recipes. Do you have any?

How would you like a light version of a secret family recipe from the oldest restaurant in Los Angeles, Tam O'Shanter, a Scottish inn that has been feeding patrons since 1922. The recipe is for honey-glazed chicken and it's no wonder they've survived six decades and many an earthquake—this chicken is simple and yet tastes spectacular.

I trimmed the oil back from ¼ cup to 1 tablespoon and doubled the sherry—always a good idea. I switched to a lower-sodium soy sauce and skinned the chicken breasts. Don't worry, the marinade coats the chicken nicely and keeps it moist and tasty while it cooks.

This chicken is so good you'll want to double the recipe so you'll have chicken left over for chicken sandwiches or salads the following day.

⚛ HONEY-GLAZED CHICKEN ⚛

Original recipe contains 384 calories, 22 grams fat, and 93 milligrams of cholesterol per serving.

Makes 6 servings

¼ cup honey
¼ cup low-sodium or light soy sauce
¼ cup sherry
1 tablespoon canola oil
3 cloves garlic, crushed or minced
1 tablespoon finely minced fresh ginger
4–8 skinless chicken breasts (with or without bone)*

1. Combine honey, soy sauce, sherry, oil, garlic, and ginger in small food processor or blender. Pulse briefly until well combined.
2. Pour marinade into a heavy-duty plastic bag or a covered bowl or dish.
3. Rinse chicken and pat dry. Place chicken in marinade and refrigerate overnight, turning occasionally if possible.
4. Preheat oven to 325 degrees. Remove chicken from marinade. Place in single layer in ovenproof dish coated with nonstick cooking spray, and bake for 60 minutes or until golden brown. You may also barbecue the chicken until cooked throughout (about 30 minutes).

*If you use boneless breasts you will have enough marinade for up to 8 half breasts; if you are using breasts with the bone you will probably have enough marinade for 4 to 6.

PER SERVING (when 6 chicken breasts are used and all the marinade is consumed): 217 calories, 28 g protein, 14 g carbohydrate, 3.8 g fat, .5 g saturated fat, 68 mg cholesterol, 0 fiber, 415 mg sodium. Calories from fat: 17 percent.

Q

Dear Recipe Doctor,

I've never made this recipe (strata) but ate it years ago and it was delicious and very rich. I would really appreciate your expert diagnosis and prescription to make this a guilt-free yet enjoyable and good-tasting dish.

A

This reader has patiently been waiting for me to lighten up this recipe (she wrote me twice about this particular recipe). I like that kind of low-fat fortitude.

In my travels I have yet to see or taste strata, but I might be the exception. I found out my neighbor's mother-in-law makes it every Christmas for brunch, a tradition which is actually quite inspired because the recipe calls for making it the night before, then letting it sit overnight in the refrigerator. The next day you just pop it in the oven. No muss. No fuss. And the result is a rich-tasting, upscale casserole.

The original recipe calls for a 9 x 13-inch baking dish and makes 12 servings. I modified it to fit a 9 x 9-inch baking dish and make 6 servings. If you are expecting a small crowd, you might want to double the ingredients and use the 9 x 13-inch dish instead.

Fat and cholesterol are coming from several different directions in this recipe. I used skinless, boneless chicken breasts for the meat ingredient; you could also use turkey breast or lean ham. Instead of ½ cup of mayonnaise, I mixed 3 tablespoons of the real thing with ⅓ cup of my favorite fat-free sour cream. But if you happen to like light or low-fat mayonnaise, go ahead and use ½ cup of light or low-fat mayonnaise instead. But I have to tell you, combining a few tablespoons of real mayonnaise with the fat-free sour cream worked quite well.

I replaced one of the two eggs called for with egg substitute and added low-fat milk instead of whole. I used Campbell's Healthy Request cream of mushroom soup to cut down the fat a smidgen and sprinkled about a cup of reduced-fat sharp cheddar cheese over the top of the casserole (Cracker Barrel light or Kraft reduced fat taste great). To add a little extra flavor, I increased the green pepper, onion, and celery slightly. The original recipe called for whole wheat bread, which I happened to have on hand, but I imagine it would work just as well with sourdough bread (although you will lose some fiber in the process).

I ran a piece of my lower-fat strata over to my neighbor (the one whose mother-in-law makes a high-fat one every Christmas) and she thought it was a winner.

≈ STRATA ≈

Original recipe contains 550 calories, 36 grams fat, and 152 milligrams of cholesterol per serving.

Makes 6 servings

> 7 slices whole wheat bread, cubed
> 2 cooked boneless and skinless chicken breasts, cubed
> $\frac{2}{3}$ cup chopped green pepper
> $\frac{2}{3}$ cup chopped onion
> $\frac{2}{3}$ cup chopped celery
> 3 tablespoons mayonnaise
> $\frac{1}{3}$ cup Naturally Yours fat-free sour cream (in a
>   cowhide container)
> 1 egg
> $\frac{1}{4}$ cup egg substitute
> 1 cup low-fat milk
> $\frac{1}{4}$ teaspoon salt (optional)
> 1 can Campbell's Healthy Request cream of mushroom soup
> 1 cup shredded reduced-fat sharp cheddar cheese

1. Place half of the bread cubes in a 9 x 9-inch baking dish that has been coated with nonstick cooking spray.
2. In medium bowl blend chicken pieces, green pepper, onion, celery, mayonnaise, and sour cream together. Spread all of it over the bread cubes.
3. Spread remaining bread cubes over the chicken mixture.

4. In mixing bowl, beat egg, egg substitute, milk, and salt together until smooth. Pour egg mixture evenly over the bread cubes. Cover dish and refrigerate overnight.

5. Preheat oven to 325 degrees. Spread condensed soup over the top of the casserole. Bake for 45 minutes. Sprinkle cheese over the top and bake 5 minutes longer.

PER SERVING: 339 calories, 23.5 g protein, 31.5 g carbohydrate, 14 g fat, 4 g saturated fat, 75 mg cholesterol, 3 g fiber, 639 mg sodium. Calories from fat: 37 percent.

Dear Recipe Doctor,

I have this recipe for Sonoma Chicken that we love to make. Is there a way to keep the flavor of the cheese filling and the golden brown crust made from frying the chicken rolls—but with less fat? Am I asking the impossible?

A   Not only can we reduce the fat, we can cut a few steps out of the recipe, too! I'm always looking for places to cut the time as well as the fat. In the original recipe the filling was processed at different stages, then chilled until firm and rolled in grated Swiss cheese. I just threw all the filling ingredients into the food processor at the same time, including the reduced-fat Swiss cheese, and spread it directly onto the chicken breast.

I switched to light cream cheese instead of regular for the filling and cut out the tablespoon of butter called for. Instead of dipping the chicken roll in an egg/milk mixture, I dipped it in an egg substitute-milk mixture. After the chicken rolls are rolled in bread crumbs, the original recipe calls for pan-frying the breasts in 4 tablespoons of olive oil and butter. I cut out the butter and was able to fry the chicken rolls in a total of 1 tablespoon of canola oil. I sprayed the tops with canola cooking spray before flipping the rolls over to brown the other side.

The chicken rolls are then baked about 25 minutes (this is a good time to cook the rice). They were crispy on the outside and tender and juicy on the inside—and loaded with flavor. My husband loved this one! And I shaved about 20 minutes of time off, not to mention 18 grams of fat, 90 milligrams cholesterol, and 150 calories per serving.

⤳ SONOMA CHICKEN ⤳

Original recipe contains 647 calories, 28.5 grams fat, and 175 milligrams cholesterol per serving.

Makes 4 servings

> 4 green onions, white and green portion, chopped
> 1/3 cup light cream cheese
> 2 teaspoons dry sherry
> pinch or two of ground nutmeg
> 1/4 cup grated reduced-fat Swiss cheese
> 4 skinless and boneless chicken breasts
> 2 tablespoons Dijon mustard
> 1/2 cup flour
> 1/4 cup egg substitute
> 1/2 cup low-fat milk
> 2/3 cup plain bread crumbs
> 1 tablespoon canola oil
> 3 cups steamed rice

1. Combine green onions, cream cheese, sherry, nutmeg, and Swiss cheese in a mini or regular size food processor (if you don't have a food processor, use a mixer) and process until completely mixed.
2. Place each chicken breast between two sheets of wax paper and pound with meat mallet until thin. Spread top side of each breast with some Dijon mustard. Then spread a fourth of the cream cheese mixture over the center portion of each chicken breast. Roll the chicken breasts up; cover and store in refrigerator until you are ready to proceed.

3. Preheat oven to 350 degrees. Place flour in medium bowl. Whisk egg substitute and milk together; pour into a second medium bowl. Put bread crumbs in a third medium bowl. Make an assembly line in this order: chicken, flour, egg mixture, bread crumbs, large nonstick frying pan.

4. Put oil in the large frying pan; spread evenly with pancake turner. Heat pan over medium heat. Holding each roll carefully, roll chicken carefully in flour, then in egg mixture, then in bread crumbs (coating all around). Place chicken breasts in frying pan. Spray canola cooking spray over the tops of each chicken roll. Once golden on the bottom, flip chicken rolls over to brown other side.

5. Place in baking dish and bake until chicken is cooked throughout (about 25 minutes). Serve each chicken roll with ¾ cup steamed rice.

PER SERVING: 493 calories, 38 g protein, 57 g carbohydrate, 10.5 g fat, 2.5 g saturated fat, 83 mg cholesterol, 1.5 g fiber, 354 mg sodium. Calories from fat: 20 percent.

Dear Recipe Doctor,

My husband and I have gotten in the habit of having chicken pot pie once a week. We buy the gourmet frozen kind, but they have 80 grams of fat or more apiece! I'm willing to make them homemade if it means fewer calories and fat. Do you have a recipe?

Many of those frozen chicken pot pies have more pastry and gravy than they have chicken and vegetables, which is why they add up to so much fat. But I understand that most people may not be too enthusiastic about making a pie crust at the end of a workday either. For one of my past cookbooks I came up with a pot pie that uses a lower fat biscuit crust. But honestly, when you are in the mood for a pastry crusted pot pie, this biscuit alternative is close, but no cigar.

So given that most people are going to prefer pastry, and given that most people don't want to make it from scratch, I called on the Pillsbury doughboy. You can cut the fat in a pot pie simply by eliminating the bottom crust, and use a refrigerated prepared crust to save yourself time.

You can also save yourself time cooking the chicken by using leftover barbecued or oven-fried chicken breast or buying roasted chicken at a supermarket or restaurant. We used 1 teaspoon of canola oil and canola cooking spray to sauté the vegetables in. Instead of making a gravy with light whipping cream or half and half, I used whole milk (which, to a veteran low-fat milk user, looks like cream).

It turned out rich tasting and savory, with a golden, flaky top crust—just like a chicken pie should.

⌐ QUICK CHICKEN POT PIE ⌐

Original recipe contains 598 calories, 39 grams of fat, and 100 milligrams of cholesterol per serving.

Makes 6 servings

> 1 teaspoon canola oil
> 1 large onion, chopped
> 1 cup fresh mushroom slices
> ³/₄ cup sliced celery
> ¹/₂ cup finely chopped red bell pepper
> ¹/₃ cup flour
> 1 teaspoon poultry seasoning
> ¹/₄–¹/₂ teaspoon freshly ground black pepper
> 14¹/₂-ounce can ¹/₃-less-sodium chicken broth (or 1¹/₂ cups broth made from packets or cubes)
> 1 cup whole milk (or 2% low-fat milk)
> 3 skinless chicken breasts, cooked and shredded into bite-sized pieces*
> 1 cup frozen peas
> 1 Pillsbury pie crust (packaged)

1. Spray a deep 9-inch cake pan with canola cooking spray. Preheat oven to 400 degrees.
2. Pour canola oil into large saucepan; bring to medium heat. Add onion, mushrooms, celery, and red pepper; spray top of vegetables with cooking spray. Cook about 5 minutes, stirring frequently. Meanwhile, combine flour, poultry seasoning, and black pepper in 1 cup measure and stir to blend.
3. Once vegetables are just tender, stir in flour mixture, then immediately add broth and milk all at once. Cook and stir until

thickened and bubbly. Turn off heat and stir in chicken and peas. Spoon into prepared pan.

4.   Lay prepared crust over the chicken mixture. You will have extra pie crust around the edges of the pan, which you can handle in three different ways. You can tuck the extra crust under to form a side crust. You can turn edges of crust under and flute to top edges of pan. Or you can trim it off with a knife, cut out small leaves or other shapes from this crust, and use it to decorate the top of the pie.

5.   Place cake pan on a large cookie sheet or jellyroll pan (in case the pot pie bubbles over—I learned this from experience) and bake for about 30 minutes or until the crust is golden brown. Cool about 15 minutes.

Note: Serve this entree with very-low-fat side dishes such as steamed vegetables, mixed bean salad, or fresh fruit salad to bring down the percentage of calories from fat for the meal.

*If you aren't using leftover chicken to make this recipe, combine the chicken broth for this recipe and the raw chicken breasts in a medium saucepan. Bring broth to boil, cover pan, and reduce heat to lowest setting. Cook until chicken is cooked throughout (about 20 to 30 minutes). Remove chicken and shred for recipe, and the chicken broth can still be used in the recipe, too.

PER SERVING: 330 calories, 18 g protein, 32 g carbohydrate, 13.5 g fat, 3.7 g saturated fat, 50 mg cholesterol, 3 g fiber, 257 mg sodium. Calories from fat: 36 percent.

Dear Recipe Doctor,

I made this recipe (penne in cream sauce with sausage) for my family and everyone loved it. We try to trim our fat and salt intake whenever possible. I know that Italian turkey sausage would lower the fat, but what do I do about the cream? Thanks.

If I could eat my way through any country in the world, it would be Italy—hands down. My husband and I even had a family-style Italian dinner at our wedding. Which is even more curious since neither one of us is even one iota Italian. I even made my own pasta and rolled my own ravioli B.K. (Before Kids). So, needless to say, I am always happy to lighten up pasta recipes.

In order to brown the onion and garlic, you will need a little bit of fat. So I kept the 1 tablespoon olive oil called for and I lost the tablespoon of butter. In terms of a lower-fat sausage, you have many choices. The original recipe calls for sweet Italian sausage with the casings removed. You can opt for turkey sausage with a little less fat (such as Jimmy Dean Light) or you can opt for turkey based sausage links with a lot less fat (such as Hillshire Farms turkey polska kielbasa or smoked sausage). Rather than remove the casings, these would probably work better cut into slices at a diagonal.

Instead of light whipping cream, you can use half-and-half and trim the fat by 7.7 grams of fat per serving. Or, you can do what I usually do, and use whole milk (which starts to look a little like cream after years of using 1 percent milk). In order to mimic the thicker texture of cream, I sprinkled in a tablespoon or two of Wondra quick-mixing flour. As far as the Parmesan cheese, I've learned not to mess with the Parmesan from years of lightening recipes. If anything, I just use a little less. In 1½ cups of grated Parmesan cheese there is a total of 45 grams of fat. So for this recipe I used 1 cup instead to bring the fat grams down a little.

PENNE IN CREAM SAUCE WITH SAUSAGE

Original recipe contains 937 calories, 60 grams of fat, and 142 milligrams cholesterol per serving.

Makes 6 servings

1 pound penne pasta
1 tablespoon olive oil
1 medium onion, thinly sliced
3 cloves garlic, minced
1 pound turkey breakfast sausage or large links
²/₃ cup dry white wine
14 ½-ounce can Italian recipe diced tomatoes
1 cup whole milk
6 tablespoons (¼ cup + 2 tablespoons) chopped Italian
   parsley, divided
pepper to taste
1 cup freshly grated Parmesan cheese, divided

1. Start water boiling for pasta. Once the water boils, add the pasta and boil until desired doneness (tender or al dente). Turn off heat. Drain pasta just before the sauce is ready.
2. Melt oil in large heavy skillet over medium-high heat. Add onion and garlic, and sauté until golden brown and tender, about 7 minutes.
3. Cut sausage links into slices at a diagonal. Add sausage slices to skillet and sauté until golden brown, about 5 minutes.
4. Add wine to skillet and boil until almost all liquid evaporates, about 2 minutes.

5. Add can of tomatoes, including liquid, and simmer 3 minutes.
6. Add whole milk and simmer until sauce thickens slightly, about 5 minutes. Stir in 4 tablespoons of parsley. Season with pepper to taste. Remove from heat. (Sauce can be prepared one day ahead; just cover at this point and refrigerate.)
7. Pour sauce over pasta. Add ¾ cup Parmesan and toss to coat. Sprinkle with remaining ¼ cup Parmesan and 2 tablespoons parsley.

PER SERVING: (using Hillshire Farm turkey polska kielbasa for the sausage) 528 calories, 26.5 g protein, 70 g carbohydrate, 13.7 g fat, 1 g saturated fat, 45 mg cholesterol, 3.3 g fiber, 831 mg sodium. Calories from fat: 23 percent.

Q

Dear Recipe Doctor,

I have a recipe for an old family favorite, sausage pie. Can you skim the fat off so we can enjoy it more often?

A

The fact that it is a "pie" means we are dealing with a flaky pie crust, and the Italian sausage means the recipe is filled with even more fat. I must admit I really scaled down this recipe to the bare minimum. I may have acted a little rash—eliminating the pie crust altogether, cutting down to 1 egg, and opting for turkey polska kielbasa sausage—but my family still really enjoyed it.

Instead of pie crust I coated a pie plate generously with canola cooking spray (you could lightly grease with butter or shortening), then coated the inside of the pie plate with seasoned bread crumbs. It ends up making a nice, browned, very thin crust. I used 1 egg blended with ½ cup egg substitute instead of 3 eggs. Because the turkey sausage I used contains only 5 grams of fat per 2-ounce serving, we could get away with using a little more sausage if desired, which helps balance the spinach flavor nicely. And I used part-skim ricotta cheese and mozzarella cheese to complete the filling.

This much leaner sausage pie makes a nice warm dinner or brunch entree.

⇐ SAUSAGE PIE ⇒

Original recipe contains 760 calories, 58 grams fat, 24 grams saturated fat, and 266 milligrams cholesterol per serving.

Makes 4 servings

> ¼ cup seasoned bread crumbs
> 8–12 ounces Hillshire Farm turkey polska kielbasa sausage links
> 1 egg
> ½ cup egg substitute
> ⅓ cup part-skim ricotta cheese
> 10-ounce package spinach, thawed and drained
> ¼ teaspoon salt
> ⅛ teaspoon pepper
> ¼ teaspoon garlic powder
> 4 ounces part-skim mozzarella cheese, shredded
> ⅓ cup shredded Parmesan cheese

1. Preheat oven to 375 degrees. Generously coat bottom and 1 inch up sides of 9-inch pie plate with canola cooking spray. Put bread crumbs in pie plate and tilt plate to evenly distribute the bread crumbs to form a light crust.
2. Remove skin from sausage links and crumble into smaller pieces. Lightly brown sausage pieces in large nonstick frying pan (about 2 minutes).
3. Combine egg, egg substitute, and ricotta cheese in mixing bowl. Blend on medium speed until smooth. Stir in spinach, salt, pepper, garlic powder, mozzarella and Parmesan cheeses, and sausage. Spoon into prepared pie plate. Bake for about 25 minutes or until knife inserted in center comes out clean.

PER SERVING: (using 8 ounces of sausage) 324 calories, 30.5 g protein, 15.5 g carbohydrate, 15 g fat, 8.5 g saturated fat, 120 mg cholesterol, 2 g fiber, 1,060 mg sodium. Calories from fat: 41 percent.

Q

Dear Recipe Doctor,

I am an avid reader of your column, and if you could lighten up this recipe my entire family would be so delighted. My husband's recent heart attack has caused us all to take more notice of the fat in food.

A

This looked like a fancy enchilada casserole recipe—just the type I like to make. Although the list of ingredients is rather foreboding, it is actually easier than it looks. I used skinless, boneless chicken breasts not only to cut some of the fat, but to shave some of the prep time off as well. This way you just place the raw breasts in their seasoned bath to cook and afterwards, the breasts only need to be shredded and they are ready to go.

I cut the 7 tablespoons of butter completely from the sauce. It is there mainly to make a paste with the flour before being blended with the milk and cream. I used the more forgiving Wondra quick-mixing flour and made a paste with some of the milk instead. I used 2 cups of whole milk as called for, but cut out the cup of heavy whipping cream and replaced it with another cup of whole milk (which, to a 1 percent milk drinker, looks like cream). The sauce also calls for 2 beaten eggs; I used 1 egg and added ¼ cup egg substitute.

I cut the amount of sliced olives in the filling in half. Three-fourths of a cup seemed like plenty to me. I used reduced-fat versions of sharp cheddar and Monterey Jack cheese (Cracker Barrel makes a super-reduced-fat sharp cheddar, and Kraft makes a reduced-fat version of both types). I thought about using less cheese than the amount normally called for (3 cups total), but decided most people probably don't like to skimp on their cheese.

Instead of using 2 tablespoons of oil to soften the tortillas in a frying pan, I used a nonstick frying pan and coated the tortillas lightly with canola cooking spray. This way, you are still coating the tortilla surface with oil, you are just making a little go a much longer way.

This yummy dish is served with salsa and sour cream. I served it with Naturally Yours fat-free sour cream (a fat-free sour cream that beat out light sour creams in a taste test) and it worked perfectly.

I know cutting all of the butter and oil seems drastic, but in this recipe the cheese is the most important fat source for flavor. I can't believe how many grams of fat, saturated fat, and cholesterol were shaved off because of these steps. Each serving was saved from almost 300 calories, 38 grams of fat, 21 grams saturated fat, and 125 milligrams of cholesterol! And it still tastes so good—amazing.

Original recipe contains 743 calories, 52.5 grams fat, 28.5 grams saturated fat, and 238 milligrams cholesterol per serving.

Makes 8 large servings

CHICKEN:
6 skinless and boneless chicken breast halves
6 large cloves garlic, minced
¾ teaspoon cayenne pepper
12 ounces Mexican or light beer

SAUCE:
½ cup Wondra quick-mixing flour
1 teaspoon ground cumin
½ teaspoon salt
½ teaspoon pepper
¼ teaspoon ground coriander
¼ teaspoon cayenne pepper
3 cups whole milk
1 egg, beaten
¼ cup egg substitute

FILLING:
¾ cup canned sliced black olives
7-ounce can diced green chilies
1½ cups grated reduced-fat sharp cheddar cheese
1½ cups grated reduced-fat Monterey Jack cheese
½ cup sliced green onions (about 6)
10 corn tortillas

SERVE WITH:
1 cup salsa
1 cup Naturally Yours fat-free sour cream (cowhide container)

1. Arrange chicken in single layer in baking dish. Sprinkle with garlic and cayenne. Pour beer over chicken. Marinate at room temperature 1 hour, turning once.

2. Pour marinade and chicken into heavy skillet and bring to a simmer. Cook over low heat, covered, until tender, about 30 minutes. Drain and cool chicken slightly; cube or shred.

3. Mix flour, cumin, salt, pepper, coriander, and cayenne in a small bowl. Pour milk into heavy medium saucepan. Gradually whisk flour mixture into milk and cook over medium-low heat until sauce thickens, about 5 minutes. Break egg into a 2-cup measure and lightly beat in egg substitute. Blend 1 cup sauce with egg mixture. Whisk mixture back into sauce and cook for 1 minute; do not boil. Adjust seasonings.

4. Preheat oven to 350 degrees. Combine chicken, olives, chilies, cheeses, and onions in large bowl.

5. Heat large heavy nonstick frying pan or skillet over medium heat. Spray one side of a tortilla lightly with canola cooking spray. Place spray side down into heated pan. Spray top lightly with canola cooking spray. After about 5 seconds, flip tortilla over to soften other side (about 5 seconds). Remove tortilla to cutting board and repeat with the rest of the tortillas. When cool, cut tortillas in half.

6. Line bottom of 9 x 13-inch baking dish with half of the tortilla halves. Cover with half of the chicken mixture. Pour half of the sauce over the chicken. Repeat layers, ending with sauce. Bake for 30 minutes or until bubbly. Cool 5 minutes and cut into squares. Serve with sour cream and salsa.

PER SERVING: 451 calories, 41 g protein, 38 g carbohydrate, 14.5 g fat, 7 g saturated fat, 113 mg cholesterol, 3 g fiber, 736 mg sodium. Calories from fat: 29 percent.

Q

Dear Recipe Doctor,

One of our favorite weeknight dinners is a skillet chicken fricassee that calls for butter, cream, mushrooms, and celery. Is there a way that we can make this lower fat and still have fork tender chicken?

A

Can you say Crock-Pot? After reading this letter I had a brainstorm. Why not put all the ingredients in the Crock-Pot and after a long day's work come home to piping hot chicken with vegetables in a savory gravy? This way the chicken breast is tender and you eliminate the need for any butter for frying. You make the creamy gravy with condensed cream of chicken soup, some broth or milk, and some flour.

My husband and I both had a bad cold when I acted on my brainstorm, but the chicken *still* tasted terrific! I know traditional chicken fricassee is served with noodles, but we served ours over steamed rice and it worked very well too. I added baby carrots into the equation to beef up the vegetables in this dish and I tripled the amount of celery and onion. I also added artichoke hearts (in place of mushrooms) just because it sounded good, and I threw in a couple teaspoons of minced garlic for good measure. After all these ingredient changes, and converting the recipe to a Crock-Pot, it may not be exactly like the chicken fricassee you've had before, but it sure is easy to fix and it sure is delicious.

☞ SLOW-COOKER CHICKEN FRICASSEE ☜

This tastes great served over steamed rice or cooked noodles.

Original recipe contains 638 calories, 44 grams fat, 17 grams saturated fat, and 172 milligrams cholesterol per serving.

Makes 4 servings

> 10 ¾-ounce can Campbell's 98% fat free cream of chicken condensed soup
> 6 ½-ounce jar marinated artichoke hearts, well drained, or 1 cup sliced mushrooms
> 2 large celery stalks, sliced at a diagonal
> 1 ½ cups baby carrots
> 1 onion, quartered then sliced
> 1–2 teaspoons minced garlic (optional)
> pinch or two of paprika (optional)
> 1 tablespoon Wondra flour
> ⅓ cup double strength (or regular) chicken broth or whole or low-fat milk
> 4 boneless and skinless chicken breasts

1. Combine soup, artichoke hearts (or mushrooms), celery, carrots, onion, garlic, and paprika in the slow cooker.
2. Blend flour with chicken broth or milk in 1-cup measure. Add to Crock-Pot and stir all the ingredients together. Lay chicken breasts on top and gently stir mixture to coat chicken breasts well. Cover, turn Crock-Pot to low, and cook about 8–10 hours (or on high for 4 hours) or until chicken is tender.
3. Serve over steamed rice or cooked noodles if desired.

PER SERVING: 278 calories, 33 g protein, 24 g carbohydrate, 6 g fat, 2 g saturated fat, 79 mg cholesterol, 5 g fiber, 890 mg sodium. Calories from fat: 19 percent. PER SERVING (including ¾ cup rice): 478 calories, 37 g protein, 67 g carbohydrate, 6 g fat, 2 g saturated fat, 79 mg cholesterol, 5.5 g fiber, 895 mg sodium. Calories from fat: 11 percent.

The Recipe Doctor column is all about me lightening up recipes that you send me—and that's what I love most about doing this column. But every now and then I am inspired to create my own recipes, which I call "Elaine Originals."

Well, the other day I just threw a few things together and this really yummy lunch or dinner salad was born. Just to show you how great this salad is on a hot summer night, we've had it twice in the past two weeks. We will throw extra chicken breasts on the barbecue just so we can have this salad the next day. Even though there really isn't anything terribly fancy about it, the natural flavors work really well together.

The only wild card in the recipe is the mango. The mango season peaks around June but runs through August, which works out well with the garden tomato season. Although it won't be quite as exotic, on the off-season, fresh, frozen, or canned peaches can be used in place of the mango.

➣ CHICKEN-MANGO-AVOCADO SALAD ➣

Makes 4 servings

4 cooked boneless and skinless chicken breasts,
   roasted or barbecued (leftover chicken from the night
   before works great)
1 mango
$\frac{1}{2}$ large avocado, peeled and pitted
$\frac{1}{4}$ cup finely chopped green onions
$1\frac{1}{4}$ cups chopped vine-ripened tomato (any type)

DRESSING:
1 tablespoon mayonnaise*
2 tablespoons fat-free sour cream
2 tablespoons orange juice
1 teaspoon finely chopped orange zest (optional)
freshly ground black pepper to taste

1. Cut cooled cooked chicken into bite-sized pieces. Cut mango into bite-sized pieces. Cut avocado into bite-sized pieces. Combine chicken, mango, and avocado in medium serving bowl. Stir in green onions and tomatoes.
2. In a small bowl, blend dressing ingredients well. Drizzle over salad ingredients and stir to blend. Chill until served.

*Most people truly prefer the taste of real mayonnaise, so I use part mayonnaise, part fat-free sour cream, and part orange juice in this dressing—and it tastes terrific. If you like light or fat-free mayonnaise, go ahead and use it. If you use light mayonnaise instead of the regular, a serving will contain 254 calories, 8.5 grams fat, and 73 mg cholesterol.

PER SERVING: 267 calories, 29 g protein, 16 g carbohydrate, 10 g fat, 1.5 g saturated fat, 75 mg cholesterol, 3.3 g fiber, 99 mg sodium. Calories from fat: 34 percent.

ENTREES

BEEF & PORK

"NO BOIL" TRADITIONAL LASAGNA

TACO SALAD

MOMMA'S SUNDAY PORK CHOPS

THE NOT-SO-CLASSIC CHEESEBURGER

4-CAN BEEF & BEAN ENCHILADAS

SKIERS' STEAKS (TOM KENNEDY'S STEAKS)

PORK CHIMICHANGAS (OVEN FRIED)

GREEN CHILI

CAJUN MEAT LOAF

Q

Dear Recipe Doctor,

We make lasagna almost every week. Can you make it lighter and easier to make? (I hate boiling the noodles.) The whole family looks forward to your column!

A

I know what you mean about the noodles. I made up a "no boil" vegetable lasagna recipe years ago. I made a few adjustments to this recipe to come up with a more traditional meat lasagna that I hope your family will love.

Don't worry if the lasagna seems a bit watery before you bake it. The extra water provides the liquid that softens the uncooked noodles. I used a low-fat bottled marinara sauce and bought preshredded part-skim mozzarella and Parmesan cheese to cut down the prep time.

I trimmed the fat everywhere I could but I tried not to go too far. I still maintained some fat so the lasagna would taste as good as the original. For example, I used part-skim ricotta cheese, part-skim mozzarella, and ground sirloin (and reduced the amount down to ³⁄₄ pound). I also used egg substitute in the cheese fillings, used a lower-fat (but great-tasting bottled tomato and basil spaghetti sauce), and reduced the Parmesan cheese a smidgen. The calories went down from 510 to 346 per serving and the fat grams went from 28 grams to 12 per serving. The cholesterol went from 123 milligrams to 38 per serving.

This is one of those dinners that you look forward to eating as leftovers the next day.

excellent (handwritten)

"NO BOIL" TRADITIONAL LASAGNA

This recipe makes about 8 servings, so if there are only two of you, freeze a couple of portions in microwave-safe containers to make your own great-tasting (and healthful) frozen entree.

Original recipe contains 510 calories, 28 grams fat, 13.5 grams saturated fat, and 123 milligrams cholesterol per serving.

Makes 8 servings

> ¾ pound ground sirloin (or very lean ground beef)
> 26-ounce jar marinara (or spaghetti) sauce
> 14 ½-ounce can vegetable or chicken broth
> 15-ounce container part-skim or low-fat ricotta cheese
> 1 cup grated part-skim mozzarella cheese, divided
> 5 tablespoons grated Parmesan cheese, divided
> 3 tablespoons chopped fresh parsley or 1 tablespoon dried parsley
> 3 tablespoons chopped fresh basil leaves (optional)
> ¼ cup egg substitute
> ½ teaspoon salt (optional)
> ¼ teaspoon pepper
> 9 wide lasagna noodles (uncooked), about 10 ounces

1. Preheat oven to 350 degrees. In large nonstick saucepan, brown ground sirloin well. Stir in marinara sauce and broth and set aside.
2. In medium bowl, combine ricotta, ¾ cup mozzarella, 3 table-spoons Parmesan cheese, parsley, basil, egg substitute, salt, and pepper.

3. In 13 x 9-inch baking dish, layer 1½ cups meat sauce, then 3 strips of uncooked noodles. Dot the noodles with ⅓ of the cheese mixture. Cover the cheese with 1½ cups meat sauce and 3 more strips of noodles. Dot the noodles with another third of the cheese mixture. Top the cheese with 1½ cups meat sauce and the last 3 noodles. Dot the noodles with the remaining cheese mixture and meat sauce. Sprinkle the remaining 2 tablespoons Parmesan and ¼ cup mozzarella over the top.

4. Spray one side of a piece of foil with canola cooking spray (so the cheese doesn't stick to the foil) and cover the lasagna tightly with the foil. Bake for 35 minutes. Uncover the lasagna and bake 15 more minutes. Let stand 10 minutes before cutting.

PER SERVING: 346 calories, 24 g protein, 34.5 g carbohydrate, 12 g fat, 6 g saturated fat, 38 mg cholesterol, 3 g fiber, 935 mg sodium. Calories from fat: 31 percent.

Q

Dear Recipe Doctor,

My family enjoys taco salad as a cool, light dinner. Do you have a lower-fat version?

A

I've been holding on to this letter for months now just waiting for the warmer weather to arrive. Taco salad can be a refreshing dinner or lunch in the warmer months. It is also a popular potluck type of dish.

Not only does this taco salad recipe have less fat; it's got a nice dose of fiber. I added some canned kidney beans into the mix. I did the obvious and used ground sirloin instead of regular and also used reduced-fat cheddar cheese instead of regular (and used less). I found some very crispy and tasty reduced-fat tortilla chips in my supermarket—those came in handy.

For the dressing I simply stirred 2 tablespoons of canola mayonnaise with ½ cup fat-free sour cream and ¼ cup mild salsa instead of mixing the salsa with a cup of mayonnaise. If you brown the beef and mix the dressing ahead of time (just store them in the refrigerator until needed) you can whip this main-dish salad up in about 15 minutes when you get home from work.

⇒ TACO SALAD ⇐

Original recipe contains 652 calories, 47 grams fat, 17 grams saturated fat, and 98 milligrams cholesterol per serving.

Makes 6 servings

1 pound ground sirloin (or very lean ground beef)
½ envelope Lawry's taco seasoning
1½ cups grated reduced-fat sharp cheddar cheese
1 head iceberg lettuce, shredded (about 6 cups)
3 tomatoes, diced
1 small sweet or mild onion, chopped
15-ounce can lower-sodium kidney beans, drained and rinsed
Sliced black olives (optional)
6 ounces reduced-fat tortilla chips (crumble chips lightly
   with hands)

DRESSING:
2 tablespoons canola mayonnaise (or similar)
½ cup fat-free or light sour cream
½ cup mild salsa

1. Brown meat with taco seasoning until cooked throughout and nicely browned. Let cool.
2. In a large bowl, toss seasoned beef with cheese, lettuce, tomatoes, onion, and beans. Add sliced olives if desired.
3. In small bowl, blend dressing ingredients. Mix until smooth. Add crumbled chips and dressing to salad right before serving.

PER SERVING: 461 calories, 28.5 g protein, 41 g carbohydrate, 20 g fat, 6.5 g saturated fat, 40 mg cholesterol, 8.5 g fiber, 580 mg sodium. Calories from fat: 39 percent.

Dear Recipe Doctor,

Here is my momma's age-old recipe for Sunday pork chops. It has always been a favorite of mine. Please help bring the recipe into the twenty-first century. I've tried switching to canola oil, but it still seems greasy. Thanks.

Sunday pork chops—doesn't that conjure up all sorts of delightful images (and smells)? Growing up my family didn't really have a "Sunday" anything, so I'm always happy to hear somebody did!

This reader was definitely started in the right direction—switching to canola oil. But we are going to use less of it than the original recipe calls for. They call for 2 tablespoons of oil in the mixture the apple slices are bathed in and it calls for oil to fry the seasoned pork chops in. I trimmed it back to 1 teaspoon for the apple bath and 1 teaspoon for browning the chops. You can also use center cut pork chops, trimmed of visible fat, to keep this entree lean and mean.

In place of the oil I took out of the apple bath, I added a tablespoon of maple syrup (always a flavor enhancer, especially when it comes to apples). If you don't want a strong maple flavor use a tablespoon of reduced-calorie pancake syrup. I also doubled the lemon juice to 1 teaspoon to add a bit of zip to the apple bath.

Instead of frying the pork chops with even more oil, I used a thick nonstick frying pan or skillet with just a hint of oil to coat the surface (1 teaspoon). I used canola cooking spray to lightly coat the top of the pork chops. These pork chops would grace my table any day of the week. We loved them at my house.

MOMMA'S SUNDAY PORK CHOPS

Original recipe contains 338 calories, 18 grams fat, and 5 grams saturated fat per serving.

Makes 5 servings

> $\frac{1}{2}$ cup flour
> 1 teaspoon coriander, divided
> $\frac{1}{4}$ teaspoon salt
> $\frac{1}{4}$ teaspoon pepper
> 1 tablespoon vanilla
> 2 teaspoons canola oil, divided
> 1 tablespoon maple syrup
> $\frac{1}{2}$ teaspoon ground cinnamon
> 1 teaspoon lemon juice
> 2 apples with peel, thinly sliced
> 5 1-inch thick center cut pork chops, trimmed of fat, and
>   split to the bone (to make a pocket)

1. Preheat oven to 350 degrees. In shallow bowl, mix together flour, $\frac{1}{2}$ teaspoon coriander, salt, and pepper. Set aside.
2. Blend vanilla, 1 teaspoon canola oil, maple syrup, cinnamon, lemon juice, and remaining $\frac{1}{2}$ teaspoon coriander in small bowl. Add apple slices and let them sit a minute or two. Arrange about 6 slices of apple in the split of each pork chop. Spoon a teaspoon of liquid (if any in the bottom of the bowl) over the apples in the middle of each pork chop.

3. Coat the outside of the chops well with the seasoned flour. Heat a thick nonstick skillet or frying pan over medium heat. Add remaining teaspoon of canola oil and spread out over bottom of pan. Add pork chops and coat tops with canola cooking spray. When underside is nicely browned, flip chops over to brown other side. Put chops in an ovenproof dish, cover, and bake for 20 minutes. Remove foil and continue baking until cooked through (about 10 more minutes).

PER SERVING: 267 calories, 23 g protein, 25.5 g carbohydrate, 8 g fat, 2 g saturated fat, 58 mg cholesterol, 2 g fiber, 150 mg sodium. Calories from fat: 25 percent.

Q

Dear Recipe Doctor,

My family has been trying to eat healthier these days (your column sure is a lifesaver), but our one problem is cheese-burgers. I thought I would write you, especially with summer arriving. We've tried ground turkey, but it just isn't doing it for us. Can you help us?

A

Some people are quite happy with turkey burgers, but others wouldn't touch them with a 10-foot spatula. To me, they're fine, but they are not hamburgers—they're turkey burgers. They look and taste completely different. Ground turkey is sometimes just as high in fat as ground round (you have to check the label). If you buy a ground turkey breast, it is most definitely going to be very low fat. But it is also most definitely going to be very dry (unless you make a mixture of ground turkey breast and moistening ingredients such as barbecue sauce—but then that's getting away from the traditional burger, isn't it). So what's a burger-loving family to do?

A hamburger is only as good as the beef that makes the burger. I can tell you to buy extra lean ground beef at the supermarket, but the truth is, I can't guarantee you will be happy with that meat. Every store makes a different extra lean ground beef. Some of the lean ground beef I've tried has had unidentified chewy things in it—which, in a word, is simply yucky! So, the first trick is finding a good extra lean ground beef.

If you have an old-fashioned meat market near you, you could ask them to grind up a sirloin steak for you (making "ground sirloin"). The supermarket near my house has a nice meat counter and I really like their "diet super lean" ground beef, which is about 9 percent fat.

All I do when I make hamburgers is use one of those patty presses to make ¼-pound burgers. Then I sprinkle freshly ground pepper and garlic salt over the top. From here you could pan-fry (use canola cooking spray to lubricate the pan), broil, or barbecue (spray the grill with canola cooking spray before putting the burgers on and they won't stick). Just be forewarned these leaner burgers will cook faster and dry out a little quicker than the ones you are used to. So just keep a closer eye on them.

Top them with Kraft 2 percent milk singles if you want (adding only 3 grams fat per slice). Assemble your burger with lettuce, fresh tomato, sliced onions, catsup, mustard, or barbecue sauce and it will stay a lower-fat option. If you just have to have mayonnaise, spread it real thin. A level tablespoon will add 11 grams of fat to the hamburger equation.

THE NOT-SO-CLASSIC CHEESEBURGER

A traditional cheeseburger with mayonnaise contains approximately 620 calories, 38 grams fat, 15 grams saturated fat, and 110 milligrams cholesterol per serving.

Makes 4 servings

> 1 pound super lean (6–9 percent fat) ground beef or freshly made ground sirloin
> freshly ground black pepper, to taste
> 1/2 teaspoon garlic salt, to taste
> 4 slices reduced-fat cheese (Kraft 2 percent milk singles)
> 4 bakery hamburger buns
> tomato and onion slices
> lettuce leaves
> mustard, barbecue sauce, or catsup (optional)

1. Divide the beef into 4 equal portions. Use a patty press to make 4 burgers. Sprinkle pepper and garlic salt over the top.
2. Pan-fry, broil, or barbecue burgers using canola cooking spray to keep it from sticking to pan or grill. When almost cooked throughout, place cheese slices on top, and finish cooking 30 to 60 seconds. Remove burgers from heat to serving plate. Cover plate with a large dome saucepan lid (or foil) to keep burgers warm and moist if you want.
3. Dress up your burger on the bun with lettuce, tomato, onion, mustard, barbecue sauce, and catsup, as desired.

PER SERVING: 397 calories, 35.5 g protein, 34.5 g carbohydrate, 13 g fat, 5 g saturated fat, 86 mg cholesterol, 2.5 g fiber, 767 mg sodium. Calories from fat: 29 percent.

Dear Recipe Doctor,

We love beef enchiladas. We order them in restaurants all the time. I was wondering if you had a quick and healthy version for making them at home?

Somehow I end up ordering chicken enchiladas at restaurants, but I do love making the following beef enchilada recipe at home. I call it 4-Can Beef & Bean Enchiladas because you use 4 cans to make them. I know that probably doesn't make it sound very appetizing, but hopefully it makes it sound easy to make—because it is. You don't even have to heat the tortillas and roll up anything—it's made like a layered casserole.

To make the beef enchiladas score higher on the nutrition index, I reduced the amount of beef a little and added some beans, always a good thing nutrition-wise. I also added some Mexican-style stewed tomatoes for a good dose of nutrients and phytochemicals.

I used a super lean ground beef and doubled the onion and garlic. To trim down the calories further, the tortillas weren't fried in oil, and reduced-fat versions of sharp cheddar and Monterey Jack cheese were used.

4-CAN BEEF & BEAN ENCHILADAS

Original recipe contains 517 calories, 15 g saturated fat, 33.5 g fat, and 100 mg cholesterol per serving.

Makes 8 servings

1 onion, chopped
1 pound super lean ground beef or ground sirloin
2 teaspoons minced garlic
15-ounce can pinquitos, pinto beans, or similar beans
15-ounce can Mexican-style stewed tomatoes, undrained
4-ounce can diced green chilies (mild, medium, or hot, according to preference)
10-ounce can enchilada sauce
12 corn tortillas
2 cups grated reduced-fat sharp cheddar and reduced-fat Monterey Jack cheese, mixed

1. Preheat oven to 350 degrees. Coat a 13 x 9-inch baking pan with canola cooking spray; set aside. Coat large nonstick saucepan generously with canola cooking spray. Add onion and beef and brown over medium heat, stirring and crumbling beef often.
2. Once beef has browned, add garlic, beans, tomatoes, chilies, and enchilada sauce. Stir until sauce is heated through.
3. Arrange 4 tortillas to cover the bottom of the pan (they will overlap some). Cover with ⅓ of meat mixture.
4. Repeat layers of corn tortillas and beef mixture twice. Top with grated cheese. Cover pan with foil; bake for 30 minutes.

PER SERVING: 383 calories, 24.5 g protein, 37.5 g carbohydrate, 15.5 g fat, 8 g saturated fat, 47 mg cholesterol, 6 g fiber, 620 mg sodium. Calories from fat: 36 percent.

Q

Dear Recipe Doctor,

We love to make these glorified hamburgers. Some call them Tom Kennedy's Steaks and some call them Skiers' Steaks. We love them because they are so moist and flavorful. Can you keep it moist and full of flavor and reduce the saturated fat a bit?

A

Anything called Skiers' Steaks has got to be worth a try. You can cook these patties over the barbecue (which is what I decided to do), or follow the directions for broiling.

I started out with some high-quality super lean ground beef, which is usually a ground sirloin. I switched to reduced-fat sharp cheddar cheese instead of regular. I used 2 tablespoons of egg substitute to replace the egg yolk and it seemed to do the job just as well. I added the onion, chopped tomatoes, green pepper, and stuffed green olives as called for.

After adding all the ingredients to the ground sirloin, I didn't know what to expect. But the patties held together very well and they were so juicy and tasty. We loved them.

SKIERS' STEAKS (TOM KENNEDY'S STEAKS)

Original recipe contains 445 calories, 33 grams fat, 15.5 grams saturated fat, and 166 milligrams cholesterol per serving.

Makes 4 servings

> 1 pound super lean ground beef (ground sirloin)
> 1 cup finely shredded reduced-fat sharp cheddar cheese
> 2 tablespoons egg substitute
> ³/₄ cup finely chopped onion
> ³/₄ cup seeded and finely chopped tomatoes
> ¹/₃ cup finely chopped green sweet pepper
> 2 tablespoons minced stuffed green olives

1. In a large bowl, combine all ingredients. Blend the ingredients well and shape the mixture into 4 patties about 4 ¹/₂ inches in diameter.
2. To broil: place the patties on the unheated rack of a broiler pan that has been coated with canola cooking spray. Broil the patties 3 to 4 inches from the heat for 13 to 15 minutes (turning patties after 6 or 7 minutes) or until cooked throughout.
3. To grill: spray grill with canola cooking spray. Grill patties directly over medium coals for 13 to 15 minutes (turning patties after 6 or 7 minutes) or until cooked throughout.

Serving suggestion: Serve steaks with grilled vegetables and grilled slices of French bread.

PER SERVING (NOT including bread or vegetables): 276 calories, 29 g protein, 6 g carbohydrate, 14.5 g fat, 7 g saturated fat, 50 mg cholesterol, 1 g fiber, 385 mg sodium. Calories from fat: 49 percent.

Q

Dear Recipe Doctor,

A Mexican restaurant near my house makes these wonderful deep-fried pork chimichangas. Is there a way to make them without frying them?

A

Yes and no. Yes, you can oven-fry them instead of deep-frying them and they will still taste delicious. But no, they probably won't be quite as crispy as the deep-fried version. Years ago I worked out a recipe for oven-fried pork chimichangas that I really liked.

I used pork tenderloin for the pork filling and added some canned vegetarian or fat-free refried beans to boost the fiber and make the pork go farther. I used a tablespoon of canola oil for browning the pork and brushed the tortillas with canola oil (or melted canola margarine) before filling and baking the chimichangas.

☞ PORK CHIMICHANGAS (OVEN FRIED) ☜

Original recipe contains 842 calories, 41 grams fat, 11 grams saturated fat, and 83 milligrams cholesterol per serving.

Makes 5 servings (2 chimichangas each)

1½ pounds pork tenderloin (about 2 tenderloins), cut into
    1-inch chunks
1 tablespoon canola oil
3 cups hot beef broth
2 tablespoons distilled white vinegar
⅓ cup finely chopped moderate chili peppers (such as Pasilla)
    or ¼ cup canned chili peppers
2 cloves garlic, minced
1 teaspoon dried oregano, crumbled
½ teaspoon ground cumin
¼ cup chopped green onion
10 home-style flour tortillas
1 tablespoon canola margarine, melted, or canola oil
1¼ cups canned vegetarian or fat-free refried beans
salsa and light or fat-free sour cream (optional)

1. Coat bottom of a large nonstick saucepan or frying pan with a tablespoon of canola oil, and brown pork pieces on all sides over medium heat (about 8 minutes). Add hot broth, scraping the bottom of pan to loosen browned bits. Bring to a boil, then reduce heat to low. Cover and simmer until meat is tender (about 30 to 40 minutes).
2. Preheat oven to 450 degrees. Uncover the pan, raise heat to high, and boil until over half of the liquid has evaporated (8 to 10 minutes). Add the vinegar, chilies, garlic, oregano, cumin,

and green onion. Stir well and continue cooking until almost all of the water has evaporated (3 to 5 minutes more). Let the pork cool completely. Shred the pork with your fingers.

3. Heat each tortilla in a nonstick frying pan, then flip over to heat other side and brush the top lightly with melted canola margarine or canola oil. Quickly flip greased side of tortilla into a 9 x 13-inch baking pan (greased side down).

4. Spread 2 tablespoons of beans in the middle of tortilla. Add about ¼ cup of pork mixture. Fold in sides, overlapping them, then fold over the ends to rest atop the seam. Place seam side down on baking sheet. Repeat with remaining nine tortillas.

5. Bake until nicely browned (about 12 to 15 minutes). If desired, serve with salsa and/or sour cream.

PER SERVING: 530 calories, 40 g protein, 54.5 g carbohydrate, 17 g fat, 2 g saturated fat, 79 mg cholesterol, 4.5 g fiber, 864 mg sodium. Calories from fat: 29 percent.

Q   *Dear Recipe Doctor,*

I've heard a lot about something called green chili. I was wondering if you had a healthful version of this southwestern favorite.

A   The original recipe for this green chili came from the *Denver Post*. But I'm sure there are different renditions in various southwestern cookbooks.

To make this lower in fat, I cut down on the oil called for and switched to canola oil. I used the leanest cut of pork I know of (which may not be the cheapest), the pork tenderloin.

The meat comes out nice and tender and the roasted peppers swimming in the tomato-based chili add a beautiful color and wonderful flavor. If you like it hot, add a little more pepper, a few more chilies, and a dash or two more of Tabasco.

≈ GREEN CHILI ≈

Original recipe contains about 630 calories, 35 grams fat, and 180 milligrams cholesterol per serving.

Makes 4 large servings

> 6 to 8 Anaheim chilies, quartered and seeded
> 1 tablespoon canola oil
> 1¹/₂ pounds pork tenderloin, cut into small cubes
> 1 large onion, coarsely chopped
> 2 large cloves garlic, minced
> ¹/₂ teaspoon salt, or to taste
> ¹/₂ teaspoon freshly ground pepper, or to taste
> 16-ounce can whole peeled tomatoes, drained and chopped,
>   reserve juice
> 12 ounces beer (nonalcoholic works well)
> 2 tablespoons all-purpose flour
> ¹/₃ cup water
> flour tortillas (optional)

1. Preheat oven to 450 degrees. Place chili peppers on a cookie sheet. Roast in oven for about 30 minutes, or until charred. Let cool slightly, then chop.
2. Meanwhile, heat oil in a large nonstick skillet or saucepan over medium heat. Add the pork, onion, garlic, salt, and pepper, and sauté until the pork browns, stirring occasionally. Add the tomatoes and reserved juice, the beer, and chopped chilies. Stir well, cover the pan, reduce the heat, and simmer for 45 minutes.
3. Blend the flour with water and stir until smooth. Add to the chili and stir until well blended. Cover and simmer for an additional 15 minutes. Serve with tortillas if desired.

PER SERVING: 350 calories, 44 g protein, 21 g carbohydrate, 10 g fat, 2 g saturated fat, 100 mg cholesterol, 4 g fiber, 460 mg sodium. Calories from fat: 26 percent.

Q *Dear Recipe Doctor,*

I make the Cajun Meat Loaf in Chef Paul Prudhomme's book every now and then. It tastes great but contains your usual high-fat, high-calorie ingredients. Is there something you can do?

A Thank goodness we're just basically chopping, mixing, and molding here because the list of twenty-some-odd ingredients looks time-prohibitive to say the least. And I have to admit, cajun anything usually scares me off, being the hot spice wimp that I am. But I tamed this version down a bit and gave you some options should you want to turn up the heat.

The original recipe calls for ground pork and ground beef. I used the leaner choice, ground sirloin, for the beef and made my own ground pork in a food processor using pork tenderloin or trimmed pork cutlets. Many butchers and chefs would argue that when you go with a leaner ground meat, you are giving up flavor and tenderness. I'm sure that is true. But if you keep the ground meat mixture well flavored and moistened with other ingredients, you are less likely to notice.

I cut the butter way back to a tablespoon, adding beer in its place, and switched to evaporated skim milk or fat free half and half instead of cream. Since the 2 eggs called for are acting mostly as a binder and not an emulsifier, I was able to get away with ½ cup egg substitute. This turned out to be a spicy meat loaf that even a spice wimp could love.

⇒ CAJUN MEAT LOAF ⇐

Original recipe contains 470 calories, 34 grams fat, and 150 milligrams cholesterol per serving.

Makes 8 servings

SEASONING MIX:
2 bay leaves
1 teaspoon salt (optional)
$1/2$–1 teaspoon cayenne pepper
$1/2$–1 teaspoon freshly ground pepper
$1/4$–$1/2$ teaspoon white pepper
$1/2$ teaspoon ground cumin
$1/2$ teaspoon ground or grated nutmeg

MEAT MIXTURE:
1 tablespoon canola margarine or butter
$1/4$ cup nonalcoholic beer
$3/4$ cup finely chopped onions
$1/2$ cup finely chopped celery
$1/2$ cup finely chopped green bell peppers
$1/4$ cup finely chopped green onions
4 cloves garlic, minced or pressed
1 tablespoon Tabasco sauce
2–3 teaspoons Worcestershire sauce
$1/2$ cup evaporated skimmed milk
$1/2$ cup catsup
$1^1/2$ pounds ground sirloin (or similar)
$1/2$ pounds pork tenderloin (or lean boneless pork chips), trimmed of any visible fat and ground by a butcher or in a food processor
$1/2$ cup egg substitute
1 cup very fine dry bread crumbs

1. Combine the seasoning mix ingredients in a small bowl and set aside.
2. Melt butter in large nonstick saucepan over medium-low heat. Add the beer, onions, celery, bell peppers, green onions, garlic, Tabasco, Worcestershire, and seasoning mix, and sauté until the mixture starts sticking to the bottom of the pan (about 5 minutes), stirring frequently. Stir in the milk and catsup and continue cooking for about 2 minutes, stirring occasionally. Remove from heat and let cool to room temperature.
3. Preheat the oven to 350 degrees. Coat two 9 x 9-inch loaf pans or a 6 x 12-inch baking pan with canola cooking spray.
4. Place the beef and pork in a large bowl and add the egg substitute, cooked vegetable mixture (remove the bay leaves), and bread crumbs. Mix with your hands to thoroughly combine. Divide in half and shape into loaves in the two prepared loaf pans.
5. Bake uncovered for 25 minutes. Increase oven temperature to 400 degrees and cook until a cut slice looks done (about 25 minutes more).

PER SERVING: 296 calories, 32 g protein, 18.5 g carbohydrate, 10 g fat, 3 g saturated fat, 84 mg cholesterol, 695 mg sodium. Calories from fat: 32 percent.

ENTREES

SEAFOOD

CRAB QUESADILLAS

CRAB CAKES
WITH QUICK JALAPEÑO-LIME MAYONNAISE

PRAWNS WITH GLAZED WALNUTS
(OR PECANS)

SIMPLE SALMON PASTA SALAD

CRAB AND SHRIMP SALAD

Q

Dear Recipe Doctor,

I ate a crab quesadilla in a restaurant recently and just loved it! Can you come up with a quick, lighter version I can make at home?

A

What a great idea! Love crab. Love quesadillas. Love quick dinner ideas. I looked at a couple of recipes and pulled what I liked about each to make one (I hope) new and improved version.

The original recipes called for lots of butter and oil. I cut out the butter completely and opted for 2 teaspoons of canola oil to sauté the garlic and onion. A wonderful crab mixture is made with crab, sautéed vegetables, jalapeños (you can buy "tamed" jalapeños in jars at most supermarkets), salt, and cilantro all blended together with a little mayonnaise and sour cream.

Did I use real mayonnaise? You bet I did (have you tasted the low-fat and fat-free alternatives?). I just used a lot less. I used a tablespoon of Best Foods mayonnaise (instead of ¼ cup) and a few tablespoons of my favorite fat-free sour cream (Naturally Yours brand).

I used Kraft reduced-fat Monterey Jack cheese to finish off the quesadillas. You can choose whatever flour tortillas you like; there are all sorts available—lard-free, light, whole wheat, or the thick home-style type (which is my favorite).

Here's the kicker. I tried these lighter quesadillas using imitation crab, thinking if I could get them to taste good with imitation crab, imagine how great they would taste with the real thing! (That, and I was too cheap to buy fresh crab.) My husband and I thought the quesadillas had a great flavor. I doubled the garlic and cilantro—that may have helped. They even tasted great the next day as leftovers.

CRAB QUESADILLAS

Original recipe contains 390 calories, 25 grams fat, 6 grams saturated fat, and 73 milligrams cholesterol per serving.

Makes about 6 quesadillas

2 teaspoons canola oil
1 teaspoon minced garlic
½ medium onion, chopped
1–2 jalapeño peppers, stemmed, seeded, and finely diced
  (or chop 2 "tamed" bottled jalapeños)
⅔ pound crabmeat, washed (imitation crab can be
  substituted) and shredded into bite-sized pieces with
  hands or a knife
1 tablespoon mayonnaise
3 tablespoons fat-free sour cream
salt to taste
2 tablespoons minced fresh cilantro
6–8 flour tortillas
4 ounces reduced-fat Monterey Jack cheese, shredded
salsa, fat-free sour cream, and avocado/guacamole (optional)

1. Heat oil in medium nonstick frying pan. Add garlic and onion and sauté over moderate heat until translucent (about 2 minutes). Remove mixture to medium bowl and stir in jalapeño, crab, mayonnaise, sour cream, salt, and cilantro; blend well.
2. Heat nonstick skillet or frying pan over medium heat for about 2 minutes. Place 1 tortilla in the skillet and let soften 30 seconds. Spray top with canola cooking spray, then flip over.

Sprinkle some cheese over the tortilla, then spoon about $\frac{1}{3}$ cup of crab mixture evenly over half of tortilla. When underside is lightly browned, fold the half without the crab mixture over and remove to serving plate.

3. Repeat step #2 with remaining tortillas, cheese, and crab mixture.
4. Serve with salsa, sour cream, and/or avocado if desired.

PER SERVING: 264 calories, 19 g protein, 23 g carbohydrate, 10 g fat, 3 g saturated fat, 62 mg cholesterol, 1 g fiber, 450 mg sodium. Calories from fat: 34 percent.

Q *Dear Recipe Doctor,*

While my family was all gathered together this past Christmas we got to wondering if you could lighten up one of our favorite recipes—the crab cake recipe in Lee Bailey's California Wine Country Cooking *(Clarkson Potter, 1991). We would appreciate it if you would try. They are great, but...*

A I wish this letter came with a pound of crab, because last I checked, crabmeat was $20 a pound! But I decided to lighten up the poor man's version of crab cakes (using shredded imitation crabmeat at $3 a pound).

The recipe started by cooking onions and celery in 2 tablespoons of butter and 2 tablespoons of peanut oil—I used 1 tablespoon of canola, which worked just fine.

The crabmeat mixture called for a beaten egg; I opted for ¼ cup of egg substitute. But if you insist on using a real egg here, go ahead, the nutritional damage won't be prohibitive. Then you get to the breading and frying part of the recipe, calling for another 4 tablespoons of peanut oil and 3 tablespoons of butter! Again, I used 1 measly tablespoon of canola oil, armed with a can of canola cooking spray just in case I needed a little extra nonstick protection.

This original recipe seemed pretty predictable, until I got to the jalapeño-lime mayonnaise. By "mayonnaise" they don't mean the kind that you buy in the store. They mean homemade mayonnaise, complete with simmering saffron (which shares the same color and cost per pound as gold) and wine, and whisking in large quantities of peanut oil and egg yolks. I hope you don't mind, but I made my own 1-minute version, blending a little real mayonnaise with a lot of fat-free or light sour cream, lime juice, jalapeño, and Dijon mustard. At the time I was fresh out of saffron, so I skipped it.

These were scrumptious—even using imitation crab! Meanwhile, I'm still waiting for that pound of crab to be delivered.

CRAB CAKES
WITH QUICK JALAPEÑO-LIME MAYONNAISE

Original recipe contains 800 calories, 65 grams fat, and 190 milligrams cholesterol per serving.

Serves 6 as an entree (12 as an appetizer)

2 tablespoons canola oil, divided
1 cup finely diced white onions
1 cup finely diced celery
1 pound fresh crabmeat (imitation crabmeat can be substituted)
¼ cup egg substitute (1 lightly beaten egg can be substituted)
1½ tablespoons Dijon mustard
1–2 tablespoons finely chopped fresh parsley
    (or 1½ teaspoons dried)
1 tablespoon finely chopped fresh thyme (or 1 teaspoon dried)
salt and pepper to taste
cayenne pepper to taste (optional)
2 cups fine white bread crumbs, divided

JALAPEÑO-LIME MAYONNAISE:
2 tablespoons real mayonnaise
½ cup fat-free sour cream (Naturally Yours brand)
2 tablespoons lime juice
½ teaspoon seeded and minced jalapeño pepper (or to taste)
½ teaspoon Dijon mustard
salt, pepper, and cayenne pepper to taste

1. Heat 1 tablespoon of the oil in a large nonstick skillet or frying pan, and cook onion and celery over medium heat until tender, about 4 minutes. Add a tablespoon or two of water if moisture is needed toward the end. Place in a food processor and pulse a few times to make mixture finer.

2. Place crabmeat in mixing bowl. Lightly mix in onion mixture; add egg substitute and mustard. Mix again very lightly, then add parsley, thyme, salt, pepper, cayenne (if desired), and 1 cup of bread crumbs.

3. Form gently into 12 small cakes, and roll in the remaining bread crumbs.

4. Heat remaining tablespoon of canola oil in same skillet or frying pan over medium heat. Lightly brown crab cakes on each side, 2 to 3 minutes, turning once (coat pan or crab cakes with canola cooking spray as needed).

5. For mayonnaise: combine mayonnaise, sour cream, lime juice, jalapeño, and mustard in a food processor or 2-cup measure. Blend until smooth. Adjust seasoning to taste.

PER SERVING: 327 calories, 22.5 g protein, 32 g carbohydrate, 11.5 g fat, 1.5 g saturated fat, 78 mg cholesterol, 1.5 g fiber, 700 mg sodium (not including salt to taste). Calories from fat: 33 percent.

Q

Dear Recipe Doctor,

One of my favorite dishes to order at Chinese restaurants is prawns with glazed pecans or walnuts. I'm enclosing a recipe from the Oriental Pearl restaurant that the Contra Costa Times *(California) ran a year or so ago. Of course, everything in this recipe is deep-fried. Please help! I look forward to your column every week.*

A

Prawns with glazed walnuts is one of *my* favorite Chinese dishes too! So, I leaped at the chance of lightening it up. The last time I ordered it at a Chinese restaurant, I noticed the menu described the dish as being fried prawns in a "white sauce." But the "white sauce" looked and tasted frighteningly similar to a cup of mayonnaise.

But in this wonderful dish the fat isn't coming just from mayonnaise, it's also coming from the fried prawns. Even the glazed walnuts are deep-fried—which to me is like spreading butter on your margarine. Nuts are already mostly fat (albeit the more helpful types of fat), so deep-frying them is, well, overkill. But there are ways around this. I cut a few steps from the original recipe. You now need only to stir the walnuts into boiling corn syrup. And instead of deep-frying the nuts in 350-degree oil, you now bake the nuts in a 350-degree oven.

As far as the deep-fried prawns go, it works well to pan-fry them in a token amount of canola oil. For the mayonnaise driven "white sauce," I used a combination of mostly fat-free sweetened condensed milk (maybe you will have some left over during the holiday season), which had the ideal texture for this dish, lemon juice, and just a touch of light, low-fat or even real mayonnaise. Egg substitute is added in place of egg yolk.

Since I happen to live near this reader, I ran a sample of this "lightened" dish over to her one cold October night (this recipe doctor will sometimes make house calls). I waited anxiously as she carefully tasted a bite. She grinned and said, "You did it again." I was so relieved. I had already tasted the dish and loved it, but sometimes my taste buds can be a little overly optimistic.

PRAWNS WITH GLAZED WALNUTS (OR PECANS)

Original recipe contains 1,032 calories, 69 grams fat, and 206 milligrams cholesterol (not including the steamed rice).

Makes 3 servings (or 2 large servings)

1 teaspoon lemon juice
3 tablespoons fat-free sweetened condensed milk
1½ tablespoons light, low-fat, or regular mayonnaise
1½ teaspoons sugar
1½ teaspoons egg substitute
10-ounce bag frozen large prawns or jumbo shrimp, deveined and shelled
½ cup flour
2 tablespoons canola oil
½–⅔ cup Glazed Walnuts or Pecans—recipe follows (if in a hurry just use toasted pecans)
3 cups steamed rice

1. In large mixing bowl, combine lemon juice, sweetened condensed milk, mayonnaise, sugar, and egg substitute. Mix thoroughly and set aside.
2. Fill a large saucepan with water and bring to a rapid boil. Blanch prawns in boiling water for 30 seconds. Remove prawns from water with slotted spoon and drain on paper towels. Dredge prawns in flour.
3. Heat canola oil in large nonstick frying pan, saucepan, or wok over medium heat. When oil is hot, add prawns to pan. Spray tops of prawns with canola cooking spray. Once bottom is golden, turn prawns over with spatula. When other side is golden, remove prawns and drain on paper towels.

4. Add hot prawns and pecans to lemon-milk mixture in mixing bowl and toss thoroughly to blend. Serve on a bed of steamed rice.

GLAZED WALNUTS/PECANS:

Warning: these nuts can be addicting! Proceed with extreme caution.

2 tablespoons granulated sugar
¼ teaspoon Chinese 5-spice blend
⅓ cup light corn syrup
6 ounces walnut halves or pecan halves (about 1½ cups)

1. Preheat oven to 350 degrees. Coat a 9 x 9-inch baking pan or cookie sheet with canola cooking spray; set aside.
2. In small bowl, blend sugar with Chinese 5-spice; set aside.
3. In small nonstick saucepan, bring corn syrup to a boil on medium heat. Boil for 1 minute without stirring. Add walnuts; stir constantly for 2 to 3 minutes with wooden spoon (nuts should be coated with the glaze). Immediately remove saucepan from heat; sprinkle the sugar mixture over the nuts and toss until nuts are evenly coated with sugar.
4. Spread walnuts out onto prepared pan, gently separating any nuts attached to each other (as much as possible). Bake until golden brown (about 8 to 10 minutes). Be careful not to burn. Stir the nuts a bit with a pancake turner, making sure the glaze is lifted up off the pan and coating the nuts well. Let cool. Store in an airtight container for up to a week.

PER SERVING (INCLUDING RICE): 750 calories, 28 g protein, 102 g carbohydrate, 25 g fat, 2.5 g saturated fat, 138 mg cholesterol, 2.5 g fiber, 80 mg sodium. Calories from fat: 31 percent.

Dear Recipe Doctor,

Do you have a light recipe for dinner pasta salad? We love eating this on hot summer days. My wife has high serum cholesterol and we would love your help in time for summer.

A

Not only do I have a yummy pasta salad for you, but it features salmon, a rich source of heart protecting omega-3 fatty acids. At the risk of making omega-3s sound like the latest panacea, omega-3s have been linked to lowering both blood pressure and serum triglyceride levels, preventing blood clots. They may even help increase HDL (good) cholesterol levels. They have also been shown to slow or prevent cancerous tumor growth. The two particular cancers that omega-3s may help prevent are colon and possibly breast cancer.

Perhaps you have even heard of the study reported in the *New England Journal of Medicine*, where the researchers reported that men who ate one to two servings of fish a week cut their risk of heart attack in half.

This is one of those dishes where you can't wait to eat the leftovers the next day. I took some over to a friend last summer to see if she liked it and she licked the bowl clean—I took that as a yes.

Try to cook or grill your salmon with little or no added fat. If you do add fat, use a little olive oil. Feel free to cook your salmon with herbs, lemon, wine, or light soy sauce. For a quick broiling sauce you can use an olive oil vinaigrette.

For the dressing in this dish, I used a touch of real mayonnaise for flavor and texture and some fat-free or light sour cream. If there is a light or nonfat mayonnaise you like, you can use that in place of the sour cream. To add some flavor to the dressing I added lemon juice, Dijon mustard, dill, and freshly ground pepper. It is so simple to put together but it looks and tastes terrific, especially served cold on a hot summer night.

⁓ SIMPLE SALMON PASTA SALAD ⁓

Makes about 4 servings

   3 cups dried bow tie or rotelle pasta, cooked al dente
   1 cup salmon flakes (freshly cooked, smoked, or grilled salmon
      fillets or steaks, broken into flakes with fork or hands with
      no bones or skin)
   1 cup almost tender (still somewhat crisp) asparagus pieces,
      steamed or micro-cooked (another vegetable can be
      substituted)
   3 green onions, finely chopped

   DRESSING:
   1 tablespoon real mayonnaise
   3 tablespoons fat-free or light sour cream or low-fat
      mayonnaise
   1 tablespoon lemon juice
   1½ teaspoons Dijon or other prepared mustard
   ½ teaspoon dillweed
   black pepper to taste

1. Combine first four ingredients in serving bowl; toss to blend.
2. Combine dressing ingredients in a measuring cup, and stir until
   smooth. Pour over pasta salad ingredients and stir to mix.

PER SERVING: 400 calories, 21 g protein, 63 g carbohydrate, 7 g fat, 1 g saturated fat, 3 g fiber, 27 mg cholesterol, 205 mg sodium. Calories from fat: 16 percent.

Dear Recipe Doctor,

When I think of summer I think of some of my favorite warm weather dinners, like crab or shrimp salad. Have you lightened one of these lately?

In the middle of summer the usual dinner standbys of spaghetti, tuna casserole, or baked chicken just don't sound good when you're driving home in your hot car, brainstorming over what you're going to fix for dinner tonight. Plan B: crab and shrimp salad. It has two things going for it on a hot summer night—it's cold, and it's quick.

I thought I would doctor up the infamous Bullock's Department Store recipe for Crabmeat and Shrimp Salad. So, I set out to my trusty fish counter the very next evening (which happened to be during a heat wave) and ordered half a pound of imitation crabmeat and half a pound of...but before I could finish my order, the man behind the counter finished it for me..."shrimp." "How did you know?" I gasped. He said it was the fourth shrimp and crab order he had filled that evening. Hmm...I thought. Maybe I'm onto something. My reader and I are not the only ones who find the thought of a chilled crab and shrimp salad refreshing on a hot summer night.

The obvious first step in lightening the traditional mayonnaise-laden crab and shrimp salad is to alter the mayonnaise somehow. I could have used light or low-fat mayonnaise, but I tried another technique I've been employing a lot lately—using one-third real mayonnaise and two-thirds Naturally Yours nonfat sour cream. This is the best tasting nonfat sour cream, bar none.

I used imitation crab instead of real crab because at almost $20 per pound for real crab, that's not crab anymore—that's caviar. I also added some sliced olives and chopped green onions for a little added flavor and color. This tastes so good I've made it twice in the past two weeks.

CRAB AND SHRIMP SALAD

Original recipe contains 502 calories, 140 milligrams cholesterol, and 45 grams of fat per serving.

Makes 3 servings

2 tablespoons real mayonnaise
⅓ cup Naturally Yours fat-free sour cream
juice from ½ lemon
1 cup shredded cooked crabmeat or imitation crabmeat (about ⅓ pound)
1 cup bay shrimp (about ⅓ pound)
½ cup chopped celery
¼ teaspoon salt
¼ teaspoon freshly ground pepper (or more to taste)
2 tablespoons sliced black olives
1 green onion, chopped
chopped lettuce (optional)
French or sourdough bread (optional)

1. Combine mayonnaise with sour cream and lemon juice.
2. Stir in crab, shrimp, celery, salt, pepper, olives, and green onion. Chill at least 1 hour.
3. Serve on bed of chopped lettuce and/or with fresh bread if desired.

PER SERVING: 202 calories, 18 g protein, 12 g carbohydrate, 9 g fat, 1.5 g saturated fat, 113 mg cholesterol, 1 g fiber, 730 mg sodium. Calories from fat: 41 percent.

ENWLINE ENTREES

MEATLESS & MORE

FETTUCCINE ALFREDO

SPAGO CALZONE (WITH BREAD MACHINE)

ANTIPASTO ITALIAN WRAP SANDWICH

Q   *Dear Recipe Doctor,*

One of my favorite pasta dishes is fettuccine Alfredo, but I recently saw in a newsletter article that it can contain over 1,000 calories and a day's worth of fat grams. Can you make a really creamy lower-fat version—or am I asking too much?

A   A day's worth of fat grams and calories—kind of takes the fun out of it, doesn't it? I have made several lower-fat fettuccine Alfredos over the years, but I think this time I have really done it. This version looks and tastes thick and creamy and has plenty of sauce to coat every single noodle.

This is one of those 10-minute dinners, too. Just start boiling the noodles when you get home from work, make the sauce while they're boiling, and if you buy the Parmesan cheese preshredded, you will be sitting down to dinner in the time it would take you to pick up the phone and order out.

The problem with regular fettuccine Alfredo is the butter and the cream, both adding tons of saturated fat grams and calories. But it wouldn't be fettuccine Alfredo without at least some butter. So, we are still using butter; we just cut it down to 1½ teaspoons per serving. You can use canola margarine if you would rather. Then, instead of whipping cream or half-and-half, we are using whole milk (which looks like cream to those of you who have switched to nonfat or low-fat milk) to make the sauce.

The thickening and creaminess of the sauce, though, comes from some added light cream cheese and Wondra quick-mixing flour. To complete the flavors of the sauce, you can sprinkle some freshly ground black pepper and/or nutmeg into the sauce.

✑ FETTUCCINE ALFREDO ✑

Original recipe contains 860 calories, 59 grams fat, 35 grams saturated fat, and 263 milligrams cholesterol per serving.

Makes 4 servings

¼ cup light cream cheese
1½ cups whole milk, divided
1 tablespoon Wondra quick-mixing flour
2 tablespoons butter (canola margarine can also be used)
6 cups hot cooked and drained spaghetti or fettuccine noodles
salt and freshly grated pepper to taste
nutmeg to taste
¾ cup shredded Parmesan cheese (add more at table if desired)

1. Combine cream cheese, ¼ cup whole milk, and Wondra flour in a mixing bowl or food processor. Beat or pulse until well blended. Slowly pour in remaining milk (1¼ cups) and beat until smooth.
2. Melt butter in large, thick nonstick frying pan or saucepan over medium heat. Add the milk mixture and continue to heat, stirring constantly, until the sauce is just the right thickness. Turn the heat to low and add the hot noodles. Toss to coat noodles well with sauce. Add salt, pepper, and nutmeg to taste. Stir in grated Parmesan and serve.

PER SERVING: 510 calories, 23 g protein, 66 g carbohydrate, 16.5 g fat, 9.5 g saturated fat, 45 mg cholesterol, 3 g fiber, 512 mg sodium. Calories from fat: 30 percent.

Q *Dear Recipe Doctor,*

I've been to Spago's in Hollywood several times and I always order the calzone with prosciutto and grilled eggplant. Although it probably isn't dripping in grease, I was wondering if you could modify the recipe for the suburban kitchen and make it a little lighter at the same time?

A On occasion, I like to buy the Spago's frozen cheese pizza. It's the closest I ever get to buying a frozen entree. Anyway, I love the crust and the combination of cheeses so I was thrilled to lighten up this recipe. Sure enough, the crust and the combination of cheeses (which includes a 50 percent less-fat goat cheese)—even after I lightened it up—was very similar to the frozen pizza I have come to enjoy. I have yet to get to a Spago restaurant, so I am afraid the frozen model is the only standard I can compare this calzone to.

The first thing I did was convert the pizza dough recipe to a bread machine format. This way the bread machine is mixing and kneading instead of you. You have better things to do—like grill eggplant and grate cheese. I added a tablespoon of olive oil to the dough instead of two, just because one will do ya.

I used part-skim mozzarella, but if there is a low-fat mozzarella that you like, go for it. I actually found a 50-percent-less-fat goat cheese at my grocery store, so that's what I used. If you can only find the real thing, use a little less. The original recipe calls for ½ cup of shredded fontina cheese (which I love but don't usually have hanging around my house), so I used ⅓ cup of shredded Parmesan.

Instead of grilling the eggplant, which may require firing up charcoals and brushing with olive oil, I simply pan-fried it in a large nonstick pan with canola cooking spray in hand. It was absolutely scrumptious. I loved every part of it—even the edge of the crust that didn't have any filling was yummy. My husband loved it, too, but he could have done without the goat cheese (that's one of those things you either love or hate).

☞ SPAGO CALZONE (WITH BREAD MACHINE) ☜

Original recipe contains 780 calories, 38 grams fat, and 50 milligrams cholesterol per serving.

Makes 4 servings

PIZZA DOUGH:
1⅛ cups lukewarm water
1 tablespoon olive oil
2 tablespoons sugar
about 3 cups bread flour (regular will also work)
2 teaspoons salt
1½ teaspoons dry yeast
flour (for rolling out dough)
1 cup shredded part-skim or low-fat mozzarella cheese
¼ cup 50-percent-less-fat coarsely chopped goat cheese
   (or regular)
⅓ cup shredded Parmesan cheese (fontina can be substituted)
½ regular eggplant (or 1 Japanese eggplant)
1 ounce prosciutto (about 2 long slices)
1 tablespoon olive oil
dash red pepper flakes (optional)
½ teaspoon crumbled dried basil

1. For pizza dough, place water, oil, sugar, flour, salt, and yeast in bread machine pan in the order recommended by manufacturer. Set bread machine to dough cycle and turn on. Let complete mixing and kneading cycle (about 10 to 15 minutes). Unplug bread machine. Remove dough from pan. Let rest on lightly floured surface for 10 to 15 minutes. Divide into 4 portions and let rest another 10 minutes.

2. While pizza dough is mixing in the bread machine, cut eggplant into round slices about ¼-inch wide. Spago's original recipe calls for grilling the eggplant. But in case you don't have a grill fired up and you just want to get this part over with, heat a large nonstick frying pan over medium heat. Generously coat pan with canola cooking spray. Cover bottom of pan with eggplant slices. Spray tops with canola cooking spray. When bottom is lightly browned, flip over and brown other side. Remove from pan to cool.

3. Preheat oven to 450 degrees. Roll each portion of dough out to a small circle, then stretch into a circle about 8 to 10 inches in diameter. Sprinkle half of the mozzarella and all of the goat cheese, Parmesan cheese, eggplant, and prosciutto over the dough circles. Top with remaining mozzarella cheese. Fold dough over to form a half circle. Moisten edges to seal. Crimp edges. Place calzones on cookie sheet.

4. Combine 1 tablespoon of olive oil with red pepper and basil. Brush top surface of dough with olive oil mixture. Bake for 15 to 20 minutes or until calzone becomes crisp underneath and golden brown on top.

PER SERVING: 583 calories, 24.5 g protein, 81 g carbohydrate, 17 g fat, 5.5 g saturated fat, 29 mg cholesterol, 3 g fiber, 920 mg sodium. Calories from fat: 27 percent.

Q

Dear Recipe Doctor,

Will you please help me recreate the new "wrap" rolled sandwiches? How do you make the flatbread?

A

Wraps are all the rage these days. The few parties I have attended (and I don't get out much) have featured sliced wrap sandwiches, and my local Italian restaurant put out a colorful sign boasting "Wrap sandwiches now served." Okay, so it is now officially a fad—but a delicious and potentially healthful fad! Probably the most healthful are the Mediterranean wraps brimming with roasted vegetables and legumes.

It's actually a case of something old becoming new again, because other cultures have been wrapping with flatbreads for centuries. How do you make flatbread? Well, are you sure you want to? Make a homemade batch of pocketless pitas or other flatbreads, even with the aid of a bread machine, and suddenly those oversized burrito tortillas you can buy in the supermarket start looking pretty good. You may also be able to find lahvash (Armenian flatbread) in a local grocery or specialty store.

My experience has been that when you finally get your hands on some of these specialty products, the lack of freshness may leave a little to be desired. So check those expiration dates carefully. I tend to opt for the burrito-sized tortillas. They seem to stay fresh longer, and I can use whatever tortillas are left for other mealtime favorites.

The trick to a lower-fat wrap has nothing to do with the flatbread (which is usually already low in fat) and has everything to do with the fillings and spreads. Most wraps have a spread on the bread. The filling ingredients are then placed evenly over the spread and the flatbread is wrapped jelly roll style into a sandwich. You can follow any wrap recipe you see, just choose lower-fat fillers when possible (reduced-fat cheese, lean ham, turkey breast, light salami, lean roast beef, etc.) and choose lower-fat spread ingredients.

Makes 2 small sandwiches

1 tablespoon low-fat or light mayonnaise
1 tablespoon sun-dried tomato spread or lower-fat pesto
  (try Armanino pesto in the frozen food section)
1 large burrito-sized flour tortilla
½ cup loosely packed fresh basil leaves (if not using pesto
  for spread)
2–3 ounces thinly sliced reduced-fat mozzarella cheese
8–10 slices lower-fat salami
2–3 pieces roasted red peppers, bottled (about 2–3 ounces) or
  ⅓ cup marinated or canned artichoke hearts, sliced

1. Blend mayonnaise with the sun-dried tomato spread or pesto
    in cup or small bowl. Spread top of tortilla evenly with may-
    onnaise mixture.
2. Arrange basil leaves evenly over spread on tortilla. Arrange
    mozzarella slices, salami, and roasted red peppers over top of
    tortilla.
3. Roll tortilla up tightly, jelly roll style. Cut in half at a slight
    diagonal for sandwiches or cut into thin diagonal slices for
    appetizers.

PER SERVING: 308 calories, 19.5 g protein, 22.5 g carbohydrate, 14.5 g fat, 5.5 g saturated fat, 45 mg cholesterol, 1.5 g fiber, 900 mg sodium. Calories from fat: 42 percent.

Chapter Four

BREADS

COFFEE HOUSE MAPLE SCONES

ALMOND POPPY SEED MUFFINS

CARROT MUFFINS

JAM MINI MUFFINS

HAM AND CHEESE MUFFINS

BANANA SQUARES

APPLE BRANDY MUFFINS

TAHITIAN LANAI BANANA MUFFINS

MOCK MARIE'S CORNBREAD

LIGHT WALNUT BREAD

ORANGE-GLAZED TROPICAL FRUIT SCONES

LEMONADE MINI MUFFINS

RAISIN BRAN MUFFINS

Q

Dear Recipe Doctor,

I am addicted to the Starbucks maple scone. The boy behind the counter told me it is loaded with fat grams. Help me! Can you make a lower-fat rendition that will satisfy my craving?

A

Well, I went to the aforementioned coffee chain and tasted the alleged addicting scone. I even did a little bit of detective work—apparently the maple scones sell out every day and are one of their most popular food items. Now I know why this reader is addicted—they taste totally terrific.

I made up my own lower-fat version that I think came pretty darn close. My husband even liked this light version better! Can you believe that? These freeze really well, too. Just make a batch and pop them into the freezer (using plastic freezer bags) and you've got a quick breakfast or a quick snack when unexpected guests arrive.

If you even barely like the taste of maple, you will find the lower-fat maple scones addicting! It has a very similar flavor and yet the dough seems moister than the Starbucks version.

I used maple syrup to replace some of the butter in the dough, and I used whole milk instead of heavy cream (but low-fat milk would work in a pinch). I even converted the recipe to a food processor to make these scones a cinch to make.

COFFEE HOUSE MAPLE SCONES

Makes 8 scones

> 1½ cups all-purpose flour
> ³/₄ cup oats
> 2 tablespoons sugar
> ½ teaspoon salt
> 1 tablespoon baking powder
> 2 tablespoons maple syrup
> 2½ tablespoons cold butter, cut into small pieces
> 1 egg
> ½ cup whole milk
> ½ teaspoon maple extract (³/₄ teaspoon if you want a stronger maple flavor in the dough)
> ²/₃ cup coarsely chopped pecans (a little smaller than pecan pieces but bigger than finely chopped pecans)

MAPLE GLAZE:
1½ cups powdered sugar
½ teaspoon maple extract
5 teaspoons water

1. Preheat oven to 425 degrees. Make an 8-inch circle with canola cooking spray on a thick baking sheet.
2. Place flour, oats, sugar, salt, and baking powder in food processor. Pulse to mix and finely grind the oats with the flour.
3. Add maple syrup and butter pieces to the flour mixture and pulse to blend the two well (the butter will be broken up into very small pieces).

4. In a separate small bowl, beat the egg lightly with the milk and
   $1/2$ teaspoon maple extract. Pour the milk mixture into the flour
   mixture in the food processor. Pulse briefly to make a dough.

5. Place dough on well-floured surface. Sprinkle pecans over the
   top and knead lightly 4 times to evenly distribute the pecans.
   Pat dough into a $7\frac{1}{2}$-inch circle. Cut into 8 wedges. Place
   wedges in a circle on prepared baking sheet. Bake in center of
   oven for about 13 to 15 minutes (top will be lightly browned).

6. While scones are baking, combine glaze ingredients in a small
   bowl and stir well until smooth. Remove scones from oven to
   wire rack and let cool about 3 to 5 minutes. Spread glaze generously over each scone. Once glaze has dried (about 15 minutes) the scones can be served. They keep well overnight in a
   plastic bag.

Note: quite a bit of the fat comes from the pecans, therefore 6
grams of the fat (per serving) comes from monounsaturated fat.

PER SERVING: 330 calories, 6 g protein, 51 g carbohydrate, 12 g fat, 3.3 g saturated fat, 2 g fiber, 38 mg cholesterol, 370 mg sodium. Calories from fat: 33 percent.

Dear Recipe Doctor,

I love almond poppy seed muffins. I have been buying the Otis Spunkmeyer type at the supermarket, but they always leave my fingers so oily. Can you make up a lower-fat version that I can whip up at home?

It's no wonder why they leave your fingers oily—one of those muffins contains 24 grams of fat (and 420 calories). If you quickly look at the label you might mistake the muffin as containing 210 calories and 12 grams of fat. But take a second glance at the serving size—½ muffin. I just have one question—who eats half of a muffin?

The first step was to find a recipe to lighten up. I figured my general cookbooks would have one—nope. I checked all my baking books. No again. Out of desperation I went to the bookstore and looked in all of those "how to bake everything" kind of cookbooks. Three strikes, I was out. They should call them "how to bake everything but almond poppy seed muffins." So I did the only thing a recipe doctor would do—I made a recipe up.

Since poppy seed muffins are so sweet and so well oiled, I figured they're more like cake anyway. So I started with a cake recipe that calls for lots of oil. I cut the oil back from 1⅛ cups to ½ cup and switched to canola oil. I made up the difference with corn syrup (which helps baked products stay moist over time) and cut the granulated sugar back accordingly.

I doubled the almond extract and vanilla called for and used the low-fat milk I had in the refrigerator instead of regular. I added my usual token egg instead of the 3 in the recipe. I added ½ cup egg substitute instead. This is one of those recipes I had to make several versions of until I got it just right. They turned out moist and flavorful without leaving grease marks on your napkin and fingers. You can make a batch and freeze some. Just pop them in the microwave and you've got breakfast on the run.

☞ ALMOND POPPY SEED MUFFINS ☜

One brand I found in the supermarket contains 420 calories and 24 grams of fat per muffin.

Makes 24 regular-sized muffins

> 3 cups unbleached all-purpose flour
> 1½ teaspoons salt
> 1½ teaspoons baking powder
> 1¾ cups sugar
> ½ cup canola oil
> ½ cup light corn syrup
> 2 tablespoons fat-free or light sour cream
> 1½ cups low-fat milk
> 1 egg
> ½ cup egg substitute
> 2 teaspoons vanilla extract
> 2 teaspoons almond extract
> 2 tablespoons poppy seeds

1. Preheat oven to 350 degrees and coat muffin pans with canola cooking spray.
2. Combine flour, salt, baking powder, and sugar in a large mixing bowl and blend well with mixer on lowest speed.
3. Add oil, corn syrup, sour cream, milk, egg, egg substitute, vanilla extract, and almond extract and mix on lowest speed of mixer until fairly smooth. Stir in poppy seeds.
4. Spoon ¼ cup of batter into each muffin cup. Bake for 20 to 25 minutes. Let cool in pan 10 minutes before serving.

PER SERVING: 190 calories, 3 g protein, 33 g carbohydrate, 5.5 g fat, .5 g saturated fat, 9 mg cholesterol, .6 g fiber, 190 mg sodium. Calories from fat: 25 percent.

Dear Recipe Doctor,

I've been wanting to make these carrot muffins from Chef Paul Prudhomme's Louisiana Kitchen *cookbook. But I was shocked that something that contains carrots also calls for a stick of butter and two egg yolks (for just 12 muffins). Is there something you can do?*

Carrot cake recipes are notorious for calling for 1½ cups of oil, so I guess even something as seemingly healthful as carrot muffins shouldn't be that different. These carrot muffins are a little like zucchini bread in taste and texture—which is just fine with me. You can freeze these and pull them out for a quick breakfast or snack. They could even accompany an entree at lunch or dinner.

Usually in muffin recipes, I use about 2 tablespoons of fat per 12 regular-sized muffins. I decided to cut this recipe back from the ½ cup of butter called for to ¼ cup canola oil. Canola oil is a plant source of omega-3 fatty acids and is mostly monounsaturated fat (both of which appear to be beneficial for the body). I added in some maple syrup instead of the lost butter. But don't worry, I cut down the brown sugar called for to help compensate.

I also cut one of the egg yolks and added an egg white instead. One egg yolk, worth 210 milligrams of cholesterol, divided by 12 muffins, computes to about 18 milligrams saved per muffin. I also thought a carrot muffin should probably have some whole grain in there. So I substituted some whole wheat flour for my usual unbleached white flour. You can use half whole wheat and half white flour if you'd like or you could use all white flour—it's up to you. If you are a bit skeptical, start by using just ½ cup of whole wheat. Trust me, you won't even know it's there. When I tested these muffins I happened to be fresh out of pecans and walnuts, so I made them without nuts. They were still good, but I think they would be even better with these little nuggets of flavor.

∼ CARROT MUFFINS ∼

Original recipe contains 235 calories, 12.5 grams fat, 5.6 grams saturated fat, and 58 milligrams cholesterol per serving.

Makes about 12 regular-sized muffins

1½ cups unbleached white flour
½ cup whole wheat flour
½ cup packed light or dark brown sugar
¾ cup coarsely grated carrot
½ cup coarsely chopped pecans or walnuts, dry roasted
2 teaspoons baking powder
¾–1 teaspoon ground cinnamon
¼ teaspoon salt
1 egg plus 1 egg white, beaten
⅔ cup low-fat milk
¼ cup canola oil
¼ cup maple syrup

1. Preheat oven to 350 degrees. Coat 12 muffin cups with canola cooking spray.
2. Combine the flours, sugar, carrots, nuts, baking powder, cinnamon, and salt in a large bowl; mix thoroughly with a spoon, breaking up any lumps.
3. Add the remaining ingredients and mix just until blended; do not overbeat.
4. Spoon batter into prepared muffin cups. Bake until golden brown and top springs back when gently touched (about 30 to 35 minutes).

PER SERVING: 198 calories, 4 g protein, 29.5 g carbohydrate, 7.5 g fat, .8 g saturated fat, 18 mg cholesterol, 1.5 g fiber, 150 mg sodium. Calories from fat: 34 percent.

Dear Recipe Doctor,

I would appreciate your help lightening up a prized family recipe for plain muffins. The original recipe came from someone's home economics class years ago. My family especially enjoys dropping jam in the middle to make jam muffins.

A good basic muffin recipe is hard to find and that's just what this reader sent me. The thought of warm moist low-fat jam muffins fresh from the oven on a cold winter's morning makes my mouth water.

I immediately set to work by cutting the oil in half and replacing the lost half with nonfat or light sour cream. I took out the egg and added ¼ cup egg substitute. Then my last act as recipe doctor was to add ½ teaspoon lemon extract to complement the flavor of the jam (2 teaspoons lemon zest would accomplish the same end).

I used a mini muffin pan to test the recipe, adding a teaspoon of jam for each mini muffin—I guess I was going for the cute look. You might notice I called for "less-sugar" jam just because it is an easy way to curb some of the extra calories. But you can use any jam you want. I tend to make a few batches of less-sugar three- or four-berry jam each summer, and that irreplaceable homemade jam flavor made these muffins even more yummy.

⇒ JAM MINI MUFFINS ⇐

Original recipe contains 178 calories, 18 milligrams cholesterol, and 5.5 grams of fat per serving.

Makes 12 servings (2 mini muffins or 1 regular-sized muffin each)

⅛ cup (2 tablespoons) nonfat or light sour cream
⅛ cup (2 tablespoons) canola oil
½ cup low-fat milk
¼ cup egg substitute (or 1 egg)
½ teaspoon lemon extract (or 2 teaspoons lemon zest, finely chopped)
1½ cups unbleached flour
½ cup granulated sugar
2 teaspoons baking powder
½ teaspoon salt (optional)
24 teaspoons less-sugar jam

1. Preheat oven to 375 degrees. Coat mini muffin cups with canola cooking spray.
2. Place sour cream in a glass mixing bowl and warm briefly in the microwave so it will blend easier. Stir in oil and milk, a tablespoon at a time. Stir in egg substitute and lemon extract.
3. Blend dry ingredients together (flour, sugar, baking powder, salt) and add all at once to liquid mixture. Stir just enough to moisten.
4. Fill each mini muffin cup with a level tablespoon of batter. Drop a level teaspoon of jam or jelly into the center of each muffin. Bake about 15 minutes (20 to 25 minutes for regular-sized muffins) or until golden brown and muffin tests done.

PER SERVING: 143 calories, 3 g protein, 27 g carbohydrate, 2.5 g fat, .2 g saturated fat, .4 mg cholesterol, 1 g fiber, 101 mg sodium. Calories from fat: 16 percent.

Dear Recipe Doctor,

These savory biscuit-like muffins are delicious at breakfast or with a bowl of soup. They call for half a cup of mayonnaise. What can I add instead?

I have to admit I've never had a ham and cheese muffin, and I don't think I've seen a muffin recipe calling for mayonnaise before (believe it or not, though I've seen a cake recipe calling for mayonnaise). But at least the ham and cheese part sounded good. This is a way to mix a little protein into your breakfast without whipping up scrambled eggs or something. I froze a batch to see if they could be popped into the microwave for a quick breakfast or side dish. It definitely worked.

In the original recipe they add mayonnaise instead of oil, so I kept 3 tablespoons of real mayonnaise, knowing a batch of muffins needs at least 2 tablespoons of oil to maintain its desirable muffin texture and taste. To replace the mayonnaise I wasn't adding, I added ⅓ cup of fat-free sour cream.

I beefed up the amount of ham a little (to turn the ham flavor up a notch) and used a hunk of very lean ham. I trimmed off a couple grams of fat per serving just by using reduced-fat sharp cheddar cheese instead of regular. I was surprised to find these muffins were light, almost like brioche but without all the egg yolks. Which reminds me, when I first noticed this recipe didn't call for any eggs, I got a little suspicious. But it still worked. Just to be safe, keep leftover muffins in the refrigerator or freezer.

⁖ HAM AND CHEESE MUFFINS ⁖

Original recipe contains 185 calories, 11 grams fat, 3 grams saturated fat, and 17 milligrams cholesterol per muffin.

Makes 12 muffins

> 2 cups self-rising flour*
> ½ teaspoon baking soda
> 1⅛ cups low-fat milk
> 3 tablespoons mayonnaise
> ⅓ cup fat-free sour cream
> ¾ cup finely chopped cooked lean ham
> ½ cup reduced-fat shredded sharp cheddar cheese

1. Preheat oven to 425 degrees. Coat 12 muffin cups with canola cooking spray or line with papers.
2. Combine flour and baking soda. Combine remaining ingredients and stir into dry ingredients just until moistened.
3. Fill muffin cups evenly (at least two-thirds full). Bake until muffins test done (about 16 minutes). Freeze or refrigerate any leftover muffins.

*Instead of self-rising flour, you can place 1½ teaspoons baking powder and ½ teaspoon salt in a measuring cup. Add enough all-purpose flour to equal 1 cup. Repeat with second cup of flour needed.

PER MUFFIN: 145 calories, 6.5 g protein, 18 g carbohydrate, 5 g fat, 1.5 g saturated fat, 10 mg cholesterol, 1 g fiber, 470 mg sodium. Calories from fat: 31 percent.

Dear Recipe Doctor,

We love these banana squares. We are all hoping you can make them a little more nutritious.

I'm always looking for a few good banana recipes because every now and then, I end up with a couple of blackened bananas sitting in my fruit basket. This recipe is so good I might start using good bananas.

Instead of shortening I used a canola margarine (with liquid canola oil as the first ingredient) and used half the amount called for. In its place I used light cream cheese. I cut down the sugar by half a cup and switched part of it to brown sugar. I used one egg and replaced the other one called for with egg substitute, just because one egg does the trick just fine and this keeps the cholesterol pretty low.

The rest of the recipe stayed pretty much the same, except I doubled the amount of vanilla extract added. Everybody who tasted these banana squares (including a handful of neighborhood children) really loved them. They stand on their own just fine; they don't need any glaze or frosting. If you want to try using half whole wheat flour, you will increase the grams of fiber a bit.

≈ BANANA SQUARES ≈

Original recipe contains 185 calories, 9 grams fat, 5 grams saturated fat, and 47 milligrams cholesterol per serving.

Makes 16 servings

> 2 egg whites (reserve one of the yolks)
> $\frac{1}{3}$ cup canola margarine (with liquid canola oil as the first ingredient)
> $\frac{1}{3}$ cup light cream cheese
> $\frac{1}{2}$ cup sugar
> $\frac{1}{2}$ cup packed brown sugar
> 1 egg yolk (reserved)
> 2 tablespoons egg substitute
> 1 cup mashed ripe banana (2 to 3 medium)
> 1$\frac{1}{2}$ cups all-purpose flour
> 1 teaspoon baking soda
> $\frac{1}{4}$ cup buttermilk or sour milk*
> 1 teaspoon vanilla extract
> $\frac{1}{2}$ cup chopped walnuts (optional)

1. Preheat oven to 350 degrees. Coat a 9 x 13-inch baking pan with canola cooking spray. In a small mixing bowl, beat egg whites until soft peaks form; set aside.
2. In large mixing bowl, cream margarine and cream cheese together well. Add sugars and beat until blended. Beat in egg yolk and egg substitute; mix well. Add mashed bananas.
3. Combine flour and baking soda; add to creamed mixture alternately with milk, beating well after each addition. Stir in vanilla. Fold in egg whites and nuts if desired.

4.   Pour into prepared pan and spread evenly with spatula. Bake until fork inserted in center comes out clean (about 35 to 45 minutes). Cool on a wire rack. Cut into 16 squares.

*You can make sour milk by placing 1 teaspoon white vinegar in a measuring cup. Add enough milk to equal ¼ cup.

PER SQUARE: 151 calories, 3 g protein, 25 g carbohydrate, 4.5 g fat, .7 g saturated fat, 15 mg cholesterol, 1 g fiber, 40 mg sodium. Calories from fat: 27 percent.

Q   *Dear Recipe Doctor,*

My entire mother's club is hoping you will lighten this recipe up! I got it from a friend and it is so delicious, but it calls for 1½ cups of oil, 3 eggs, and marscarpone cheese. It is a great way to use leftover apples. Please help us; everyone in my mother's group loves these!

A   Inevitably a few apple slices come home every day in my daughters' lunchboxes. If this happens to you, too, just keep them in a bag in the refrigerator, and in a few days, you will have the apples you need to make this fabulous muffin/cake. I know the recipe says these are muffins, but they are truly too delicious and sport too delicate a crumb to hold the name muffin. It just doesn't do it justice. (Not that there is anything wrong with muffins.)

I think I should warn you, this is a rather large recipe. It makes 24 cupcakes/muffins. These freeze real well so maybe this is a good thing.

Given the fact that this recipe makes 24 muffins, I reduced the oil down to ½ cup. I replaced the cup I took out with fat-free sour cream. I could have gone the apricot brandy route, but decided the fat-free sour cream was more kid-friendly. If kid-friendly isn't in your vocabulary, you could use ½ cup apricot brandy and ½ cup fat-free sour cream. You could even add ½ cup applesauce in place of the fat-free sour cream. But frankly, the sour cream worked so well, I'm sticking with it.

I thought 1 egg per 12 muffins would work well, so I replaced the third egg called for with egg substitute. I replaced the mascarpone cheese with a mixture of honey-sweetened low-fat ricotta cheese. I also added a little vanilla extract and ground nutmeg to add a little depth to the flavors. Now all I needed to do was chop up my three-day supply of recycled lunchbox apple slices.

All this brought the fat down from 16 grams to 5.5 and the cholesterol from 32 milligrams to 19. The calories went from 275 to 196—25 percent calories from fat.

APPLE BRANDY MUFFINS

Original recipe contains 275 calories, 16 grams fat, and 32 milligrams cholesterol per serving.

Makes 24 muffins/cupcakes or 12 Texas-size muffins

- ½ cup canola oil
- 1 cup fat-free or light sour cream
- 1½ cups sugar
- ½ cup brown sugar
- 2 large eggs
- ¼ cup egg substitute
- 3 cups flour
- 2 teaspoons ground cinnamon
- 1 teaspoon baking soda
- ½ teaspoon ground nutmeg
- ½ teaspoon salt
- ¼ cup low-fat ricotta cheese
- 2 tablespoons honey
- 2 teaspoons vanilla extract
- 2 teaspoons brandy extract
- 3½ cups minced peeled apples

1. Preheat oven to 350 degrees. Coat thick muffin pans with canola cooking spray, then lightly flour each muffin cup.
2. Combine oil, sour cream, and sugars in mixing bowl. Beat until well blended. Add eggs one at a time, then add egg substitute and beat until the mixture thickens slightly.
3. Combine dry ingredients together in another bowl and add to batter a third at a time; mix just until blended. Beat in the ricotta, honey, and vanilla extract and brandy extract on low speed just until blended. Fold in the apples.
4. Pour about ¼ cup of batter into each muffin cup (use ½ cup for Texas-size pans). Bake until center of a muffin springs back when gently pressed (about 12 minutes for regular size and 18 for Texas size).

PER SERVING: 196 calories, 3.5 g protein, 34 g carbohydrate, 5.5 g fat, .8 g saturated fat, 1 g fiber, 19 mg cholesterol, 125 mg sodium. Calories from fat: 25 percent.

Q *Dear Recipe Doctor,*

I love all your muffin recipes. I think your Marie Callender's Mock Corn Muffins were even better than the restaurant's! I haven't seen you do a banana muffin, though. Would you mind lightening up my favorite banana muffin recipe?

A I don't know, maybe I had a bad banana as a child, but as long as I can remember, I have gone out of my way to avoid them. I'll even pick them out of fruit salads. But for some reason, banana bread I can do. So I waited till I had a few blackened bananas in my fruit basket and I went to work on Sheila's recipe.

The original recipe called for ¾ cup butter; I brought it down to ¼ cup. So now I was looking for ½ cup of some fat replacement to make up the difference. I looked at the rest of the ingredients and noticed they were only calling for ½ cup of mashed bananas, but at the same time it called for banana extract. Operating on the applesauce-as-fat-replacement hypothesis, I figured, "Why not add mashed banana in place of the ½ cup of butter?" Get more banana flavor from bananas instead of banana extract.

I increased the vanilla extract a little to complement the added bananas, and I switched from granulated sugar to brown sugar to add a little more flavor. I kept one of the eggs and added ½ cup of egg substitute to replace the two I tossed out. The recipe also called for cake flour, but I happened to be out of it at the time. So I used unbleached all-purpose flour and it worked great.

The recipe also called for sifting the flour, baking soda, and salt not once, but three times. As you may have already guessed, I am generally opposed to sifting. I will do so under protest only when absolutely necessary. Banana muffins didn't qualify. I didn't sift. The result? These muffins were full of flavor and the texture was perfectly light and moist. What can I say? This banana hater happened to love these banana muffins!

The fat went down by two-thirds and the cholesterol went from 56 milligrams to 18. These muffins freeze well, too.

☞ TAHITIAN LANAI BANANA MUFFINS ☜

When I ran this column, I received several letters from people who had enjoyed these in Hawaii. They wrote me because they wanted the original recipe. I told them to try the light version, and if they didn't come close, to write me and then I would give them the original. They never wrote back.

Original recipe contains 170 calories, 9 grams fat, and 56 milligrams cholesterol per muffin.

Makes 18 regular-sized muffins (or 32 mini muffins)

- ¼ cup butter or margarine, softened
- 1 cup mashed ripe bananas, divided
- 1 cup packed brown sugar
- 1 egg
- ½ cup egg substitute
- 1 teaspoon vanilla extract
- 2 cups cake flour (all-purpose flour may also be used)
- 1 teaspoon baking soda
- ¼ teaspoon salt

1. Preheat oven to 350 degrees. Coat 18 muffin cups with canola cooking spray.
2. Cream together butter, ½ cup of the bananas, and the brown sugar until light and well blended. Add the egg, egg substitute, remaining ½ cup of mashed bananas, and vanilla. Mix well.
3. Stir flour, baking soda, and salt together in medium bowl. Stir into banana mixture until just mixed (being careful not to overmix).
4. Spoon into prepared muffins cups and bake for about 18 to 20 minutes (about 8 to 10 minutes for mini muffins) or until golden brown.

PER MUFFIN (OR TWO MINI MUFFINS): 123 calories, 2.5 g protein, 21.5 g carbohydrate, 3 g fat, 2 g saturated fat, 18 mg cholesterol, 1 g fiber, 144 mg sodium. Calories from fat: 22 percent.

Q

Dear Recipe Doctor,

I have a challenge for you. I love cornbread, particularly Marie Callender's cornbread. I would love it if you could come up with a light version! I read your column every week.

A

Northerners and southerners have different ideas of how cornbread should be. Northerners seem to prefer their cornbread sweet and with a cakelike crumb. All I know is Marie Callender's cornbread is coveted by many a northerner. It is unmistakably the best cornbread and honey-butter I've ever tasted.

So, my goal here was to maintain that fluffy texture and sweet taste while cutting the fat. I started by beating a blend of butter or canola margarine, fat-free cream cheese (I used the Philadelphia type in the block), and sugar for 8 minutes. That's right, 8 minutes. This way the starting batter is nice and fluffy.

Next I added 2 eggs in place of 3. I was going to add ¼ cup egg substitute to make up the difference, but frankly, I forgot to. And the cornbread turned out so good that now I don't want to change a thing. I also added 1 percent lowfat milk in place of whole milk or half-and-half.

The texture was moist and light, just like Marie Callender's, and I could hardly notice a difference in taste. But this version has fewer calories, half the fat and saturated fat, and almost half the cholesterol. These muffins are so healthful you could stir in some blueberries and call it breakfast!

☞ MOCK MARIE'S CORNBREAD ☜

Original recipe contains 260 calories, 10.5 grams fat, 6 grams saturated fat, and 78 milligrams cholesterol per serving.

Makes 12 servings (2 regular-sized muffins each)

   ¼ cup butter, softened
   ¼ cup fat-free cream cheese
   ½ cup sugar
   1½ cups unbleached all-purpose flour
   1½ cups stone-ground or regular yellow cornmeal
   2 tablespoons baking powder
   ¾ teaspoon salt
   1½ cups low-fat milk
   2 large eggs

1. Preheat the oven to 425 degrees. Coat 2 muffin pans (12 muffin cups each) with canola cooking spray. Two mini muffin pans (24 mini muffin cups each) can also be used.

2. In a large mixing bowl, cream the butter, cream cheese, and sugar together for about 8 minutes with a standing mixer. While this is mixing, stir together the flour, cornmeal, baking powder, and salt in medium bowl or 8-cup measure. Measure the milk and set aside.

3. Once the butter mixture has been beaten for 8 minutes, beat in the eggs, one at a time. Add dry ingredients to butter-egg mixture alternately with the milk, beginning and ending with the dry ingredients. Beat just until nicely blended.

4. Spoon into prepared muffin cups and bake until bread is browned lightly on top and toothpick or fork inserted in center comes out clean (about 10 to 12 minutes for mini muffins and 15 minutes for regular-sized muffins). Serve with honey-butter (see below) if desired.

For optional honey-butter: blend 2 tablespoons honey with 2 tablespoons softened butter or canola margarine.

PER SERVING: 218 calories, 6 g protein, 36 g carbohydrate, 5.5 g fat, 3 g saturated fat, 47 mg cholesterol, 2 g fiber, 470 mg sodium. Calories from fat: 23 percent.

Q

Dear Recipe Doctor,

We love this rich walnut bread recipe from the Rancho Bernardo Inn in San Diego. I hope you can transform it for us.

A

I'm going to assume this reader still wants this bread to taste rich. He probably just wants some of the calories and fat to take a hike. To maintain the rich taste and texture, I stuck with butter as the fat of choice (the original recipe called for one stick)—I just used 4 tablespoons of it. I could have cut back to 2 tablespoons, but I wanted to make sure the richness was preserved. I whipped the reduced amount of butter in a mixer with ¼ cup of fat-free cream cheese to make up the difference.

Instead of the 2 eggs called for, I used 1 egg and ¼ cup egg substitute (or 2 egg whites). I know this usually shocks people, but nuts are high in fat—walnuts being no exception. Did I decrease the walnuts then? Heck no! This is a walnut bread after all. Besides, walnuts contain the beneficial type of fat anyway.

The original recipe called for adding a cup of sour cream toward the end of the mixing process; I used my favorite fat-free sour cream, of course. It also called for vanilla extract, which I doubled to make sure the vanilla flavor (which delightfully complements the walnuts) came through.

I often taste the batter before I bake it to make sure all the flavors are in balance (risking salmonella poisoning in the presence of raw eggs, so don't try this at home). The batter was finger-licking good. Always a good sign.

It tasted so good fresh from the oven. The rich taste and texture was indeed preserved. In fact, this bread reminded me of those Snowball or Mexican Tea Cookies that have the chopped nuts mixed into the batter. Yum yum!

☞ LIGHT WALNUT BREAD ☜

Original recipe contains 309 calories, 17 grams fat, and 65 milligrams cholesterol per serving.

Makes 12 servings

- ¼ cup butter or canola margarine, softened
- ¼ cup fat-free cream cheese
- 1 cup sugar
- 1 egg
- ¼ cup egg substitute
- 2 cups flour
- ¼ teaspoon salt
- 1 teaspoon baking soda
- ¾ cup chopped walnuts
- 2 teaspoons vanilla
- 1 cup fat-free sour cream

1. Preheat oven to 350 degrees. Coat a 9 x 5-inch loaf pan with canola cooking spray (or lightly grease and flour).
2. Cream butter, cream cheese, and sugar until fully blended. Slowly beat in egg and egg substitute.
3. Blend flour, salt, and baking soda together, then slowly beat the dry mixture into egg mixture.
4. Slowly beat in nuts, vanilla, and sour cream. Beat only until blended. Pour into prepared loaf pan. The batter is a bit thick so you will probably need to level off the top with a rubber spatula.
5. Bake about 45 minutes (or until tester inserted in center comes out clean). Cool in pan 10 minutes, then invert onto wire rack.

PER SERVING: 255 calories, 7 g protein, 38 g carbohydrate, 9 g fat, 3 g saturated fat, 28 mg cholesterol, 1 g fiber, 244 mg sodium. Calories from fat: 30 percent.

Q   *Dear Recipe Doctor,*

We love fresh-baked scones. Do you have any hints as to how to lower the fat content?

A   I'm one of those people who drools over the freshly baked breads, not the cakes or cookies, when I walk by a bakery. I am usually more than happy with one cookie, but one slice of freshly baked bread? Not bloody likely.

So I couldn't resist trying my hand at the Pillsbury Bake-Off winning recipe in the breads, coffee cake, and sweet roll category: Orange-Glazed Tropical Fruit Scones. These scones taste so good by themselves they really don't need the orange glaze called for in the original recipe. But I have to admit the orange glaze, which adds a nice tangy flavor without adding any fat (since it is basically orange juice and powdered sugar), finishes the scones off perfectly.

Scones seem innocent enough to most health-conscious eaters. But, like biscuits, underneath their fine crumb exterior is a dough laced with tiny bits of butter, more butter, and sometimes cream.

So the first thing I did was slash the butter in half and cut in fat-free cream cheese to make up the difference. I used ¼ cup egg substitute instead of one of the eggs, and I used low-fat buttermilk instead of whole milk for a thick and flavorful alternative.

And my final nutrition act was to reduce the vanilla chocolate chips from ½ cup to ⅓ cup. Experience has taught me that a little chocolate goes a long way. Now I know why this recipe was a winner—the combination of white chocolate and dried fruit is fantastic!

Could I have reduced the fat even more and made this a fat-free scone? Yes. Would I want to? No. I would have had a scone with a different texture and no chocolate chips. These lower-fat scones can even be frozen and defrosted with little change in texture and flavor, while a fat-free scone would have to be served warm, otherwise it would start to dry and crumble.

ORANGE-GLAZED TROPICAL FRUIT SCONES

Original recipe contains 430 calories, 70 milligrams cholesterol, and 14 grams of fat per scone.

Makes 8 scones

2 cups Pillsbury Best all-purpose flour
2 tablespoons sugar
1 tablespoon baking powder
1 teaspoon salt
1½ teaspoons grated orange peel
2 tablespoons butter or margarine
2 tablespoons fat-free cream cheese
⅓ cup buttermilk
1 egg, beaten
¼ cup egg substitute
1 cup tropical medley dried fruit or dried fruit bits
⅓ cup vanilla chocolate chips

GLAZE:
1 cup powdered sugar
2 to 3 tablespoons orange juice

SPREAD:
⅓ cup less-sugar apricot preserves

1. Preheat oven to 400 degrees.
2. Lightly spoon flour into measuring cup; level off. In large bowl, combine flour, sugar, baking powder, salt, and orange peel; mix well. With pastry blender or fork, cut in butter and cream cheese until mixture resembles coarse crumbs.
3. Add milk, egg, and egg substitute; blend well. Stir in dried fruit and vanilla chips until well mixed.
4. On lightly floured surface, knead dough 6 or 7 times until smooth. Divide dough in half. Pat each half into a 6-inch circle. With floured knife, cut each circle into 4 wedges. Place wedges 2 inches apart on ungreased cookie sheet.
5. Bake for 10 to 14 minutes or until golden brown. Cool 1 minute.
6. Meanwhile, in small bowl, combine powdered sugar and enough orange juice for desired consistency; blend until smooth. Drizzle mixture over top and sides of each scone. Cool 5 minutes. If desired, split each scone and spread with 2 teaspoons preserves.

PER SCONE: 328 calories, 7 g protein, 62 g carbohydrate, 6 g fat, 3.5 g saturated fat, 36 mg cholesterol, 2 g fiber, 539 mg sodium. Calories from fat: 17 percent.

AN ELAINE ORIGINAL

"To die for" is the phrase that comes to mind when I remember tasting these lemonade mini muffins. I first tasted these muffins when a friend brought samples of them to a Saturday morning Jazzercise class. While all the Jazzercise participants were oohing and aahing around the refreshment table, I found my friend and asked her how much butter was in the recipe. She responded "one stick," and the disappointment could be heard all around me.

I couldn't get those muffins off my mind—I was determined to make them low in fat if it was the last thing I did.

The original recipe specifies Meyer lemons, which have a unique sweetness and tartness all their own (and besides, they are much easier to squeeze juice from). After using a few Meyer lemons from my friend's tree, I decided to go out and buy one myself.

Instead of the stick of butter originally called for, I creamed 3 tablespoons of butter with ⅓ cup of nonfat cream cheese. I replaced one of the eggs with fat-free egg substitute, used low-fat milk instead of whole milk, and decreased the sugar slightly in both the batter and the lemonade syrup. I just needed to reduce the fat in the muffins as much as possible while preserving the light texture because the flavor really comes from the lemonade syrup soaked into the cooked muffin.

The new lower-fat muffins were a hit at Easter dinner and a hit when I brought the light version back to the same Jazzercise class. I was thrilled to hear tasters comment that the low-fat muffins were "to die for" just like the original muffins. I just love happy endings.

LEMONADE MINI MUFFINS

Original recipe contains 243 calories, 9 grams of fat, and 56 milligrams of cholesterol per serving.

Makes 24 mini muffins or 10 regular-sized muffins

> 3 tablespoons butter, softened
> 1/3 cup nonfat cream cheese
> 1 cup sugar
> 1 egg
> 1/4 cup egg substitute
> juice and finely chopped lemon zest of 1 lemon
> 1 1/2 cups flour
> 1 teaspoon baking powder
> 1/2 teaspoon salt
> 1/2 cup 1% low-fat milk
>
> LEMONADE SYRUP TOPPING:
> juice and finely chopped lemon zest of 2 lemons
> 1/3 cup sugar

1. Preheat oven to 350 degrees. Coat mini muffin cups with canola cooking spray.
2. Blend butter and cream cheese together with mixer. Cream butter mixture and sugar together with mixer. Beat in egg. Beat in egg substitute. Beat in juice and lemon zest of 1 lemon (about 3 tablespoons juice and 1 teaspoon finely chopped lemon zest).
3. In another bowl, blend dry ingredients together. Add half of flour mixture to butter mixture, then half of milk. Add in remaining flour mixture, then remaining milk.

4. Fill mini muffin cups almost full. Bake about 10 to 12 minutes or until middle springs back when pressed with finger.
5. While muffins are baking, blend lemonade syrup ingredients together. Poke the top of each muffin with toothpick or fork. Pour lemonade syrup over muffins using a $\frac{1}{2}$ teaspoon measuring spoon until it all soaks in. Let it stand an hour or so.

PER 2 MINI MUFFINS: 136 calories, 3 g protein, 25 g carbohydrate, 3.5 g fat, 2 g saturated fat, 26 mg cholesterol, .5 g fiber, 224 mg sodium. Calories from fat: 22 percent.

Q

Dear Recipe Doctor,

I really like this recipe for bran muffins, but it bothers me that it doesn't call for some whole wheat flour. Can you tweak this recipe so it is a little more nutritious?

A

Elaine is my name and tweaking recipes is my game. Lately I'm putting ground flaxseed into just about everything brown and baked, so that was the first thing I did. I reduced the flour by ¼ cup and added ¼ cup of ground flaxseed. Flaxseed is a potent source of one of the phyto-estrogens (plant estrogens), it contributes one of the plant forms of omega-3 fatty acids, and it is rich in soluble fiber.

Then I replaced ¾ cup of the flour with whole wheat flour just because bran muffins shouldn't call for all white flour—that's all there is to it. I reduced the oil called for from ½ cup to ¼ cup and switched to canola oil (a source of monounsaturated fat and one of the plant forms of omega-3 fatty acids). I added some maple syrup to make up the difference and decreased the granulated sugar accordingly. You can add ½ teaspoon of maple extract if you want to give the maple flavor a boost.

I also added 2 egg whites instead of one of the eggs called for to keep the cholesterol low. The result? Great tasting muffins with just the right amount of sweetness and almost two times the fiber (some of which is now from soluble fiber) of the original recipe. The vitamin and mineral content is also now higher, along with phytochemicals (protective plant chemicals).

⤙ RAISIN BRAN MUFFINS ⤚

Original recipe contains 235 calories, 1.5 grams fiber, 8 grams fat, and 27 milligrams cholesterol per muffin.

Makes 18 regular-sized muffins

> ¼ cup ground flaxseed (you can find flaxseed at health food stores)
> ¾ cup whole wheat flour
> 1½ cups unbleached white flour
> 1¼ cups sugar
> 2½ teaspoons baking soda
> 1 teaspoon salt
> 3 cups Raisin Bran cereal
> 2 cups low-fat buttermilk
> ¼ cup canola oil
> ¼ cup maple syrup
> 1 large egg
> 2 egg whites

1. Preheat oven to 425 degrees and coat 18 muffin cups with canola cooking spray.
2. Combine flaxseed, flours, sugar, baking soda, and salt in large mixing bowl and beat on low to blend well. Add Raisin Bran and beat on low speed of mixer until blended in.
3. Combine buttermilk, oil, maple syrup, and eggs in another bowl and whisk with fork to blend well. Pour into dry ingredients and beat on low speed briefly just to blend.

4, Spoon ¼ cup batter into each prepared muffin cup and bake until tester inserted in center of muffins comes out clean (about 15 minutes). Transfer to rack and cool.

Note: You can cover the mixing bowl and chill the muffin batter in refrigerator for up to a week. The mixture will thicken, though.

PER MUFFIN: 197 calories, 4.5 g protein, 37 g carbohydrate, 4 g fat, .5 g saturated fat, 12 mg cholesterol, 2.7 g fiber, 370 mg sodium. Calories from fat: 18 percent.

Chapter Five

BREAKFAST & BRUNCH

RESTAURANT-STYLE BUTTERMILK PANCAKES

OVERNIGHT (EASIER-THAN-IT-LOOKS)
LIGHTER CINNABON-LIKE ROLLS

MEXICAN QUICHE

QUICHE MONTEREY

CINNAMON CRUMB COFFEECAKE

SPINACH QUICHE MUFFINS

BLENDER SWEDISH PANCAKES

CHRISTMAS EGGS

APPLE-WALNUT COFFEECAKE

Q

Dear Recipe Doctor,

I saw this recipe for restaurant-style buttermilk pancakes in the newspaper recently and would love for you to improve on it nutritionally since we eat pancakes often.

A

I had so much fun playing with this recipe. We have pancakes often, too, but I admit to using the reduced-fat Bisquick recipe for fluffy pancakes on the back of the box most of the time.

So I delighted in trying this homemade recipe, what with its 2 cups of buttermilk, cake flour, teaspoon of vanilla, and stick of butter—what! A stick of butter? That's right. Well, we can't have that, can we?

I thought 2 tablespoons of melted butter should suffice (you could substitute canola margarine or canola oil if you prefer) and I added ¼ cup of reduced-calorie pancake syrup in its stead. I cut the eggs from 3 to 2 and used low-fat buttermilk.

The original recipe calls for sifting the dry ingredients together, and, let's put it this way, I don't sift unless my arm is being twisted, tightly. I didn't sift, and everything turned out great. So there. I also cut the salt in half because otherwise a serving would contain more than 1,000 milligrams.

The cake flour gives the pancakes a finer crumb and I thought it was a nice touch. But then, that's easy for me to say—I always have a box of cake flour in my kitchen. My family truly loved these pancakes. This is a recipe I will keep close by, believe me.

～ RESTAURANT-STYLE BUTTERMILK PANCAKES ～

Original recipe contains 396 calories, 20.5 grams fat, 180 mg cholesterol per serving.

Makes 5 servings (about 3–4 pancakes each)

> 2 cups cake flour
> 2 teaspoons baking powder
> 1 teaspoon baking soda
> 1/2 teaspoon salt
> 2 tablespoons sugar
> 2 large eggs
> 2 cups buttermilk
> 1 teaspoon vanilla
> 2 tablespoons butter, melted
> 1/4 cup reduced-calorie pancake syrup

1. Combine flour, baking powder, baking soda, salt, and sugar in medium bowl and blend well with fork.
2. Beat eggs, buttermilk, and vanilla in mixing bowl on medium-low speed until smooth.
3. Add melted butter, pancake syrup, and dry ingredients to egg mixture in mixing bowl and beat on lowest speed, scraping with rubber spatula, just until blended. Do not overmix.
4. Let batter rest for 20 minutes. Spray griddle lightly with canola cooking spray. Preheat griddle until water skittles.
5. Pour 1/4 cup batter onto griddle. Cook over medium heat until bubbles form in pancake (30 to 60 seconds). Turn over with spatula and cook another 30 to 60 seconds or until golden brown. Serve pancakes with your preferred toppings.

PER SERVING: 292 calories, 9 g protein, 46 g carbohydrate, 7.8 g fat, 4 g saturated fat, 100 mg cholesterol, 1 g fiber, 870 mg sodium. Calories from fat: 24 percent.

Q

Dear Recipe Doctor,

I look forward to cinnamon rolls every time I go to the mall. I'm sure they are loaded with calories and fat. Can you come up with a light Cinnabon-like cinnamon roll for me?

A

I've probably purchased a Cinnabon roll or two myself over countless trips to the mall. And as far as cinnamon rolls go, they are hard to beat—moist and buttery with more icing than you know what to do with. In a word: decadent.

Fat, saturated fat, and calories invade your cinnamon roll from three directions—the rich dough, the butter filling, and the creamy icing. Needless to say, I had a lot of work to do.

I started with the taste-alike Cinnabon recipe from *More Top Secret Recipes* by Todd Wilbur (Plume, 1994). I started by modifying the recipe for the bread machine. Then I used half as much butter as the original recipe called for and added a little more milk to compensate. And I used one egg and some egg substitute instead of two eggs.

In the original recipe, the icing called for 1 stick of butter and 2 ounces of cream cheese. I cut the butter down to 2 tablespoons and doubled the amount of cream cheese (and switched to light cream cheese).

My daughter asks for these cinnamon rolls periodically (and she is one of those borderline picky eaters). Granted, homemade cinnamon rolls take a bit of effort, but using a bread machine and letting them rise in the refrigerator overnight certainly cut down on the hassle, and the results are mouth-watering!

OVERNIGHT (EASIER-THAN-IT-LOOKS) LIGHTER CINNABON-LIKE ROLLS

The original mock Cinnabon recipe contains 480 calories, 22 grams fat, and 92 milligrams cholesterol per serving.

Makes 12 rolls

DOUGH:
1 cup plus 2 tablespoons warm milk (105–110 degrees)
3 tablespoons melted butter
1 egg, lightly beaten
¼ cup egg substitute
½ cup sugar
4 cups unbleached flour
1 teaspoon salt
4 teaspoons active dry yeast

FILLING:
1 cup packed brown sugar
2 tablespoons cinnamon
¼ cup good-tasting diet margarine (like I Can't Believe It's Not Butter Light) or canola margarine

ICING:
½ cup light cream cheese
2 tablespoons butter or canola margarine, softened
1½ cups powdered sugar
½ teaspoon vanilla extract

1. Place dough ingredients in a 2-pound bread machine in the order recommended by manufacturer. Set machine to dough cycle and press start.
2. When dough cycle is complete, roll dough out on lightly floured surface until it is about 21 inches long and 16 inches wide. It should be about ¼ inch thick.
3. Combine the brown sugar and cinnamon in a bowl. Spread the diet margarine evenly over the surface of the dough, and then sprinkle the cinnamon mixture evenly over the surface.
4. Working carefully from the 21-inch side, roll the dough down to the bottom edge. Cut the rolled dough into 1¾-inch slices and place in a 9 x-13-inch pan that has been coated with canola cooking spray. You can cover and let rise in the refrigerator overnight, or let rise at room temperature for an hour.
5. Bake in a preheated 400-degree oven for about 10 minutes, or until the rolls are light brown on top and cooked throughout. While the rolls bake, beat the icing ingredients with an electric mixer until fluffy.
6. When the rolls come out of the oven, coat each generously with icing.

PER ROLL: 370 calories, 7.5 g protein, 66 g carbohydrates, 8.5 g fat, 4.5 g saturated fat, 35 mg cholesterol, 1.5 g fiber, 330 mg sodium. Calories from fat: 21 percent.

Q

Dear Recipe Doctor,

My friends have passed this recipe around quite a bit over the years, but now we would all love to reduce the dietary damage from this old family favorite.

A

It's the type of recipe you love to serve when you're expecting company. You know the type—it never ceases to receive rave reviews every time you serve it. It looks and tastes like you spent all morning in the kitchen, when it really took just five to ten minutes of your time. In this case, it's a throw-together Mexican quiche recipe.

The first thing I did was eliminate the stick of butter called for. I really didn't need to add anything in its place—I just cut it out. Save the butter for the biscuits or toast you might be serving on the side. I then cut the number of eggs in half and used egg substitute to replace the lost eggs. Of course, you could always cut out the real eggs completely, but the result would taste about as good as the name "100 Percent Egg White Quiche" sounds. If you just cut the number of eggs in half, you still have a quiche that looks and tastes a lot like the original, but with less fat and half the cholesterol!

I used low-fat milk and low-fat cottage cheese to blend with the egg mixture. If you want to use nonfat milk and fat-free cottage cheese, go ahead. I prefer to use at least 1 percent low-fat products. And last but not least, the cheese. To help cut the fat in half you have two options. You can use half as much of the regular fat Monterey Jack cheese, or you can add just as much as the original recipe, but use reduced-fat Monterey Jack cheese. I prefer the latter option, because the Kraft reduced-fat Monterey Jack leaves nothing to be desired. And frankly, serving a quiche that oozes with cheese is what this recipe is all about.

I want to thank the reader and her friends for sending me this recipe; it has now become one of my favorite recipes, too.

⮞ MEXICAN QUICHE ⮜

Original recipe contains 468 calories, 35 grams fat, and 351 milligrams cholesterol per serving.

Makes 8 servings

> 5 eggs
> ½ cup flour
> 1 teaspoon baking powder
> dash salt
> 1¼ cups egg substitute
> ½ cup low-fat milk
> 2 4-ounce cans chopped green chilies, mild, medium, or hot
> 2 cups low-fat cottage cheese, whipped in food processor
>   until smooth
> 12 ounces reduced-fat Monterey Jack cheese, grated
> salsa

1. Preheat oven to 400 degrees. Coat a large casserole pan (or 9 x 13-inch baking pan) with no-stick cooking spray; set aside.
2. In mixer bowl, combine the eggs, flour, baking powder, and salt and beat until blended. Add egg substitute and milk and beat until smooth. Stir in green chilies, cottage cheese, and grated cheese.
3. Pour into prepared pan and bake for 15 minutes, then reduce heat to 350 degrees and bake for 30 minutes more. Serve with salsa.

PER SERVING: 259 calories, 12 g carbohydrates, 27 g protein, 11 g fat, 6 g saturated fat, 161 mg cholesterol, .3 g fiber, 610 mg sodium. Calories from fat: 38 percent.

Q

Dear Recipe Doctor,

I dearly love the Nancy's Quiche Monterey you buy in super-markets. However, as you can see from the label, it is not exactly what you would call a healthy diet dish. Could you please cut down somewhat on the calories and fat while still retaining the great Mexican flavor? I would be eternally grateful.

A

Whenever you lighten up a quiche you come down to the same question, "To crust or not to crust, that is the 200-calorie question." If you really like pie crust and can't imagine quiche without it, you will probably need to make this using pie crust. Otherwise, I whipped up a reduced-fat biscuit crust that you can use instead. Just blend some reduced-fat Bisquick with some low-fat buttermilk and knead and roll on a floured surface, just as you would a pastry dough.

In Nancy's quiche she used part cheddar cheese and part red pepper jack cheese. I couldn't find a reduced-fat pepper jack cheese so I used a reduced-fat jack cheese (you can sprinkle some pepper flakes into the grated cheese if you would like) and a reduced-fat sharp cheddar. It's no secret that I do not like my food hot-spicy, so I made this recipe with a little tiny zing. If you like smoke blowing out of your ears, then you will have to blend in a few pinches of red pepper flakes.

For the egg mixture, I cut the eggs in half and used egg substitute to make up the difference. I added low-fat milk instead of whole milk or cream to the beaten eggs, along with garlic salt, chili powder, and onion powder.

You can add some chopped green onions to the quiche instead of the onion powder; I just happen to be caught in the kitchen without green onions at the time I was making this. Nancy's Quiche Monterey also contains green chilies, so I added a can of Ortega diced chilies. The result was a very tasty Mexican quiche with a lot fewer calories, two-thirds less fat, and half the cholesterol of the one you can buy in the store.

ↀ QUICHE MONTEREY ↀ

Original recipe contains around 425 calories, 195 milligrams cholesterol, and 30 grams fat per serving.

Makes 6 servings

BISCUIT CRUST:
1½ cups reduced-fat Bisquick baking mix
½ cup (+1 tablespoon if needed) low-fat buttermilk
    (low-fat milk can be used in a pinch)
flour for dusting surface and rolling pin
2 large eggs
½ cup egg substitute
1 cup 1% low-fat milk
½ teaspoon garlic salt
½ teaspoon onion powder
¼ teaspoon chili powder
4 ounces reduced-fat Monterey Jack cheese, grated
4 ounces reduced-fat sharp cheddar cheese, grated
4-ounce can Ortega diced green chilies
pepper flakes (optional)

1. Preheat oven to 425 degrees. Coat a 9-inch cake or pie pan with nonstick cooking spray.
2. In a small bowl, blend the Bisquick with the buttermilk. Add an extra tablespoon of milk if needed. Turn out onto a lightly floured cutting board and knead until smooth, adding flour as needed. Roll out with a flour-dusted rolling pin into an 11-inch circle. Press into prepared pan.
3. In a medium bowl, with a wire whisk or electric mixer, beat eggs, egg substitute, milk, garlic salt, onion powder, and chili powder until well blended. Blend grated cheeses, diced

chili peppers, and a couple pinches of pepper flakes (if desired) together and spread over crust in pan. Pour egg mixture into crust.

4. Bake for 15 minutes. Reduce oven temperature to 325 degrees and bake for about 30 minutes longer, or until a knife inserted in the center comes out clean. Let stand for 10 minutes before serving.

PER SERVING: 290 calories, 19.5 g protein, 27.5 g carbohydrate, 10.5 g fat, 5.5 g saturated fat, 93 mg cholesterol, 1 g fiber, 750 mg sodium. Calories from fat: 33 percent.

Q *A charming restaurant in Lafayette, California (Millie's Kitchen), makes the most delicious old-fashioned coffeecake with a crumb topping. I've begged for the recipe with no success. Can you help? If you could lighten it up I know lots of people who would be forever grateful.*

A I begged, too. Apparently when the current owner purchased the restaurant, she agreed not to share the original recipes. National magazines have even called requesting the coffeecake recipe. No matter. I've recreated a few famous recipes in my time—I can certainly tackle a crumb coffeecake. Or so I thought.

After about five different versions, I finally came up with a lower-fat coffeecake that comes darn close to Millie's (just in time, too—I was beginning to tire of coffeecake). I used an old-fashioned jam crumb cake recipe from way back as my muse. I used a combination of canola margarine or butter and light corn syrup instead of butter in the cake batter. One of my problems in earlier versions was that the coffeecake would become too dry by the next day or two. Corn syrup, due to its molecular structure, appears to release moisture in a baked product over time. I thought this would cure my drying out problem. I was right.

I increased the vanilla extract a pinch and reduced the eggs from three to two. I added two egg whites to make up the difference. I used cake flour to encourage a tender crumb, and I switched to a low-fat milk instead of whole milk or cream (you could use whole milk, though, if that's what you have).

For the crumb topping I used a combination of brown sugar, cinnamon, and cake flour and blended it with the minimum of melted butter and reduced-calorie pancake syrup to make it crumbly.

I won't bore you with all the details of how I changed the recipe. Just know it is pretty quick to make and a pleasure to eat and, in this case, not too high in fat calories either.

CINNAMON CRUMB COFFEECAKE

Makes 12 large servings

⅓ cup canola margarine or butter, softened
½ cup light corn syrup
1 cup sugar
1½ tablespoons vanilla extract
2 whole large eggs
2 large egg whites
3 cups cake flour
4½ teaspoons baking powder
¾ teaspoon salt
1½ cups low-fat milk

CRUMB TOPPING:
1 cup packed brown sugar
1½ cups cake flour
2 teaspoons ground cinnamon
3 tablespoons butter (canola margarine can also be used)
1 tablespoon reduced-calorie pancake syrup

1. Preheat oven to 375 degrees. Lightly grease and flour a 9 x 13-inch baking pan using canola margarine or butter or canola cooking spray.
2. For cake batter, cream ⅓ cup canola margarine or softened butter and light corn syrup with electric mixer until smooth. Add sugar, vanilla, eggs, and egg whites, and beat until smooth and creamy.
3. Combine cake flour, baking powder, and salt in an 8-cup measure and stir to blend. (You can sift the dry ingredients here if

you are so inclined—I personally don't sift unless I absolutely have to.)

4. Add dry ingredients to creamed mixture alternately with the milk. Beat on low just until blended. Pour into the prepared baking pan.

5. For topping, combine brown sugar, 1½ cups cake flour, and 2 teaspoons cinnamon in a small bowl and stir with fork to blend. Melt butter in microwave using a small microwave-safe dish. Stir in the tablespoon of syrup. Drizzle the melted butter mixture over the dry ingredients and stir with fork to blend (should form a dry crumb mixture). Sprinkle it evenly over the coffeecake batter in pan. Spray the top with canola cooking spray.

6. Bake for about 30 minutes or until fork inserted in center comes out clean.

PER SERVING: 380 calories, 6 g protein, 69.5 g carbohydrate, 9 g fat, 3 g saturated fat, 44 mg cholesterol, .5 g fiber, 455 mg sodium. Calories from fat: 22 percent.

Q

Dear Recipe Doctor,

I'm looking for a recipe for spinach quiche muffins. I tried the spinach quiche muffin at the nearby mall and it was very tasty. I've looked through all my recipe books and can't find anything. Any help would be appreciated.

A

My neighbor informs me she is also addicted to spinach quiche muffins. For research purposes I had to try them out first hand and now I think *I'm* addicted to them!

I tried to get the original recipe but after weeks of making phone calls, still had nothing to go on. So I tasted the muffin myself and whipped up a lighter version, which my neighbor and I think comes darn close.

Paradise Bakery, a chain in California, has the right idea making quiche "muffins" because in doing so you automatically cut out the pastry crust, which cuts out all those flaky grams of fat. They also must add a smidgen of flour because the texture is a tad toward muffins versus the traditional cheese custard.

I used half real eggs and half egg substitute (I find this proportion usually works well). I used reduced-fat sharp cheddar cheese (Kraft and Cracker Barrel make the best-tasting reduced-fat versions). And instead of cream I used whole or low-fat milk. Paradise Bakery says they add Parmesan cheese, so I added some token Parmesan cheese. (I never need an excuse to add Parmesan.)

After two batches I think I got the taste and texture right. I love these things! They freeze well, too, in a plastic freezer bag—just pop them in the microwave when you want one. They particularly come in handy for breakfast on the run, to accompany a salad for a quick dinner, or for hors d'oeuvres (use a mini muffin pan instead).

❧ SPINACH QUICHE MUFFINS ❧

Makes about 16 muffins

1¾ cups whole or low-fat milk, divided
2 eggs
½ cup egg substitute
¼ teaspoon salt
⅛ teaspoon white pepper
⅛ teaspoon ground nutmeg
½ cup flour
10-ounce box frozen chopped spinach, thawed, gently
squeezed of extra moisture, and coarsely chopped with a
knife (about 1 cup)
1½ cups (packed) shredded reduced-fat sharp cheddar cheese
½ cup finely shredded Parmesan cheese

1. Preheat oven to 350 degrees. Coat a thick (cushion-air type) muffin pan generously with canola cooking spray.
2. Beat 1¼ cups of the milk together with the eggs, egg substitute, salt, pepper, and nutmeg. Stir ½ cup milk with flour to make a paste. Beat paste into the egg mixture until smooth. Stir in spinach and cheeses.
3. Fill each muffin cup with ¼ cup of batter. Bake until cooked throughout (about 12 to 15 minutes).

PER SERVING: 86 calories, 7.5 g protein, 6 g carbohydrate, 3.5 g fat, 2 g saturated fat, 36 mg cholesterol, .5 g fiber, 195 mg sodium. Calories from fat: 39 percent.

Q

Dear Recipe Doctor,

My husband likes to make "Swedes" (Swedish pancakes) and he makes them with 3 eggs and oodles of butter. Can you give us a lighter recipe for these tasty pancakes?

A

I consulted my trusty Scandinavian cookbook and easily found a recipe for Swedish pancakes. Maybe your husband and I have the same book, because the recipe I found also called for 3 eggs and almost an entire stick of butter, which definitely qualifies as oodles. I hope you don't mind, but I converted the recipe for a blender. This way all you do is dump the ingredients in the blender and your thin, smooth pancake batter is only a whirl away.

According to this cookbook, though, Swedish pancakes are small, like our pancakes, but much thinner and they use a special pancake pan to make them. If you like to make them this way, just use a tablespoonful of batter for each one (and make about 4 at a time) using your large nonstick frying pan. Personally I like them big, so I use a ¼-cup measure for each pancake and make them one at a time.

I used 1 egg and ½ cup of egg substitute to cut down on the cholesterol. The fat is really coming from two places—the cup of light cream and the 6 tablespoons of butter.

I used 2 cups of low-fat milk and it worked out well. You could also use 2 cups of whole milk, which is still going to give you a lot less fat than the original recipe (the original recipe calls for a cup of whole milk and a cup of light cream). The milk isn't as thick as the cream so I would normally use a little less in order to maintain the same batter consistency. But I also cut the butter from 6 tablespoons to 2, without adding anything. So I left the amount of milk alone. With less butter the batter is going to stick to the pan easier than it normally would. If you use canola cooking spray and a nonstick frying pan you won't find it a problem.

☞ BLENDER SWEDISH PANCAKES ☜

Original recipe contains 356 calories, 28 grams fat, and 187 milligrams cholesterol per serving.

Swedish pancakes are served with lingonberries or berry preserves as a dessert following Thursday pea soup (a Swedish tradition). A group of ten children and I made these blender Swedish pancakes and only one child didn't like them—the rest licked their plates, they loved them so much!

Makes 6 servings (about 2 large pancakes each)

    2 tablespoons butter
    1 egg
    ½ cup egg substitute
    2 cups low-fat milk (1% or 2%)
    1 cup flour
    1 tablespoon sugar
    ½ teaspoon salt
    ¼ teaspoon ground cinnamon (optional)
    jam
    powdered sugar (optional)

1. Melt butter in microwave-safe cup or in saucepan.
2. Place first eight ingredients in blender. Mix on medium speed until batter is smooth (about 1 to 2 minutes).
3. Heat skillet until very hot. Coat nonstick skillet or frying pan with canola cooking spray. To make each pancake, drop ¼ cup of batter into skillet; tilt pan to coat the pan evenly and make a circle. In about a minute, the edges will brown lightly. Turn the pancake over and cook other side for about a minute. Remove pancake with spatula to holding plate.
4. Repeat with remaining batter. Scoop a little jam onto each pancake. Sprinkle powdered sugar over the top with a sifter if you want.

PER SERVING: 166 calories, 8 g protein, 20 g carbohydrate, 5.7 g fat, 3 g saturated fat, 49 mg cholesterol, 1 g fiber, 302 mg sodium. Calories from fat: 31 percent.

Dear Recipe Doctor,

I've been reading your column for months now and I thought maybe you could help us with a dish that I call Christmas Eggs. My mother made this dish every Christmas morning when I was growing up in Maryland (it was my grandmother's recipe originally). My wife finally got the recipe, but we're hoping you can do something with it first.

 I'm glad the tradition of cooking special dishes for Christmas morning is still going strong. Some would say, Why lighten a dish that you only have a couple times a year? But if you can do it without a noticeable difference in taste, then why not? Then you can even make it more often.

This dish calls for croutons and lots of cheddar cheese, so I used the lower-fat croutons now available and reduced-fat sharp cheddar cheese and a bit less of it. It calls for bacon, so I used what my family considers to be "bacon"— Louis Rich turkey bacon. If you cook it gently over medium-low heat, turning the strips frequently, it will end up nice and crisp.

Instead of 4 eggs and cream, I used 2 eggs, ½ cup of egg substitute, and low-fat or whole milk.

CHRISTMAS EGGS

excellent 8-01

Original recipe contains 358 calories, 25 grams fat, 12 grams saturated fat, 198 milligrams cholesterol.

Makes 6 servings

> 2 cups low-fat seasoned croutons (e.g., Mrs. Cubbison's Restaurant Style Caesar Salad Croutons)
> ½ cup grated reduced-fat sharp cheddar cheese
> 2 eggs
> ½ cup egg substitute
> 2 cups low-fat or whole milk
> ½ teaspoon salt
> 1 teaspoon prepared mustard
> ⅛ teaspoon onion powder
> pepper to taste
> 2 tablespoons grated Parmesan cheese
> 6 slices Louis Rich turkey bacon, cooked to crisp and crumbled (optional)

1. Preheat oven to 325 degrees. Coat 8-inch square baking pan with canola cooking spray. Line the bottom of the pan with the croutons and grated cheddar cheese.
2. Blend next seven ingredients together in mixer and pour into prepared pan over croutons and cheese. Sprinkle Parmesan cheese and bacon (if desired) over the top.
3. Bake for about 50 to 55 minutes.

Note: Opting for the turkey bacon will add about 2.5 grams fat, .5 grams saturated fat, and 10 mg cholesterol per serving.

PER SERVING: 160 calories, 12.5 g protein, 13 g carbohydrate, 6.5 g fat, 3 g saturated fat, 81 mg cholesterol, .5 g fiber, 570 mg sodium. Calories from fat: 37 percent.

Q *Dear Recipe Doctor,*

I was given this recipe for Apple-Walnut Bundt Coffeecake by my aunt, who lives in Minnesota. It won a ribbon at the Minnesota State Fair in 1996. I've made it a few times and it is delicious—but what about that cup of vegetable oil?

A I know you probably won't believe it, but that cup of oil can be cut down to ¼ cup without you noticing a big difference in taste and moistness. The crumb might be less greasy to the touch, but I'm hoping that's a good thing. Let's put it this way, a slice of this cake won't leave grease marks when placed on a napkin or doily. Of course, I did have to add something in place of the ¾ cup of oil I just cut out—I chose buttermilk.

Buttermilk just sounded like it would complement the apples and walnuts. I was right, it worked wonderfully. I also traded two of the three eggs for ½ cup of egg substitute. I find that one egg yolk often does the trick. The primary job for an egg yolk in this recipe is to emulsify or blend fatty ingredients with nonfatty ingredients into a smooth batter.

To boost the flavor of the batter a bit, I increased the cinnamon a smidge and doubled the vanilla extract. This is a wonderful dessert, snack, or breakfast cake—take your pick! And the optional lemon glaze makes this coffeecake even more yummy.

☞ APPLE-WALNUT COFFEECAKE ☜

Original recipe contains 388 calories, 19.5 grams of fat, and 40 milligrams cholesterol per serving.

Makes 16 servings

    3 cups all-purpose flour
    1 teaspoon baking soda
    1 teaspoon salt
    1 teaspoon baking powder
    1 tablespoon ground cinnamon
    ¾ teaspoon ground nutmeg
    1 egg
    ½ cup egg substitute
    ¼ cup canola oil
    ¾ cup low-fat buttermilk
    2 cups shredded, cored and peeled apple (Granny Smith, Pippin, or Braeburn)*
    2 cups granulated sugar
    1 tablespoon vanilla
    ½ cup black walnuts, regular walnuts, or pecans, chopped
    3 tablespoons lemon juice (optional)
    1 cup powdered sugar (optional)

1. Preheat oven to 325 degrees. Coat a 10-cup bundt pan or fluted cake pan with canola cooking spray.
2. Blend flour, baking soda, salt, baking powder, cinnamon, and nutmeg together in large bowl; set aside.
3. Beat egg, egg substitute, and oil in large mixing bowl. Add buttermilk, apple, sugar, and vanilla; beat 1 minute on low speed. Beat in flour mixture on low speed until blended. Increase

speed to medium-low and beat for 2 minutes, scraping down side of bowl occasionally. Stir in nuts.

4. Pour into prepared pan. Bake for 40 minutes or until wooden pick inserted in center comes out clean. Cool cake in pan on wire rack for 20 minutes. Remove cake from pan and place upside down on serving plate.

5. For optional lemon glaze, blend lemon juice with powdered sugar. Spread over cake once cake has cooled slightly.

*Grating the apple slices by hand can be done easily by cutting the apple into quarters, cutting out the core, then rubbing the apple flesh against the grater—holding on to the peel part of the apple. The peel protects your fingers from the grater and it cuts one step out—peeling the apple.

PER SERVING: 272 calories, 5 g protein, 50 g carbohydrate, 6.4 g fat, .6 g saturated fat, 14 mg cholesterol, 1.5 g fiber, 270 mg sodium. Calories from fat: 21 percent.

Chapter Six

HOLIDAY RECIPES

HEIRLOOM PUMPKIN COOKIES

MATZO-LEMON SPONGE CAKE

GRANDMA'S TRADITIONAL BREAD STUFFING

PENNSYLVANIA DUTCH PUMPKIN CAKE

LEFTOVER TURKEY SHEPHERD'S PIE

GINGERBREAD HEARTS AND SANTA CLAUS COOKIES

QUICK PANATONE

Q

Dear Recipe Doctor,

This is one of the best cookies I know! My grandmother made these cookies every holiday and they are so moist and the butterscotch frosting tops them perfectly. The only problem is the 3 sticks of butter! Is there any way to make them heart healthy?

A

Ironically, "pumpkin cookies" sound like they should be healthy. But using 3 sticks of butter to make 32 cookies isn't going to do it. I propose cutting the butter out completely and using a little canola oil, a little apple butter, and a lot of fat-free cream cheese in its place. Once combined, this mixture even starts to resemble butter.

I wouldn't get away with switching to canola oil for every cookie recipe that comes my way, though—it wouldn't work as well with cookies more dependent on butter for their characteristic taste or texture (such as butter cookies or chocolate chip cookies). But in the case of pumpkin cookies, canola oil creates their distinguished moist cake texture just as well as butter does.

I changed the frosting recipe quite a bit. I took one look at the directions to boil the frosting ingredients and my enthusiasm for butterscotch frosting quickly evaporated. So I eliminated the milk normally called for in the boiling step and achieved a similar texture by blending some diet margarine with some brown sugar, powdered sugar, vanilla, and fat-free sweetened condensed milk in a small food processor. The cookies were absolutely yummy (I had some for breakfast one morning). I brought the calories down from 180 to 120, the fat from 8.2 to 2.5 grams, and the cholesterol from 28 to 7 milligrams. But the best part is the saturated fat goes way down to a mere .3 gram per cookie!

∼ HEIRLOOM PUMPKIN COOKIES ∼

Original recipe contains 180 calories, 8.2 grams fat, and 28 milligrams cholesterol per serving.

Makes 32 large cookies

1/4 cup canola oil
1/2 cup nonfat cream cheese
1/4 cup apple butter
1 cup sugar
1 cup canned pumpkin
1 large egg
1 1/2 teaspoon vanilla
2 cups all-purpose flour
2 teaspoons pumpkin pie spice
1 teaspoon baking powder
1 teaspoon baking soda
1 teaspoon ground cinnamon
1 teaspoon salt
1/2 teaspoon ground cloves
1/2 cup dark raisins
1/2 cup chopped pecans (optional)

FROSTING:
1 cup packed dark brown sugar
3 tablespoons diet margarine
1 1/2 teaspoons vanilla
1 cup powdered sugar
1 1/2 to 2 tablespoons fat-free sweetened condensed milk

1. Preheat oven to 325 degrees. In large mixer bowl, cream the canola oil, cream cheese, and apple butter together until smooth. Add the sugar and beat for 3 minutes. Add pumpkin, egg, and vanilla and mix well.
2. In another bowl, blend flour, pumpkin pie spice, baking powder, soda, cinnamon, salt, and cloves together. Slowly add flour mixture to the pumpkin mixture; mix until combined. Stir in raisins and pecans by hand.
3. Drop tablespoonfuls (or use a cookie scoop) of dough onto a cookie sheet that has been coated with cooking spray. Bake about 10 to 12 minutes, or until top of cookie springs back when tested with a finger. Transfer to wire racks to cool.
4. For frosting, place brown sugar, margarine, vanilla, powdered sugar, and 1½ tablespoons of sweetened condensed milk in small food processor. Process until smooth and of spreadable consistency (add another 1 to 2 teaspoons of sweetened condensed milk if needed). Frost cooled cookies with this butterscotch frosting.

PER SERVING: 122 calories, 2 g protein, 24 g carbohydrate, 2.5 g fat, .4 g saturated fat, 7 mg cholesterol, .7 g fiber, 150 mg sodium. Calories from fat: 18 percent.

Every Passover I go to make a cake and can't believe the number of eggs needed. Is there anything you can do to lighten a Passover cake using kosher ingredients?

I thumbed through a few Jewish cookbooks (trying hard not to wince when I saw recipes calling for 12 egg yolks) and found a recipe for matzo-lemon sponge cake that impressed me because it only called for 8 eggs. This recipe seemed simple, calling for eggs, sugar, a pinch of salt, a lemon, and sifted matzo cake meal. The only problem I ran into was trying to find matzo *cake* meal in local supermarkets. In early February I could only find matzo meal. I'm hoping this is a special item supermarkets stock around Passover time. But, I happened to have a box of matzo meal in my cabinet so I figured I could grind it up into a cake crumb using my handy dandy food processor.

Since traditional leavens cannot be used during Passover, the air in cakes is made by whipping egg whites, which are usually folded into the cake batter. I have no problem with the egg whites. It's the large quantity of egg yolks beaten into the batter that I take some issue with. Not that I have a problem with a couple of egg yolks here and there, but it is the sheer quantity used in Passover cakes that makes each slim serving of cake pack a cholesterol wallop that rivals a serving of liver. That can't be a good thing.

Since I probably couldn't replace half the yolks with egg substitute (which has a few other ingredients added to it so it looks more like beaten whole eggs instead of what it really is, which is pasteurized egg whites), I replaced half the yolks with lemonade. And to give the cake a nice strong lemon flavor, I doubled the amount of lemon juice and rind called for too. The pinch of salt, matzo meal, and sugar stayed the same.

It turned out real spongy and moist with a nice lemon flavor.

⇜ MATZO-LEMON SPONGE CAKE ⇝

For a smaller cake (with 6 servings) you can cut the recipe in half and line the bottom of a loaf pan with parchment paper to make a pound cake-shaped cake.

Original recipe contains 225 calories, 4 grams fat, 1 gram saturated fat, 140 milligrams cholesterol per serving.

Makes 12 servings

> 8 egg whites
> 4 egg yolks
> $\frac{1}{2}$ cup lemonade
> 1$\frac{1}{2}$ cups sugar
> pinch of salt
> grated rind and juice of 1 lemon
> 1 cup sifted matzo cake meal (in a pinch, grind regular matzo
>   meal for a minute in a food processor, then sift and
>   measure 1 cup)
> strawberries and whipped cream (optional)

1. Preheat oven to 350 degrees. Line just the bottom of 10-inch springform pan with parchment or waxed paper (or line the bottom of 2 loaf pans). Beat egg whites until stiff; set aside.
2. Beat egg yolks and lemonade until light. Add sugar and beat for a minute. Add a pinch of salt, the lemon juice and rind, and the matzo cake meal, and beat on low until nicely blended. On low speed, gently beat in the egg whites (or fold in with a spatula).
3. Once well mixed, pour into prepared pan(s) and bake until golden (about 45 minutes for the springform pan or around 20 minutes for loaf pans).

4. Invert pan until cake is cool. Use knife to cut around edges and remove cake from pan. Cut with serrated knife into layers if desired. Serve with strawberries between the layers and top each serving with a dollop of whipped cream if desired.

PER SERVING (not including optional whipped cream and strawberries): 171 calories, 4.5 g protein, 36 g carbohydrate, 1.8 g fat, .5 g saturated fat, 70 mg cholesterol, .5 g fiber, 41 mg sodium. Calories from fat: 9 percent.

Q *Dear Recipe Doctor,*

I'm looking for a good bread stuffing recipe to make for the holidays. Can you help?

A Most of us make our bread stuffing with those bags or boxes of seasoned bread cubes you find in the supermarket. I've even been known to mix up a batch of Stove Top Stuffing on occasion. Make my bread stuffing totally from scratch? I've got better things to do—like make pumpkin pie.

Then I saw this quaint recipe for Grandma's bread stuffing, where you toast your slices of bread to dry them out, and I thought, "I can do this." The best part of making your stuffing from scratch is you can decide what type of bread to use. If you want a sourdough bread stuffing, use sourdough slices. If you are diabetic and need to boost your soluble fiber, use oat bran bread. And if someone at your Thanksgiving table is watching their sodium, you can easily make this an even lower-sodium stuffing just by using low-sodium chicken broth (I already deleted the $1/2$ teaspoon salt Grandma added).

Grandma must have liked her butter, too, because the original recipe called for two whole cubes. I cut it down to 3 tablespoons. I know this sounds drastic, but it really doesn't need more than this. The only step you really use the butter for is sautéing the celery and onions. Three tablespoons is plenty. I just drizzled chicken broth over the bread cubes until I had the desired moistness.

I doubled the onions and added garlic and grated carrots to make the stuffing a little more interesting. If you like a little sausage in your stuffing, crumble and brown some light Jimmy Dean sausage and add it in along with the parsley. Now you are ready to stuff your bird or serve it on the side.

GRANDMA'S TRADITIONAL BREAD STUFFING

Original recipe contains 413 calories, 33 grams fat, and 83 milligrams cholesterol per serving.

Makes 6 servings

> ½ loaf bread of your choice (about 11 slices)
> 3 tablespoons butter or margarine
> 1 small onion, finely chopped
> 1 cup chopped celery
> 2 cloves garlic, minced or pressed
> ⅛–¼ teaspoon pepper
> 2 teaspoons poultry seasoning
> 1 cup grated carrot
> 1 tablespoon chopped fresh parsley or 2 teaspoons dried
>   chervil or parsley
> up to 1 cup chicken broth

1. Toast bread lightly in toaster. Dice into medium-sized pieces. Toast more bread if need be to make a total of 8 cups of toasted bread cubes.
2. Melt butter in large skillet. Add onion, celery, garlic, pepper, and poultry seasoning. Simmer until celery is almost tender. Stir in the grated carrot and simmer a couple more minutes. Add parsley, and mix in bread cubes.
3. Drizzle ½-cup chicken broth over the top and stir. If more chicken broth is needed for desired moistness of stuffing, add ⅛ cup more, and so on. Cover pan and turn off heat. Let stuffing sit for 5 to 10 minutes to blend flavors.

PER SERVING (using oat bran bread): 207 calories, 27 g carbohydrates, 7 g protein, 8.5 g fat, 4 g saturated fat, 15 mg cholesterol, 6 g fiber, 435 mg sodium. Calories from fat: 36 percent.

Q

Dear Recipe Doctor,

I look forward to your column every week; I even send your column to members of my family who don't live in the area! Here is a bunch of my family's all-time favorite recipes. If any of them appeal to you, maybe you could try your "magic" on them.

A

This reader sent me many wonderful recipes, but the Pennsylvania Dutch pumpkin cake seemed perfect for the holiday season. The original recipe calls for 1 cup of shortening and 4 large eggs. These were the two ingredients I focused my attention on because the rest were fairly innocent: canned pumpkin, flour, spices, and sugar.

I cut the shortening down to ⅓ cup. I needed to add something to replace the ⅔ cup of shortening I just took out. I tried beating ⅓ cup of fat-free cream cheese and ⅓ cup of maple syrup (reduced-calorie pancake syrup can be substituted) in with the shortening. I reduced the granulated sugar called for to compensate for the sweetener I now was adding with the syrup.

Instead of 4 eggs, I used 1 token egg and ½ cup of egg substitute.

The original recipe calls for sifting the dry ingredients together. As a rule, I don't sift unless absolutely necessary. So I chose not to sift and the cake turned out just fine. The other option you have is using half whole wheat flour and half white flour. This will change the color and texture of the crumb, so be prepared.

PENNSYLVANIA DUTCH PUMPKIN CAKE

Instead of adding (and buying) allspice, cloves, nutmeg, and ginger, you can add 4 teaspoons of pumpkin pie spice instead.

Original recipe contains 430 calories, 19 grams fat, 5 grams saturated fat, and 70 milligrams cholesterol per serving.

Makes 12 servings

3 cups unbleached all-purpose flour
1½ teaspoons baking powder
1½ teaspoons baking soda
1 teaspoon allspice
1 teaspoon ground cloves
1 teaspoon ground nutmeg
½ teaspoon ground ginger
⅓ cup butter-flavored (or regular) shortening
1¾ cups sugar
⅓ cup maple syrup or reduced-calorie pancake syrup
⅓ cup fat-free cream cheese
1 large egg
½ cup egg substitute
15-ounce can pumpkin
1½ teaspoons vanilla extract
powdered sugar (optional)

1. Preheat oven to 350 degrees. Coat a bundt or angel food cake pan with canola cooking spray.
2. Combine first seven ingredients in a medium bowl; stir to blend.
3. In mixing bowl, beat shortening, sugar, maple syrup, and cream cheese together. Add egg and egg substitute (adding $\frac{1}{4}$ cup at a time), beating after each addition.
4. Add pumpkin and vanilla and beat until combined. Stir in dry ingredients (or beat briefly on low speed). Transfer batter to prepared pan. Bake until done, about 50 to 60 minutes. Cool cake in pan on a rack for 20 minutes. Turn out onto a rack and cool completely. Sift powdered sugar over the top if desired.

PER SERVING: 330 calories, 6 g protein, 62.5 g carbohydrate, 6.5 g fat, 1.5 g saturated fat, 18 mg cholesterol, 2 g fiber, 590 mg sodium. Calories from fat: 17 percent.

Q

Dear Recipe Doctor,

I wonder if you have a recipe for one of my favorite comfort foods—shepherd's pie?

A

Shepherd's pie (also called cottage pie) is often made in Ireland and England on Mondays with leftover minced meat and vegetables from the Sunday family lunch—which are then mixed with gravy and topped with mashed potatoes.

I saved this letter from this reader for November because this recipe is a great way to incorporate many leftovers from the Thanksgiving table (turkey, mashed potatoes, vegetables, gravy). This is so delicious it may well become a post-Thanksgiving dinner tradition at my house!

In the original recipes, butter and fat is added in just about every layer—the mashed potatoes, the gravy, sautéing the vegetables—and then even more butter is spread on top of the finished pie. To make a lower-fat shepherd's pie, start with turkey breast, low-fat mashed potatoes, and gravy. Sauté the onions with canola cooking spray. Once you've done all that, you can use a token tablespoon of butter to melt and brush over the top of the pie.

☞ LEFTOVER TURKEY SHEPHERD'S PIE ☜

Makes 4 servings

1 mild or sweet onion, chopped
2 cups leftover roasted turkey, cut or shredded into
    bite-sized pieces
leftover vegetables (depending on taste preferences;
    I like to use about 1 to 2 cups of peas or broccoli, green
    beans, or carrots)
2 cups leftover gravy
Worcestershire sauce (optional)
2 cups leftover mashed potatoes
salt and freshly ground pepper to taste
1 tablespoon butter

1. Preheat oven to 400 degrees. Coat deep-dish pie plate with canola cooking spray.
2. Coat medium, nonstick frying pan generously with canola cooking spray, and sauté onion until lightly browned. Turn off heat. Stir turkey, leftover vegetables, and gravy into onions. Add a few shakes of Worcestershire sauce if desired. (If you don't have time to sauté the onion, just mix onion, turkey, vegetables, and gravy together and go on to step 3.)
3. Spread mixture evenly in prepared pie plate.
4. If you don't already have leftover mashed potatoes, make mashed potatoes with electric mixer by combining 3 cups cooked potato pieces, ½ cup low-fat milk, and a couple sprinklings of salt and black pepper and other spices (if desired) in

mixing bowl. A potato masher can also be used if you want to make the mashed potatoes by hand. Spread mashed potatoes evenly over meat mixture in pan.

5. Make a design in the mashed potatoes with a fork. Melt butter in microwave-safe custard cup. Brush potatoes with melted butter using a pastry brush. Put pie dish in oven until heated through and golden on top (about 25 minutes).

PER SERVING: 286 calories, 28 g protein, 33.5 g carbohydrate, 5.5 g fat, 2.8 g saturated fat, 72 mg cholesterol, 6 g fiber, 900 mg sodium. Calories from fat: 17 percent.

Q

My German grandmother used to make gingerbread cookies every Christmas. Please lighten this recipe so I can make them this Christmas. Thank you so much.

A

This is a great cookie recipe for children because it is very easy to roll and cut into shapes. Typical German recipes use honey or part honey and part molasses to sweeten the cookie dough and shortening as the fat ingredient. For tradition, I used butter-flavored shortening, but cut it in half and substituted fat-free cream cheese. I also switched to egg substitute, which is pasteurized, just in case one of the kids decides to taste the raw cookie dough (no risk of salmonella).

Use a thick, even-heating cookie sheet or baking stone to bake the cookies. This way they won't burn and will stay nice and moist. A glaze can be made with powdered sugar, extract, and a tablespoon or two of milk or half-and-half. Decorate the cookies immediately after you glaze because once the glaze hardens a little, the decorations will tend to run off the cookie.

☞ GINGERBREAD HEARTS ☜
AND SANTA CLAUS COOKIES

Nuremberg, a Bavarian city in Southern Germany, is famous for its toy manufacturing and gingerbread making. Gingerbread is made and shipped from Nuremberg to cities all over the world.

Children in Germany most often make gingerbread cookies cut in the shape of little Santa Clauses or hearts. White icing and sprinkles are used to decorate the cookies.

Original recipe contains 95 calories, 3.5 grams fat, 1 gram saturated fat, and 7 milligrams cholesterol per serving.

Makes about 36 (2½-inch) cookies

    4 tablespoons (¼ cup) shortening (butter flavored if desired)
    4 tablespoons (¼ cup) fat-free cream cheese
    2½ cups all-purpose flour
    ½ cup sugar
    ¼ cup molasses
    ¼ cup honey
    ¼ cup egg substitute
    1 tablespoon baking powder
    1 teaspoon ground ginger
    ½ teaspoon ground cinnamon
    ½ teaspoon ground cloves
    ½ teaspoon ground cardamom (optional)

    POWDERED SUGAR ICING:
    1 cup sifted powdered sugar
    ¼ teaspoon vanilla
    1 tablespoon (or slightly more) milk
    decorative candies (optional)

1. In a mixing bowl, beat shortening and cream cheese with electric mixer on medium speed for 30 seconds.
2. Add about half of the flour. Then add the sugar, molasses, honey, egg substitute, baking powder, ginger, cinnamon, cloves, and cardamom (if desired). Beat till combined, scraping bowl occasionally.
3. Beat or stir in the remaining flour. Cover and chill about 3 hours (until the dough is easy to handle). Divide chilled dough in half.
4. Preheat oven to 375 degrees. Coat cookie sheets generously with canola cooking spray.
5. On lightly floured surface, roll each half of dough to about $\frac{1}{8}$-inch thickness. Using $2\frac{1}{2}$-inch cookie cutter, cut dough into hearts and Santa Clauses (or other desired shapes). Place 1 inch apart onto prepared cookie sheets. Bake for 5 minutes or till edges are lightly browned. Cool on cookie sheets for 1 minute. Remove cookies and cool on wire racks.
6. Prepare icing by mixing sugar, vanilla, and milk in a small mixing bowl. Add a teaspoon or so more milk if needed to make an icing of drizzling consistency. Decorate cookies with icing and decorative candies (if desired).

PER SERVING: 83 calories, 1 g protein, 16 g carbohydrate, 1.8 g fat, .5 g saturated fat, 0 mg cholesterol, .3 g fiber, 43 mg sodium. Calories from fat: 20 percent.

Q

Dear Recipe Doctor,

This Panatone bread recipe is an Easter and Christmas family tradition in my family. I just know there has got to be a way to make it with fewer calories. What do you think?

A

I can't resist Panatone bread. It always looks and tastes so festive. That darkened sweet bread crumb flecked with bits of green and red and dusted with powdered sugar is reminiscent of a light holiday snowfall. Most of the Panatone bread recipes I've come across over the years are prohibitive when it comes to the time and effort involved. I was happy to see something titled "Quick Panatone."

I really didn't have to do too much here at all. I still used real butter, but used a third of the original amount. I replaced the lost moisture with corn syrup and some dark rum, which I thought would complement the other flavors nicely. I cut the number of eggs in half and added some egg substitute.

⌒ QUICK PANATONE ⌒

Original recipe contains 278 calories, 65 milligrams cholesterol, and 8.5 grams fat per serving.

Makes 20 slices

1 cup low-fat milk, divided
¼ cup butter
¼ cup corn syrup
¼ cup dark rum
⅛ cup brandy (any flavored brandy can also be used)
1 teaspoon anise extract
1 teaspoon almond extract
4 cups flour
1¼ cups sugar
3 heaping teaspoons baking powder
2 large eggs
⅓ cup egg substitute
½ cup walnut or pecan pieces
1 cup golden or dark raisins
1 cup mixed glazed fruit
powdered sugar (optional)

1. Preheat oven to 350 degrees. In small saucepan, melt butter in ½ cup of milk. Stir in corn syrup and set aside to cool.
2. While milk mixture is cooling, combine remaining ½ cup milk, rum, brandy, anise extract, and almond extract in large mixing bowl. Once milk mixture has cooled, add to mixing bowl too.
3. Sift flour, sugar, and baking powder together (or blend together in food processor). Add flour mixture to milk and liquor mixture in mixing bowl on low speed. Add eggs and egg substitute, continuing to beat at low speed until blended. Add nuts, raisins, and mixed glazed fruit, beating until blended.
4. Pour into a greased tube pan or two 9 x 5-inch loaf pans (or coat pans generously with no-stick cooking spray). Bake in center of oven for about 60 minutes (tube pan) or 45 to 50 minutes for loaf pans. The bread is done when toothpick inserted in center comes out clean. Once cooled, you can dust bread with powdered sugar.

PER SERVING: 252 calories, 4.5 g protein, 46.5 g carbohydrate, 5 g fat, 1.8 g saturated fat, 28 mg cholesterol, 1.3 g fiber, 160 mg sodium. Calories from fat: 19 percent.

Chapter Seven

CAKES, COOKIES, & BROWNIES

CAKES

LEMON POUND CAKE

QUICK SHERRY CAKE
(WITH HOT BUTTERED SHERRY GLAZE)

LIGHT CHOCOLATE RASPBERRY
SACHER TORTE

MACADAMIA FUDGE TORTE
WITH HALF THE FAT

GRANDMOTHER'S CARROT CAKE

MOCK MISS GRACE'S LEMON CAKE

GERMAN APPLE CAKE

GERMAN CHOCOLATE CAKE

UPSIDE-DOWN BLACK FOREST CAKE

HARVEY WALLBANGER CAKE

MIDORI CAKE AND GLAZE

PEACH SCHNAPPS CAKE

BAILEY'S IRISH CREAM CAKE

UPSIDE-DOWN GERMAN CHOCOLATE CAKE

NO-BAKE CHEESECAKE

Q *Dear Recipe Doctor,*

I've been dying to send you my recipe for lemon pound cake. I've been making it for years and years. I wouldn't trust this recipe with just anybody. So, I am hoping you can lower the calories and such without a big change in flavor.

A Well, I love lemon, and I love pound cake. So, when I received this recipe for lemon pound cake, I got right on the case. Even better, it called for a box cake mix. The recipes that call for cake mixes are a recipe doctor's dream because these recipes usually turn out great the first time. All the additives in the cake mix somehow make those things near foolproof. They always seem to turn out great no matter how much I mess with the original recipes.

This original recipe called for the lemon cake mix plus a package of lemon pudding. These ingredients remain the same. From here on out though, I went to work. I cut the number of eggs in half and used ½ cup of egg substitute in their place. I usually can cut the eggs down to just 1 or use 3 egg whites or all egg substitute. But since this was a pound cake recipe I thought I'd better just cut the eggs in half and leave it at that.

I didn't add any of the vegetable oil called for and used my favorite fat-free sour cream instead. I thought sour cream would be a natural fat replacement for a pound cake since some pound cake recipes actually call for sour cream.

My greatest challenge in lightening this pound cake was not the cake at all, but the glaze on top. You see, this glaze called for an entire cube of butter. You mix the softened cube of butter with powdered sugar, then add lemon juice and lemon zest. I reduced the amount of butter to 2 tablespoons. I had to use a little less lemon juice and powdered sugar, though, to get the right consistency. I still had plenty of great tasting glaze to frost the cake with.

☞ LEMON POUND CAKE ☜

Original recipe contains 484 calories, 91 milligrams cholesterol, and 19 grams fat per serving.

Makes 12 servings

- 1 box Lemon Supreme cake mix
- 1 box (4-serving size) instant lemon pudding mix
- 2 eggs
- $\frac{1}{2}$ cup egg substitute
- 1 cup water (or the amount of water called for on box directions)
- $\frac{1}{3}$ cup fat-free sour cream (or the amount of oil called for on box directions)

LEMON GLAZE:
- 2 tablespoons butter, melted
- 2 $\frac{2}{3}$ cups powdered sugar
- 5 tablespoons fresh lemon juice
- 2 tablespoons lemon zest, finely chopped

1. Preheat oven to 350 degrees. Coat a 10-inch bundt pan or tube pan with nonstick cooking spray. Lightly flour the pan.
2. Combine cake mix, pudding mix, eggs, egg substitute, water, and sour cream in large mixing bowl. Beat at medium speed with mixer for 2 minutes. Pour into prepared pan.
3. Bake for 35 to 45 minutes or until toothpick inserted in center comes out clean.
4. Cool in pan 30 minutes. Invert onto serving plate and cool completely.
5. While cake is cooling, combine melted butter, sugar, lemon juice, and lemon zest in small mixing bowl. Blend until smooth. Add a tablespoon or two of extra powdered sugar if necessary for the desired consistency. Drizzle the glaze over the cooled cake.

PER SERVING: 335 calories, 4 g protein, 68 g carbohydrate, 6 g fat, 2 g saturated fat, 40 mg cholesterol, 1 g fiber, 367 mg sodium. Calories from fat: 16 percent.

Dear Recipe Doctor,

Here is a family favorite I got from a friend in 1969—it really is quick to make! Can I reduce the eggs and oil? I think Duncan Hines (without the pudding in the mix) makes a lighter and higher cake.

I have fond memories of a sherry cake I tasted years ago. So I was more than happy to oblige Elsie and lighten up the recipe she sent me. Even better—it calls for cake mix. You may have noticed how much I like to cut corners by using cake mixes.

I tried the Duncan Hines butter recipe golden cake mix because Elsie highly recommended it and because it doesn't have pudding in the mix and the original recipe called for adding a box of vanilla pudding. This recipe must have preceded the pudding in the mix trend.

Anyhoo, this one called for plenty of sherry, of course, along with 4 large eggs, ¾ cup oil, and a few other ingredients. I used 1 token egg (a little egg yolk goes a long way) and added ½ cup of egg substitute. This brings the cholesterol way down (from 71 milligrams a serving to 20) and trims off more than a gram of fat per serving.

I decided to reduce the oil to just 2 tablespoons. On my first try at lightening up this recipe, I replaced the lost oil with pear purée. I thought I would try getting a little fancy. The cake tasted very good (my husband personally polished off a fourth of it) but the texture left a little to be desired. So on my next trial run, I used my standby fat replacement, fat-free sour cream. It might have been my imagination, but this version seemed to have a more velvety texture. So, I stuck with the fat-free sour cream. But you can use puréed pears if that strikes your fancy. Either way, this new lighter version reduces the calories by 77 per serving and the fat grams go from 20 to 7.5 per serving.

On the second time around I also made up a glaze to drizzle over the top while the cake is still warm. This seemed to be the icing on the cake, so to speak. It finished the cake off very nicely. I blended a tablespoon of sherry with a tablespoon of melted butter and ½ cup of powdered sugar. Mmmm good. This time my husband polished off half of it—always a good sign.

QUICK SHERRY CAKE
(WITH HOT BUTTERED SHERRY GLAZE)

Original recipe contains 390 calories, 71 milligrams cholesterol, and 20 grams of fat.

Makes 12 servings

1 box Duncan Hines moist deluxe butter recipe golden cake mix (or similar)
1 package (4-serving size) instant vanilla pudding mix
½ teaspoon ground nutmeg
1 large egg
½ cup egg substitute
¾ cup cream sherry
2 tablespoons canola oil
½ cup + 2 tablespoons fat-free sour cream

GLAZE:
½ cup powdered sugar
1 tablespoon cream sherry
1 tablespoon melted butter

1. Preheat oven to 375 degrees (if using a metal or glass pan) or 350 degrees (if using a dark or coated pan—add 3 to 5 minutes to bake time). Coat sides and bottom of a bundt or tube pan with nonstick cooking spray.
2. Combine cake mix, pudding mix, nutmeg, egg, egg substitute, sherry, oil, and sour cream in large mixing bowl. Blend at low speed until moistened (about 30 seconds). Scrape sides of bowl.
3. Beat at medium speed for exactly 3 minutes. Pour batter in prepared pan and bake immediately (place pan in center of oven).
4. Bake for about 33 to 35 minutes. Cake is done when toothpick inserted in center of cake comes out clean. Cool in pan on rack for 15 minutes.
5. While cake is cooling, blend glaze ingredients in 1 cup measure. Poke holes in top of cake with fork. Drizzle glaze over the top of cake and enjoy!

PER SERVING: 313 calories, 6 g protein, 50 g carbohydrate, 7.5 g fat, 1.5 g saturated fat, 20 mg cholesterol, .6 g fiber, 267 mg sodium. Calories from fat: 22 percent.

Dear Recipe Doctor,

*Sacher torte is one of the foods I really enjoy and occasion-
ally crave. I usually get them at bakeries. Maybe I'm asking
the impossible but could you lighten up a Sacher torte recipe
for me to try at home?*

The only thing better than a light Sacher torte recipe that
tastes sinfully delicious is a light Sacher torte recipe that cuts
corners by using a chocolate cake mix. This Recipe Doctor
recipe is both light and convenient. I first tried my hand at
lightening up a Sacher torte scratch recipe—whipping egg
whites, melting chocolate over a double boiler, whisking
yolks . . . you get the picture.

It occurred to me while elbow deep in dirty pots and
pans that perhaps most people would take one look at this
recipe and then turn right around and drive to a bakery for
their Sacher torte. So for my second try, I used a chocolate
cake mix. It worked! Of course, I changed the ingredients
and amounts to duplicate more of a chocolate torte texture.

After the cake is cooled, the original recipe calls for a
thin layer of apricot jam to be spread on top. Don't get me
wrong, this tastes good. But I thought using *raspberry* jam
would be, well, perfection. I was right. The raspberry complements the rich chocolate glaze that glides over the top
and sides of the torte very well.

Which brings me to the distinctive chocolate laden
Sacher torte glaze, which is basically chocolate, butter, sugar,
and water. Well, I kept the chocolate and lost the butter. The
trickiest part to this recipe is adding the sugar to the water
and boiling the mixture until a certain temperature is
reached. I tried to cut corners here, too, but I never met with
the same melt-in-your-mouth success as the boiling sugar

and water version. So dust off that candy thermometer. I did notice that there was more than enough chocolate glaze, so I reduced all the glaze ingredients by a fourth.

I passed out a sample of this torte to several innocent bystanders who crossed my path that day. They all raved about it, shouting declarations like, "to die for," "awesome," "this tastes so sinful it needs horns." All I can say is I passed out so many samples because I couldn't keep my fork off it when it was sitting in *my* kitchen. So my advice to you is to make it when you know company is coming.

☞ LIGHT CHOCOLATE RASPBERRY ☜ SACHER TORTE

Original recipe contains 390 calories, 25 grams fat, and 140 milligrams cholesterol per serving.

Makes 12 servings

> 1 box devil's food cake mix
> ⅓ cup Kahlúa
> ½ cup chocolate syrup
> ½ cup nonfat sour cream
> ⅓ cup egg substitute
> 1 large egg
> ⅓ cup raspberry or apricot jam + 1 tablespoon water
> ½ cup + 1 tablespoon sugar
> ¾ cup water
> ¾ cup semi-sweet chocolate chips

1. Preheat oven to 350 degrees. Coat a springform pan generously with nonstick cooking spray.
2. Combine cake mix, Kahlúa, chocolate syrup, sour cream, egg substitute, and egg in mixing bowl. Blend at low speed until moistened (about 30 seconds), scraping sides of bowl. Beat at medium speed for 2 minutes.
3. Pour batter into prepared pan and bake immediately. After 40 minutes, check cake (it is done when toothpick inserted 2 inches from the edge of pan comes out clean).
4. Cool in pan on rack for 25 minutes. Remove sides from pan and lay a plate on top of the cake. Then flip the cake over so the plate is underneath the cake. Remove the bottom of the pan. Cool completely before frosting. (The center of the torte does tend to stick slightly as it cools.)

5. When cake has cooled, melt the jam with 1 tablespoon of water over low heat (or in microwave). Strain for a smooth consistency if you desire (but I used the raspberry jam seeds and all and nobody seemed to mind); set aside.

6. Melt chocolate in a 2-cup glass measure in microwave on 50 percent power until smooth and completely melted, stirring every minute (it will probably take about 3 minutes). Brush warm jam evenly over the top of the cake. Refrigerate to harden the jam about 30 minutes.

7. Dissolve sugar in ³/₄ cup of water in a small, heavy saucepan over low heat (water will be clear when sugar is dissolved). Increase the heat and boil until the mixture reaches 220 degrees on a sugar or candy thermometer. Immediately set the pan in a cold water bath for exactly 1 minute. Pour the sugar water into the chocolate mixture and stir to blend well. Let cool slightly before using.

8. Starting in the center, pour the chocolate glaze over the cake, working outward in a circular motion. Use a spatula for the sides of cake and to even out the top if needed. Let set overnight (or a few hours in the refrigerator).

PER SERVING: 350 calories, 4.5 g protein, 67 g carbohydrate, 8 g fat, 2.5 g saturated fat, 18 mg cholesterol, 1 g fiber, 380 mg sodium. Calories from fat: 20 percent.

Q

Dear Recipe Doctor,

Can you work on this Pillsbury Bake-Off winning recipe from a few years ago?

A

This past February, Kurt Wait of Redwood City, California, won $1 million for adding seven ingredients to your basic chocolate cake mix (only two of which were even novel or interesting). But here's my question, If the original winning recipe was worth $1 million, and I cut the fat in half with only a slight difference in taste and texture, wouldn't my revised recipe be worth half a million dollars? Well, I can dream, can't I?

But *you* don't have to dream about a light version of the recipe—here it is! All I did was replace most of the oil with non-fat sour cream and switched to fat-free sweetened condensed milk. I also reduced the amount of chocolate chips in the filling, increased the sweetened condensed milk by 2 tablespoons, and added a tablespoon of cocoa for good measure. And I replaced one of the eggs with fat-free egg substitute.

The recipe also calls for you to serve each slice on a blanket of warmed caramel sauce. You'll notice I didn't switch to a fat-free caramel sauce. There are two good reasons for this. First, I haven't found a fat-free caramel sauce yet that actually tastes good. And second, there is no difference in calories between the regular and fat-free version, and 2 tablespoons of the regular kind only adds 1.5 grams of fat. So I did what any taste-oriented dietitian would do—I simply used less of the real thing. I used 1 cup of the caramel sauce where the original recipe called for 1 ½ cups.

The result is absolutely delicious. If you are careful not to overcook it, the cake will turn out nice and moist while the topping is slightly crunchy. The filling will still be fudgey, too. So you see, you can't miss with this $500,000 recipe!

MACADAMIA FUDGE TORTE WITH HALF THE FAT

(The million dollar Pillsbury Bake-Off winning recipe)
Original recipe contains 460 calories, 35 milligrams cholesterol, and 16 grams of fat per serving.

Makes 12 servings

FILLING:
$\frac{1}{3}$ cup + 2 tablespoons fat-free sweetened condensed milk
$\frac{1}{3}$ cup semi-sweet chocolate chips
1 tablespoon cocoa

CAKE:
1 box Pillsbury Moist Supreme devil's food cake mix
$1\frac{1}{2}$ teaspoons ground cinnamon
1 tablespoon canola oil
$\frac{1}{3}$ cup nonfat sour cream
1 tablespoon fat-free sweetened condensed milk
16-ounce can sliced pears in juice or light syrup, drained
1 egg
$\frac{1}{4}$ cup egg substitute
$\frac{1}{3}$ cup chopped macadamia nuts or pecans
2 teaspoons water

SAUCE:
1 cup butterscotch caramel fudge ice cream topping
2 tablespoons low-fat or skim milk

1. Preheat oven to 350 degrees. Spray 9- or 10-inch springform pan with canola cooking spray.
2. In small saucepan, combine filling ingredients. Cook over low heat until chocolate is melted, stirring occasionally.
3. In large bowl, combine cake mix, cinnamon, oil, sour cream, and 1 tablespoon sweetened condensed milk; blend at low speed for 20 to 30 seconds or until crumbly. (Mixture will be a little dry.) Place drained pears in blender or food processor; cover and blend until smooth.
4. In large bowl, combine 2 ½ cups of the cake mix mixture, puréed pears, egg, and egg substitute; beat at low speed until moistened. Beat 2 minutes at medium speed. Spread batter evenly in springform pan. Drop filling by spoonfuls over batter.
5. Stir nuts and water into remaining cake mixture. Sprinkle evenly over filling. Bake for 40 to 45 minutes or until top springs back when touched lightly in center. Cool 10 minutes. Remove sides of pan. Cool completely.
6. In small saucepan, combine sauce ingredients. Cook over low heat for 3 minutes or until well blended, stirring occasionally. To serve, spoon about 1 ½ tablespoons of warm sauce onto each serving plate; top with wedge of torte.

PER SERVING: 360 calories, 5.5 g protein, 68 g carbohydrate, 7 g fat, 2 g saturated fat, 18 mg cholesterol, 2 g fiber, 398 mg sodium. Calories from fat: 18 percent.

Q

Dear Recipe Doctor,

I'm sending you my great-grandmother's carrot cake recipe. I'm certain you can make it better for us. Although this is a favorite family recipe, we never make it anymore due to its being so heart-unhealthy.

A

Carrot cake is really a bottle of oil in disguise. The typical carrot cake calls for at least 1 ½ cups of oil. Stacked up against the 3 measly carrots called for, this cake is more on the line of an oil cake than a carrot cake. But boy does it hit the spot.

My plan was to reduce the oil dramatically, replacing the lost oil with canned crushed pineapple in juice (chunky applesauce could also be used) and also corn syrup or maple syrup to maintain the moistness and boost the flavor a bit. I reduced the amount of the sugar called for, though, to compensate for the added corn syrup. I then used 2 egg yolks instead of 4 and added ¼ cup fat-free egg substitute. And for a little extra spice, I doubled the amount of ground cloves and added 1 teaspoon more cinnamon.

What's a carrot cake without the cream cheese frosting on top? I immediately cut the total amount of frosting in half. Then I used light cream cheese and some good-tasting diet margarine instead of butter or stick margarine.

My hope was to create a carrot cake that was sufficiently low in fat to be more like a carrot muffin nutritionally—something you could feel free to enjoy more often than just on the occasional birthday.

GRANDMOTHER'S CARROT CAKE

Original recipe, with half the amount of frosting normally called for, contains 664 calories, 91 milligrams of cholesterol, and 36 grams of fat!

Makes 12 large servings

4 egg whites
1½ cups sugar
¼ cup canola oil
¼ cup corn syrup (or maple syrup)
8-ounce can crushed pineapple (in juice)
2 egg yolks
¼ cup egg substitute
2 cups flour
2 teaspoons baking soda
1 tablespoon ground cinnamon
½ teaspoon ground cloves
1 teaspoon salt
3 cups grated carrots (finely grated if possible)

LIGHT CREAM CHEESE FROSTING:
½ cup light cream cheese
¼ cup diet margarine (e.g., I Can't Believe It's Not Butter Light)
¾ teaspoon vanilla extract
about 3 ½ cups powdered sugar

1. Preheat oven to 350 degrees. Coat a 13 x 9 x 2-inch pan with canola cooking spray. Whip egg whites in mixing bowl until stiff. Spoon into another bowl and set aside.

2. Cream sugar, oil, syrup, and crushed pineapple with juice in mixing bowl. Beat in egg yolks and egg substitute. Add flour, baking soda, cinnamon, cloves, and salt to mixing bowl and beat on low speed until blended. Fold in egg whites. Stir in grated carrots.

3. Spoon into prepared pan. Bake about 40 minutes or until a toothpick inserted in center comes out clean. Cool before frosting.

4. For frosting, beat cream cheese, margarine, and vanilla together until smooth. On low speed, beat in enough powdered sugar for desired consistency. Spread evenly over cake. Cover cake and keep chilled in refrigerator until needed.

PER SERVING (including frosting): 432 calories, 5 g protein, 85 g carbohydrate, 9 g fat, 2 g saturated fat, 1.5 g fiber, 35 mg cholesterol, 475 mg sodium. Calories from fat: 19 percent.

Q

Dear Recipe Doctor,

I love the heavily glazed lemon cake that you can buy in fancy stores around the holidays. Do you have such a recipe? I would love to make it at home. I don't care whether it is light or not.

A

I can appreciate your yearning for such a recipe. What people like most about this commercial product is that it is so very moist—as if it was soaked with lemon glaze.

I found a recipe that the *LA Times* featured many years ago as a lemon cake "like Miss Grace's." Their recipe calls for a 23.7-ounce bundt cake mix, which is now unavailable. So I modified the recipe for your basic 18.25-ounce box of yellow cake mix.

Instead of 3 eggs, I added 1 token egg with $\frac{1}{2}$ cup egg substitute. Instead of $\frac{1}{3}$ cup softened butter, I added 3 tablespoons lemon curd and 3 tablespoons fat free sour cream. The original recipe calls for plenty of lemon juice and lemon extract, but I kept it all in, even though we were using a smaller-sized mix. I figured we could use the extra kick of lemon.

The mini cakes turned out positively moist and full of flavor. But the best was yet to come. The cakes are then doused with a lemon glaze, made from powdered sugar, lemon juice, and grated lemon peel.

You can make one big lemon cake using a bundt pan or tube pan, or you can make many mini loaves. You'll have to watch the time if you use a different size pan. This recipe also works well with those fancy miniature bundt pans. After giving these lemon cakes away this past Christmas, people are already putting their orders in for next Christmas—I guess they were a hit.

⇌ MOCK MISS GRACE'S LEMON CAKE ⇌

Original recipe contains 295 calories, 12 grams fat, and 53 milligrams cholesterol per serving.

Makes 12 servings

1 yellow cake mix
1 egg
½ cup egg substitute
1 cup water
¼ cup lemon juice
1 tablespoon lemon extract
3 tablespoons lemon curd (a lemon jelly found in the jam section of most supermarkets)
3 tablespoons fat-free sour cream

LEMON GLAZE:
2 tablespoons lemon juice
1 cup powdered sugar
1 teaspoon finely grated lemon peel

1. Preheat oven to 325 degrees. Coat a tube pan or about 6 petite loaf pans (2 ½″ x 3 ½″) with canola cooking spray.
2. Combine all the cake ingredients in large mixing bowl. Beat on low until moistened. Scrape sides of bowl, then beat 2 minutes at medium speed of mixer (or highest speed of portable mixer).
3. Pour into prepared pan(s) and bake until toothpick or tester inserted in center comes out clean. If you are using petite loaf pans, which can hold about ½ cup of batter each, it will take about 22 minutes to cook. If you are using one tube pan, it will take about 35 minutes to cook.

4. Cool until lukewarm. Turn cake out onto serving platter. I like to place the mini loaves in pretty papers before going on to the glazing step.

5. To make glaze, measure lemon juice into 2-cup measure or small bowl. Sprinkle powdered sugar slowly into the lemon juice and blend until smooth. Stir in lemon peel. Spoon lemon glaze over cake(s) and chill until set.

PER SERVING: 250 calories, 4 g protein, 47 g carbohydrate, 5.5 g fat, 1 g saturated fat, 23 mg cholesterol, 1 g fiber, 318 mg sodium. Calories from fat: 20 percent.

Q

Dear Recipe Doctor,

This German apple cake sounds great, except for all the fat! Can you help?

A

Several people I know are always looking for recipes to help use apples from their trees. This one sounded easy and versatile—it can be a brunch or breakfast cake or an à la mode dessert at the end of the day.

It calls for a cup of oil. I used ¼ cup and substituted ⅓ cup light pancake syrup and some low-fat buttermilk. I thought both of those should complement the other flavors nicely. The texture and the flavor of the apple cake were absolutely perfect. I cut the sugar called for from 2 cups to 1 ½ to compensate for the extra sweetener from the pancake syrup, and just because I thought I could get away with it.

The original recipe calls for 2 eggs; I used 1 plus ¼ cup egg substitute. The recipe also called for some chopped walnuts—only ⅔ cups—but it adds 51 calories and 4.7 grams fat per serving. So it is up to you. If you think you can take them or leave them—leave them.

The icing on the original cake is made from cream cheese, butter, vanilla, and powdered sugar. I made it from light cream cheese, a token tablespoon of diet margarine, vanilla, and the same amount of powdered sugar. But honestly, my family's favorite way to enjoy this cake was warm from the oven with a scoop of light Breyers (or Dreyers) vanilla ice cream! So you may want to skip the icing altogether.

☞ GERMAN APPLE CAKE ☜

Original recipe contains 540 calories, 36 grams fat, and 67 milligrams cholesterol per serving.

Makes 10 large servings

1 egg
¼ cup egg substitute (or 2 egg whites)
¼ cup canola oil
⅓ cup light pancake syrup
7 tablespoons (½ cup – 1 tablespoon) low-fat buttermilk
1½ cups sugar
2 cups unbleached all-purpose flour
1 teaspoon baking soda
2 teaspoons ground cinnamon
4 cups thinly sliced apples (peeled or unpeeled)
⅔ cup chopped walnuts (optional)

ICING: (OPTIONAL)
¾ cup light cream cheese
1 tablespoon diet margarine
1 teaspoon vanilla
1 cup powdered sugar

1. Preheat oven to 350 degrees. Coat a 9 x 13-inch baking dish with canola cooking spray.
2. Combine egg, egg substitute, oil, pancake syrup, buttermilk, and sugar in large mixing bowl. Beat until smooth.
3. In 8-cup measure or medium bowl, mix flour, baking soda, and cinnamon together, then gradually add it to the egg mixture, beating until combined.
4. Fold in apples and nuts if desired using a wooden spoon or spatula. Spoon batter into the prepared pan, spreading so batter is even in the pan. Bake 40 to 45 minutes or until fork inserted in center comes out clean. Remove from oven and cool in pan on a rack.
5. To make the icing, beat cream cheese, margarine, and vanilla until blended. Add the powdered sugar and beat until smooth. Spread icing over cooled cake. Cut into squares.

Note: Walnuts add 51 calories, 4.7 g fat, 2 g protein, 1 g carbohydrate, and .5 g fiber per serving. Icing adds 59 calories, 1.2 g protein, 10.5 g carbohydrate, 1.5 g fat, 4 mg cholesterol, and 47 mg sodium per serving.

PER LARGE SERVING: 374 calories, 6.5 g protein, 64 g carbohydrate, 11 g fat, 1 g saturated fat, 21 mg cholesterol, 3 g fiber, 180 mg sodium. Calories from fat: 29 percent.

Dear Recipe Doctor,

I just read how many calories German chocolate cake has—848! It is my husband's favorite, but after seeing how many calories it has, I sure won't be making it very much. Could you lighten it up for us?

What a coincidence—German chocolate cake is my husband's favorite, too!

I hope you don't mind, but I used a German chocolate cake mix (I figured we'll make the frosting from scratch). The first thing I did was change the directions on the box mix. I added ⅓ cup fat-free sour cream (instead of the oil called for), and 1 token egg and ⅓ cup egg substitute (instead of the 3 eggs called for). I added the same amount of water called for on the box.

You see, the cake mix already contains 4 grams or more of fat per serving of mix, even before you've added anything. Trust me, this is plenty. All you have to do is add something in place of the oil called for and the cake will be just as moist and great tasting as if you had added that oil.

Now for the yummy homemade coconut pecan frosting. I used fat-free sweetened condensed milk (which works great in recipes), and I cut down the egg yolks from 3 to 2. I added 3 tablespoons of butter instead of 8. But I increased the vanilla extract from 1 teaspoon to 2. I didn't need to add anything to replace the butter I took out. It just seemed to thicken quicker with this reduced amount of fat, so I changed the simmering time from 10 minutes to 5 minutes. I only reduced the coconut slightly (from 1⅓ cups to 1 cup) and left the pecans alone, because where would coconut pecan frosting be without the coconut and pecans?

I served this cake to all the German chocolate cake lovers within a 1-mile radius of my house and it received very high ratings.

☞ GERMAN CHOCOLATE CAKE ☜

Original recipe contains 450 calories, 28 grams fat, and 104 milligrams cholesterol per serving.

Makes 16 servings

> 1 box Betty Crocker German chocolate cake mix (or similar)
> ⅓ cup fat-free sour cream
> 1 egg
> ⅓ cup egg substitute
> 1¼ cups water
>
> COCONUT PECAN FROSTING:
> 14-ounce can fat-free sweetened condensed milk
> 2 egg yolks, beaten
> 3 tablespoons butter
> 2 teaspoons vanilla extract
> 1 cup flaked coconut, packed
> 1 cup chopped pecans

1. Preheat oven to 350 degrees. Coat two 9-inch round pans or one 13 x 9-inch pan with canola cooking spray.

2. Combine cake mix, sour cream, egg, egg substitute, and water in mixing bowl. Beat on low speed for 30 seconds. Beat on medium speed 2 minutes. Pour into pan(s).

3. Bake until toothpick inserted in center comes out clean (27 to 32 minutes for round cake pans and 30 to 36 minutes for 13 x 9-inch pan). Cool completely.

4. In heavy 2-quart saucepan combine sweetened condensed milk, egg yolks, and butter. Cook, stirring constantly, over medium heat until mixture is noticeably thickened, about 5 minutes. Remove from heat and stir in vanilla, coconut, and pecans. Cool about 15 minutes. Spread frosting on cake(s) as desired.

PER SERVING: 315 calories, 6 g protein, 45.5 g carbohydrate, 12.5 g fat, 5 g saturated fat, 45 mg cholesterol, 1 g fiber, 334 mg sodium. Calories from fat: 36 percent.

Q

Dear Recipe Doctor,

I love Black Forest cake! Do you have a fast and lower-fat version of this classic dessert? Love your column!

A

The minute you say "fast" and "cake" in the same breath, I think of a boxed cake mix. And the best part is they can be lightened so easily. I have found that cake mixes are a lot more forgiving than scratch recipes when it comes to cutting the fat.

I decided to make an upside-down Black Forest cake, so I spread a can of cherry pie filling in the bottom of a 9 x 13-inch baking pan. If you want to try the light cherry filling (with less sugar), go ahead, but I found that it has an off, almost tinny flavor, and doesn't taste half as good as the real thing.

I added cherry brandy or cranberry liqueur to the cake mix in place of the ½ cup oil. The liqueur complements the chocolate nicely and at the same time replaces the moistness lost by the ½ cup of oil we just cut out.

The mix also called for adding 1 ⅓ cups water and 3 eggs. I added 1 cup water, ¼ cup nonfat sour cream, 1 token egg, and 3 egg whites.

The cake turned out very moist and seemed to have just the right amount of pie filling per square inch of chocolate cake. Now we get to the question of how to frost or top the cake. I am fully aware that the traditional Black Forest cake comes with real whipped cream. And don't get me wrong, I am a big fan of whipped cream. But if I top the cake with 3 cups of the real thing, I add 103 calories, 11 grams of fat, and 41 milligrams of cholesterol to each serving! If I top it with 3 cups of light Cool Whip, I add 41 calories and 2 grams of fat to each serving. It's up to you. You can top the cake with 3 cups of light Cool Whip or each serving can be topped with a dollop (⅛ cup) of real whipped cream (adding about 50 calories and 5 grams fat per serving).

⮞ UPSIDE-DOWN BLACK FOREST CAKE ⮜

Original recipe contains 350 calories, 15 grams fat, and 45 milligrams cholesterol per serving even *without* frosting or topping.

Makes 12 servings

> 21-ounce can premium "more fruit" cherry pie filling or topping
> 1 box Duncan Hines moist deluxe devil's food cake mix (or similar)
> ½ cup cherry brandy or cranberry liqueur
> 1 cup water
> ¼ cup nonfat sour cream
> 1 egg
> 3 egg whites (or ⅓ cup egg substitute)
> 8-ounce tub light Cool Whip or 1½ cups whipped cream

1. Preheat oven to 350 degrees (for metal or glass pans) or 325 degrees (for dark or coated pans). Coat a 9 x 13-inch baking pan with canola cooking spray. Spread the pie filling evenly in the bottom of prepared pan.
2. Blend dry cake mix, liqueur or brandy, water, sour cream, egg, and egg whites in large mixing bowl at low speed until moistened (about 30 seconds). Beat at medium speed for exactly 2 minutes. Pour batter into pan and bake in center of oven.
3. Cake is done when toothpick or fork inserted in center comes out clean (about 35 to 40 minutes). Cool completely. Spread top of cake with Cool Whip or whipped cream if desired.

PER SERVING (with light Cool Whip): 333 calories, 4 g protein, 59 g carbohydrate, 6.5 g fat, 3.7 g saturated fat, 18 mg cholesterol, 1 g fiber, 380 mg sodium. Calories from fat: 17.5 percent.

Dear Recipe Doctor,

My husband's favorite drink is a Harvey Wallbanger. I got this recipe for Harvey Wallbanger cake from a friend of a friend who got it from a neighbor. I was hoping to make it for his birthday and was so wishing you would lighten it up.

I love recipes that call for cake mixes because you just throw all the ingredients together in the mixing bowl and mix.

Generally you don't have to add ANY fat or oil to the mix (just substitute nonfat ingredients for the oil you were supposed to add) because the mix already contains at least 4 grams of fat per serving. I usually keep 1 of the eggs called for, but the other 2 are tossed in favor of ⅓ cup fat-free egg substitute (or 3 egg whites).

This Harvey Wallbanger cake recipe was no exception. I replaced the ⅓ cup of oil called for with fat-free sour cream (you could also use vanilla- or orange-flavored yogurt if you prefer). I suspect the orange juice, vodka, and Galliano liqueur are important ingredients for the cake as well as the drink, so I didn't touch these. I did, however, decide to add a glaze using the Galliano liqueur, orange juice, and powdered sugar to give the flavor a boost.

This cake worked out better than I could have imagined. It has a velvety pound cake type texture with a terrific taste. People who tasted this first light version told me "Don't change a thing!" So I didn't.

⇒ HARVEY WALLBANGER CAKE ⇐

Original recipe contains 302 calories, 14.5 grams fat, and 53 milligrams of cholesterol per serving.

Makes 12 servings

> 1 box deluxe yellow cake mix
> ¾ cup orange juice
> ⅓ cup Galliano liqueur
> ¼ cup vodka
> 1 egg
> ⅓ cup egg substitute
> ⅓ cup fat-free sour cream
> powdered sugar (optional)
>
> GLAZE: (OPTIONAL)
> 2 tablespoons Galliano liqueur
> 2 tablespoons orange juice
> 1 cup powdered sugar

1. Preheat oven to 350 degrees. Coat 10-inch bundt pan or tube pan with canola cooking spray and a light dusting of flour.
2. Place cake mix, orange juice, Galliano, vodka, egg, egg substitute, and sour cream in large mixing bowl. Beat 4 minutes at medium speed. Turn batter into prepared pan and spread evenly.
3. Bake for 40 minutes or until cake tester inserted comes out clean. Dust with powdered sugar or top with optional glaze (directions follow).
4. To make glaze, blend glaze ingredients together in small bowl until smooth. Poke top of cake with large fork many times. Pour glaze over warm cake (still in pan), continuing to spread glaze over the top until all is absorbed.

PER SERVING (without glaze): 241 calories, 4 g protein, 41.5 g carbohydrates, 4.5 g fat, 1 g saturated fat, 17 mg cholesterol, .7 g fiber, 280 mg sodium. Calories from fat: 17 percent.

Q *I love Midori liqueur! I always have a bottle of it in my kitchen cabinet. I found a recipe for Midori cake in a booklet that came with the bottle. Can you make it light but moist?*

A I had no idea what Midori liqueur was like. If I could have just had a clue—like "it is the bright green liqueur, you can't miss it" or it is a "melon" liqueur. After perusing the entire liquor department for what seemed like hours, I finally found it.

Because the recipe calls for a box of yellow cake mix, which already has 4 grams of fat per serving of the mix, we don't have to add the $1/2$ cup oil in the recipe. Instead, I added $1/4$ cup more yogurt and $1/4$-cup more Midori. Instead of 4 eggs I added 2 eggs and $1/2$ cup egg substitute. I bumped the coconut extract up a notch (from $1/2$ teaspoon to 1 teaspoon). The cake turned out very flavorful and best of all, very moist.

Now for the Midori glaze. The original glaze is made with powdered sugar, Midori, cream cheese, butter, and coconut flavoring. I switched to light cream cheese and cut out the butter. It worked out great—you'll never miss the butter. If the consistency seems a little stiff, just beat in a little Midori, $1/2$ teaspoon at a time, until your desired consistency is achieved.

I must warn you, this recipe uses almost the entire bottle of Midori. It makes a whole heck of a lot of glaze, too. You could get away with making half as much glaze and it would still be enough to decoratively glaze the cake.

☞ MIDORI CAKE AND GLAZE ☜

This cake is green from the inside out—a great cake for St. Patrick's Day. Original recipe contains 504 calories, 20.5 grams fat, 6 grams saturated fat, and 87 milligrams cholesterol per serving.

Makes 12 servings

1 box yellow cake mix
1 3-ounce box Jello Instant Pistachio Pudding
2 eggs
½ cup egg substitute
¾ cup plain yogurt (key lime or lemon flavor can be substituted)
1 cup Midori liqueur
1 teaspoon coconut extract

MIDORI GLAZE:
2 cups powdered sugar (1 cup if making half the glaze)
6 tablespoons Midori (3 tablespoons if making half the glaze)
½ cup light cream cheese (¼ cup if making half the glaze)
½ teaspoon coconut extract (¼ teaspoon if making half the glaze)

1. Preheat oven to 350 degrees. Coat a bundt or tube pan with canola cooking spray.
2. Combine all cake ingredients in mixing bowl and beat for 4 minutes at medium speed (scrape sides of bowl at least once). Pour into prepared pan.
3. Bake for 50 to 55 minutes or until cake tester comes out clean. Cool about 15 minutes in pan, then turn out onto cooling rack.
4. Mix and beat all glaze ingredients at high speed until smooth and spreadable. Glaze cake while slightly warm.

PER SERVING (with half the glaze): 376 calories, 8 g protein, 68 g carbohydrate, 6 g fat, 2 g saturated fat, 38 mg cholesterol, .5 g fiber, 443 mg sodium. Calories from fat: 14 percent.

Dear Recipe Doctor,

A relative in Nebraska sent me this recipe for peach Schnapps cake. She claims it is one of the best cakes she has made. However, as I look at 4 eggs and ½ cup of oil I am hesitant to make it. Would you please lighten it for me?

I have to say peach Schnapps is not one of the liqueurs I happen to keep handy in my kitchen cabinet. But a quick survey of this recipe convinced me that it was well worth the $5 investment for the peach Schnapps.

The original recipe calls for a cake mix with pudding in the mix, which already contains 4 grams of fat per serving, so the ½ cup of oil called for is really not necessary. You do need to add something in its place to add moisture and keep the batter the same consistency. I noticed that ½ cup of granulated sugar was also called for, so I decided to kill two birds with one stone and add corn syrup to replace both the sugar and the oil.

There is something about the chemical makeup of corn syrup that enables it to release small amounts of moisture into the baked product over time. This cake should stay nice and moist for almost a week.

I also replaced 2 of the 4 eggs called for with ½ cup of egg substitute. Now for the tricky part. The recipe also calls for a cup of chopped pecans. Sounds innocent enough, but even if you reduce the pecans to ¾ cup, each serving will still total 10 grams of fat, 5 of which come directly from the pecans. So here's what I propose. Delete the chopped pecans in the batter, and just add pecan halves as garnish on the cooled, glazed cake. If you use ½ cup of pecan halves, each serving will contain 8 grams of fat. If you delete the pecans altogether, the fat will go down to 5 grams per serving. So it's your choice.

The cake was very moist and very delicious even though I did cut one little corner in the original recipe—after I had already heated up the oven (and the kitchen) I noticed the original recipe called for letting the mixture of peaches, Schnapps, orange juice, and sugar sit overnight. I let it sit exactly 5 minutes and went on with the recipe.

← PEACH SCHNAPPS CAKE →

Original recipe contains 518 calories, 22 grams fat, and 71 milligrams cholesterol per serving.

Makes 12 servings

> 16-ounce can peaches, well drained and chopped
> ½ cup peach Schnapps
> ¼ cup orange juice
> ½ cup light corn syrup
> 1 yellow cake mix with pudding in the mix
> 2 eggs
> ½ cup egg substitute
>
> GLAZE:
> 2 tablespoons orange juice
> 2 tablespoons peach Schnapps
> 2 cups powdered sugar
>
> GARNISH:
> ½ cup pecan halves (optional)

1. In mixing bowl, combine peaches, Schnapps, orange juice, and corn syrup. Let sit for a few minutes or overnight if possible.
2. Preheat oven to 350 degrees. Coat a tube pan or bundt pan with canola cooking spray, then lightly coat with flour.
3. Add cake mix, eggs, and egg substitute to mixing bowl with peach mixture. Beat on low speed for 2 minutes.

4. Pour into prepared pan and bake for 45 to 50 minutes until tester inserted in center comes out clean.

5. In small bowl, stir glaze ingredients together until smooth. Pour glaze over cooled cake. Decorate top with pecan halves if desired.

PER SERVING (WITH ½ CUP OF PECANS): 403 calories, 5 g carbohydrate, 74 g carbohydrate, 8 g fat, 1 g saturated fat, 1.5 g fiber, 35 mg cholesterol, 316 mg sodium. Calories from fat: 18 percent. PER SERVING (NO PECANS): 370 calories, 4.5 g protein, 73 g carbohydrate, 5 g fat, 1 g saturated fat, 1 g fiber, 35 mg cholesterol, 316 mg sodium. Calories from fat: 12 percent.

AN ELAINE ORIGINAL

A few months ago I was inspired by a yellow cake mix and a bottle of light Bailey's Irish Cream. My mission, since I chose to accept it, was to make two cakes to sell at my daughter's school bake sale. I played with the cake mix instructions a little, made up a lower-fat Bailey's Irish Cream frosting, garnished the top with pecan halves, and all I know is that my cakes were gone by the time I got to the cake table. I did mark the cakes as "lower-fat" Bailey's Irish Cream Cakes. So maybe there is a market for fancy lower-fat cakes.

So I decided to share the recipe with all of you. Since the cake mix already includes 4 grams of fat per serving in just the mix, I didn't add any of the oil the mix instructions called for. I did, however, add ½ cup of light Bailey's Irish Cream and added a little less water. Instead of the 3 eggs called for, I added 1 egg and ⅓ cup of egg substitute.

Don't get me wrong, the cake is delicious. But the frosting is, well, it's the frosting on the cake! It looks rich and creamy and tastes even better than it looks. And the best part is, it's composed of only three ingredients: powdered sugar, Bailey's Irish Cream, and butter. You might be thinking, "What's butter doing in a lower-fat recipe?" Well, it's doing quite well, thank you. I only used 3 tablespoons to frost the entire cake. I think that's 3 tablespoons well spent.

If you pour the batter into two 9-inch square or round cake pans, you will make about 18 servings (9 servings per pan). This translates into 6 ½ grams of fat per serving altogether (frosting and all). Not bad for a cake that's "to die for."

❧ BAILEY'S IRISH CREAM CAKE ❧

Makes 18 servings (or 12 large servings)

1 box Pillsbury Moist Supreme yellow cake mix (or similar)
1 cup water
½ cup light Bailey's Irish Cream
1 egg
⅓ cup egg substitute

FROSTING:
3 tablespoons butter or canola margarine, softened
3 tablespoons light Bailey's Irish Cream
1½ cups powdered sugar

pecan halves for garnish

1. Preheat oven to 350 degrees. Coat two 9-inch round or square baking pans with canola cooking spray.
2. Mix cake mix, water, ½ cup Bailey's, egg, and egg substitute in large bowl at low speed until moistened. Beat 2 minutes at high speed. Pour batter into prepared pans.
3. Bake for about 25 minutes or until cake tests done (it springs back when lightly touched in center). Cool in pan on cooling rack.
4. Add all three frosting ingredients to mixer bowl. Beat with mixer until smooth. Spread frosting evenly over both cakes. Arrange a pecan half on frosting to designate each serving.

PER SERVING (if 18 per recipe): 205 calories, 2 g protein, 37 g carbohydrate, 6.5 g fat, 3 g saturated fat, 20 mg cholesterol, .5 g fiber, 230 mg sodium. Calories from fat: 28 percent.

AN ELAINE ORIGINAL

Did you ever have a certain dish or dessert you like to make that's just perfect for large gatherings or parties? And every time you bring it, at least three people beg you for the recipe? Well, this happens to me every time I make this lightened version of an upside-down German chocolate cake.

In fact, I was just at a bridal shower and was listening to several women proclaim that if you're going to have dessert, it should be full fat—desserts should be protected from any lightening or fat-reducing nutrition acts. After all, it's a once-in-a-while thing. To this I calmly mentioned that if you can reduce the fat in a dessert without anyone noticing a difference, then why *not* reduce the fat? Blank faces—I could tell I had some disbelievers in the crowd. I served this lower-fat upside-down German chocolate cake shortly after this conversation and it received rave reviews. I couldn't resist mentioning that I had cut the fat in half from the original. I tried very hard to hide my "I told you so" smirk.

I didn't add any of the oil the cake mix called for and added fat-free sour cream instead. I used light cream cheese for the cream cheese filling instead of regular cream cheese. The filling also called for ½ cup of butter and 3 cups of powdered sugar, so I cut the butter completely and added ⅓ cup of corn syrup instead. I was then able to cut the powdered sugar by a cup. Some fat and calories are also coming from the pecans and coconut, but those, to me, are non-negotiable ingredients in a German chocolate cake. You could reduce them from 1½ cups each to 1 cup, though, if you insist. This would shave an additional 24 calories and 2 grams of fat from every serving.

This cake is so fabulous it really doesn't need frosting. If you are a confessed chocoholic, you will probably be tempted to add a handful or two of chocolate chips to the batter. So I went ahead and listed this as an optional ingredient.

UPSIDE-DOWN GERMAN CHOCOLATE CAKE

Original recipe contains 325 calories, 18 grams fat, and 37 milligrams cholesterol per serving.

Makes 24 small servings

1½ cups flaked sweetened coconut
1½ cups pecan pieces
1 box German chocolate cake mix
⅓ cup fat-free sour cream
1 egg
½ cup egg substitute
1¼ cups water
¾ cup chocolate chips (optional)
8 ounces light or fat-free cream cheese
⅓ cup light corn syrup
2 cups powdered sugar

1. Preheat oven to 350 degrees. Coat 9 x 13-inch baking pan with canola cooking spray. Sprinkle coconut and pecans onto bottom of prepared pan.
2. Prepare cake mix according to directions except add sour cream in place of oil or butter and add 1 egg and ½ cup egg substitute in place of 3 eggs normally called for. Don't forget to add the water (mixes usually call for 1¼ cups water).
3. Stir in chocolate chips if desired. Pour batter over coconut and pecans.
4. In small mixer bowl, combine cream cheese, corn syrup, and powdered sugar and beat until smooth. Drop by large spoonfuls onto cake batter.
5. Bake for about 40 minutes or until cake tester comes out clean. Serve as is or dust powdered sugar over the top, or spread a little chocolate frosting over the top.

PER SERVING: 226 calories, 4 g protein, 35 g carbohydrates, 8 g fat, 3 g saturated fat, 10 mg cholesterol, 1 g fiber, 275 mg sodium. Calories from fat: 32 percent.

Q *Dear Recipe Doctor,*

Do you have a lower calorie no-bake cheesecake recipe?

A There's nothing more yummy than a thin slice of cold, creamy cheesecake topped with fresh summer fruit, but who wants to turn their kitchen into a summer sauna by baking a cheesecake for an hour or two? That's when a recipe for no-bake cheesecake comes in handy. And how about a delicious low-fat one—based on mostly cottage cheese instead of cream cheese?

I used Knudsen's No-Bake Cheesecake as a guide and lightened it up even more by making a graham cracker crust with 1 tablespoon melted butter and 2 tablespoons honey instead of 3 tablespoons butter and 2 tablespoons granulated sugar. I used 1 percent cottage cheese in place of full fat to save about 15 grams of fat altogether. But then I also replaced one of the cups of cottage cheese called for with light cream cheese (you can use fat-free if you want). Call me a purist, but I think a cheesecake should have *some* token cream cheese in it. I also used egg substitute in place of two egg yolks, not only to drastically reduce the cholesterol and cut out 10 grams of fat, but also to reduce the risk of salmonella food poisoning (egg substitute is pasteurized and presents no risk of salmonella).

If you blend the soft formed gelatin with the cottage cheese-cream cheese mixture using a food processor, it will turn out to be more of a chiffon-type cheesecake (I learned this by accident), which some tasters found highly desirable. The original recipe calls for 1 cup of liquid whipping cream and 2 egg whites, both to be whipped and folded into the cottage cheese mixture. Of course, the egg whites aren't the problem—it's the wonderful whipped cream. I tried using 2 cups of light Cool Whip and that worked great. But, if you just can't bring yourself to use anything but real whipped cream, you could reduce the fat a little by using ²/₃ cup whipping cream (instead of 1 cup) and whipping 3 egg whites instead of 2.

This chiffon cheesecake stands alone just fine, but I topped it with some just-made less-sugar triple berry jam. Any fresh fruit will do, though. If you decide to serve this dessert at a family gathering or party, I must warn you about one thing—this is the type of recipe that people want a copy of right then and there.

≈ NO-BAKE CHEESECAKE ≈

A serving of regular cheesecake contains approximately 355 calories, 25 grams of fat, 61 milligrams of cholesterol per serving.

Makes 10 servings

> 2 envelopes unflavored gelatin
> 1 cup sugar, divided
> ¼ teaspoon salt
> ¼ cup egg substitute
> 1 cup low-fat milk
> juice and zest from 1 lemon
> 1½ teaspoons vanilla extract
> 2 egg whites
> 2 cups light Cool Whip
> 2 cups low-fat cottage cheese (nonfat can also be used)
> 1 cup light cream cheese (nonfat can also be used)
>
> GRAHAM CRACKER CRUST:
> 1 tablespoon butter, melted
> 2 tablespoons honey or corn syrup
> 1 cup graham cracker crumbs
> ½ teaspoon ground cinnamon
> ½ teaspoon ground nutmeg

1. Mix gelatin, ¾ cup sugar, and salt in mixer bowl. Add egg substitute and milk and beat until well blended. Place mixture into top of double boiler. Cook over simmering water, stirring constantly, until gelatin is dissolved (about 5 minutes). Remove from heat. Stir in lemon juice, lemon zest, and vanilla extract. Refrigerate, stirring occasionally, until mixture mounds slightly when dropped from spoon (about 45 minutes).

2. Meanwhile, combine graham cracker crust ingredients and press into bottom of a 9-inch springform pan that has been coated with canola cooking spray (or lightly greased). If you sprinkle a little powdered sugar over the top of the crumb mixture, it is easier to press down into the pan without it sticking to the palm of your hand.

3. Beat egg whites until frothy. Gradually add ¼ cup sugar and continue beating until stiff and glossy. Stir in Cool Whip and set aside.

4. Blend cottage cheese and cream cheese in food processor until smooth. Stir gelatin mixture into cottage cheese mixture until well blended (or use the food processor if desired). Fold in egg white mixture.

5. Pour into crumb-lined pan. Refrigerate about 4 hours or until firm.

PER SERVING: 297 calories, 12.5 g protein, 40.5 g carbohydrate, 9 g fat, 6 g saturated fat, 18 mg cholesterol, .3 g fiber, 89 mg sodium. Calories from fat: 27 percent.

CAKES, COOKIES, & BROWNIES

COOKIES

CHOCOLATE MACADAMIA NUT BISCOTTI

THE ALLEGED $250 CHOCOLATE CHIP
COOKIE (LIGHTENED)

VERY CHOCOLATE, OATMEAL
AND CHOCOLATE CHIP COOKIES

LEMON POPPY SEED COOKIES

SUGAR AND SPICE
AND EVERYTHING NICE COOKIES

Q

Dear Recipe Doctor,

Please help! I've lost my recipe for my favorite biscotti—I would appreciate your help. I had a vanilla and chocolate recipe, but both were accidentally lost when cleaning out my files.

A

To say I love biscotti is an understatement. Perhaps it is because I love a good cup of coffee so much, and the two together are like a perfect symphony playing in your mouth. After pricing gourmet biscotti in the supermarket, I decided to try my hand at making it. But I didn't want to make just any biscotti.

The idea of making a chocolate macadamia nut biscotti haunted me for days. I don't know why, because I had never seen or tasted such a thing. I just thought this combination of flavors sounded like a biscotti made in heaven. A day or two later I made up a chocolate biscotti dough and kneaded in some macadamia nuts we had left over from a Hawaiian sympathy gift. (You know the type—"We got to go to Hawaii and you didn't so here are some macadamia nuts.")

Anyway, it was the holiday season so I splurged and dipped one side of the biscotti in melted white chocolate. In a word? They were addicting. I ended up making many batches before Christmas was over—they were out the door as fast as I could make them. So although I can't give this reader her favorite biscotti recipe, I can give her mine.

⌐ CHOCOLATE MACADAMIA NUT BISCOTTI ⌐

Makes about 28 large biscotti cookies

1/2 cup macadamia nuts, roasted
2 3/4 cups all-purpose flour
1 1/2 teaspoons baking powder
1/4 teaspoon salt
6 tablespoons cocoa
2 1/2 tablespoons butter, softened
2 tablespoons fat-free or light cream cheese
1 cup granulated sugar
1 tablespoon crème de cacao
2 large eggs plus 1 large egg white
1 1/2 teaspoons vanilla extract
1/2 teaspoon almond extract
about 1/4 cup powdered sugar
1 cup white chocolate chips

1. Make sure rack in oven is in the center position. Preheat oven to 350 degrees. Coat two cookie sheets down the center with cooking spray.
2. Place nuts in a heavy zip-type plastic bag and crush into coarse pieces with the bottom of a bottle or glass (or place in mini food processor and just barely pulse to coarsely chop); set aside.
3. Combine flour, baking powder, salt, and cocoa to bowl or 8-cup measure and stir to blend.
4. In large bowl, using electric mixer, cream the butter, cream cheese, sugar, and crème de cacao until light and fluffy. Add the eggs and egg white one at a time, beating well after each addition.

5. Beat in the vanilla and almond extract. With electric mixer off, add the flour mixture all at once, then beat on low until blended, scraping the sides of bowl.

6. Beat in nuts just until blended. Form dough into two balls. Add about ¼ cup powdered sugar if dough is too sticky. Place a ball on each of the cookie sheets and shape into a roll about 12 inches long, 1½ inches high, and 3 inches wide. Gently flatted the top of each roll to form a slightly domed shape (about 1 inch high).

7. Bake for 20 minutes, or until fork inserted in center of roll comes out nearly clean (rolls are dry on top and firm). Remove pan from oven and reduce heat to 300 degrees. Transfer rolls to a cutting board and let cool 5 minutes.

8. Cut the rolls into ¾- to 1-inch thick slices (you can cut it on the diagonal if desired). Place slices cut side down on one of the baking pans. Bake another 15 minutes, or until the slices are dry and crisp. Transfer the biscotti to wire racks to cool.

9. Place white chocolate chips in 1-cup glass measure. Microwave on high 2 minutes, then stir. Microwave 1 minute longer; stir. If chocolate chips are not completely melted, microwave another 30 seconds until completely melted.

10. Pour melted chocolate into a small, flat bottom bowl (biscotti should fit flat in bottom). Dip one side of biscotti cookies lightly into chocolate. Place biscotti chocolate side up on cutting board or wire rack to harden chocolate. Store in plastic bags.

PER SERVING: 146 calories, 3 g protein, 22.5 g carbohydrate, 5.3 g fat, 2 g saturated fat, 19 mg cholesterol, 1.3 g fiber, 76 mg sodium. Calories from fat: 32 percent.

Q

Dear Recipe Doctor,

Years ago I saw this recipe printed in the paper—some lady unknowingly spent $250 dollars getting the Neiman-Marcus chocolate chip cookie recipe. This is the very best chocolate chip cookie recipe ever! We mix a batch up weekly. Please help! I would love to know if there is a way to bring down the fat and cholesterol.

A

I've seen this recipe before, too—attached to many different recipe names and stories. I think the one I've got stained and folded in one of my cookbooks is called Million Dollar Cookies. However this recipe came to be and however much was originally paid for it, we all definitely benefited. This is an amazing cookie.

What makes this chocolate chip cookie recipe unique is that it calls for grinding rolled oats and some semisweet chocolate into a powder using your food processor. I switched to bittersweet chocolate and took it down an ounce. Bittersweet chocolate usually contains a higher percentage of chocolate liquor and has a more intense flavor, so theoretically I should be able to get by with less.

I used 10 tablespoons butter instead of 16 and substituted ⅓ cup of fat-free cream cheese. I replaced both eggs with egg substitute. Not only does this cut out 10 grams of fat and over 400 milligrams cholesterol (for the recipe), it eliminates any risk of salmonella poisoning should anyone accidentally find their fingers in the raw cookie dough (and they will).

I doubled the vanilla extract and cut the chocolate chips (stirred in at the end) in half. This may be a little severe for you; if so, just add 1½ or 1⅓ cups of chips instead of just 1. These cookies are absolutely moist and chewy and full of that addicting chocolate chip cookie flavor. They freeze well in plastic bags, too. Even without all the fat and cholesterol, they still taste like a million bucks!

THE ALLEGED $250 CHOCOLATE CHIP COOKIE (LIGHTENED)

I made these with a baking stone and also with a thick air-cushion cookie sheet—they worked out equally well. The trick is taking them out of the oven even though they don't look completely ready. Follow the instructions exactly; you won't be sorry.

Original recipe (without nuts) contains 221 calories, 11.2 grams fat, 6.5 grams saturated fat, and 31 milligrams cholesterol per serving.

Makes 32 bakery size cookies

2 $\frac{1}{2}$ cups old-fashioned rolled oats
3 ounces bittersweet chocolate (semisweet chocolate can also be used)
10 tablespoons ($\frac{1}{2}$ cup + 2 tablespoons) butter, softened
$\frac{1}{3}$ cup fat-free cream cheese (light can also be used)
1 cup sugar
1 cup packed light brown sugar
$\frac{1}{2}$ cup egg substitute
2 teaspoons vanilla extract
2 cups all-purpose flour
1 teaspoon baking powder
1 teaspoon baking soda
$\frac{1}{2}$ teaspoon salt
1 cup chocolate chips, the largest and best quality possible (I like to use milk chocolate chips)
1 cup chopped nuts (optional)

1. Preheat oven to 375 degrees. Line two large baking stones or thick air-cushion cookie sheets with parchment paper or coat with canola cooking spray.
2. Put oats in food processor and pulse until reduced to a fairly fine powder. Coarsely chop the bittersweet chocolate and add to the oats; process until the pieces become as fine as possible.
3. Cream the butter, cream cheese, and sugars together in a large mixing bowl. Add the egg substitute and vanilla and mix well. In another bowl, combine the flour, baking powder, baking soda, and salt. Gradually beat the flour mixture into the butter mixture.
4. If you are using a heavy-duty standing mixer, go ahead and beat the oat mixture in on low speed. If not, work the oat mixture in with your hands. Mix thoroughly.
5. Work the chocolate chips into the dough with your hands or with a strong wooden spoon. If you want to add a cup of chopped nuts, do it now.
6. Use a cookie scoop to scoop out balls of dough about the size of golf balls and place 12 balls on each cookie sheet, spacing them evenly. Lightly coat the bottom of a flat-bottomed drinking glass with canola cooking spray and press gently on balls to flatten slightly. Respray after flattening about 3 cookies and continue until all balls are completed.
7. Bake one cookie sheet at a time on the middle rack in oven. Bake until the surfaces of the cookies are covered with small cracks, but inside the cracks, the cookies will still look wet (about 7 minutes). The cookies will not appear done at this point, but take them out anyway. Let the cookies cool right on the cookie sheet. Once the cookies are cool, store them in plastic bags. They keep well in the freezer.

PER COOKIE (without nuts): 170 calories, 3.5 g protein, 26 g carbohydrate, 6.5 g fat, 3.9 g saturated fat, 11 mg cholesterol, 1.2 g fiber, 137 mg sodium. Calories from fat: 34 percent.

Q *Dear Recipe Doctor,*

I tried the recipe for Very Chocolate Oatmeal and Chocolate Chip Cookies on the bag of Safeway Select jumbo semi-sweet chocolate chips and my family loved them. Can you reduce the fat in such a way that my family will still love them? I've tried taking some of the fat out before, but the cookies came out bready, and we like them chewy.

A Who doesn't love warm, chewy chocolate chip cookies fresh from the oven? Nothing beats them on a cold, rainy day. I like this recipe that was sent to me because it actually calls for more oats than it does flour (I often try to work oats into recipes because they add soluble fiber, along with other vitamins and minerals).

The trick with cookies is knowing just how far to cut the fat. With this recipe, cutting the butter back by 3 tablespoons, from the original 8 tablespoons, seemed to work perfectly. I creamed the remaining 5 tablespoons with 3 tablespoons of my favorite fat replacement for cookies—fat-free cream cheese.

I used egg substitute instead of eggs for two reasons. First of all, with every egg yolk you yank out, you cut the fat by 5 grams and the cholesterol by 250 milligrams. But probably more importantly, when you use egg substitute you eliminate any potential risk of salmonella poisoning from eating raw egg, and I have yet to meet a person who can resist sampling the raw cookie dough. Baking cookies is a perfect activity to do with children, and when baking with children it is always better to play it safe by using egg substitutes.

I added a bit more vanilla extract and a little less chocolate. If you like your cookies loaded with chocolate chips, use the full cup of chocolate chips called for. I skipped the sifting step (the original recipe calls for sifting the flour, baking soda, and salt). It works out just fine if you just throw these ingredients into the mixing bowl and blend.

Now for my last bit of advice. If you like your cookies chewy, undercook the cookies ever so slightly. Watch your cookies carefully and pull them out while the center is still a little soft.

VERY CHOCOLATE, OATMEAL AND CHOCOLATE CHIP COOKIES

Original recipe contains 155 calories, 8.6 grams fat, and 26 milligrams cholesterol per serving.

Makes 18 large cookies

5 tablespoons butter, softened
3 tablespoons fat-free cream cheese
½ cup packed brown sugar
¼ cup white sugar
¼ cup egg substitute
¾ cup white or whole wheat flour
½ teaspoon baking soda
½ teaspoon salt
1 teaspoon pure vanilla extract
1 cup Safeway Select very chocolate jumbo chocolate chips
1 cup quick-cooking oatmeal
½ cup chopped pecans or walnuts (optional)

1. Preheat oven to 375 degrees.
2. In mixing bowl, cream together butter, cream cheese, and sugars. Add egg substitute and beat well.
3. Add flour, soda, salt, and vanilla to butter mixture and beat until well blended. Stir in chocolate chips, oatmeal, and nuts if desired. Blend thoroughly.
4. Use a cookie scoop to drop cookie dough onto a cookie sheet coated with nonstick cooking spray. You can spray the bottom of a flat-bottomed glass with nonstick cooking spray and press onto the cookie dough balls to make a flatter cookie.
5. Bake in center of oven for about 8 minutes. Remove cookies and let cool on wire rack.

PER COOKIE: 134 calories, 2 g protein, 19 g carbohydrate, 6.3 g fat, 3.5 g saturated fat, 8 mg cholesterol, 1 g fiber, 135 mg sodium. Calories from fat: 40 percent.

Dear Recipe Doctor,

Do you have a good lemon cookie recipe?

I don't know about you, but I love just about anything lemon—lemon muffins, lemon pie, lemon chicken, lemonade. . . . Last summer I lightened up the recipe for Lemon Poppy Seed Cookies from *Mrs. Fields Cookie Book*. They were so flavorful and moist, I thought I should share this recipe with you.

I was able to cut the fat in half by using half as much butter and substituting fat-free cream cheese. Since this recipe originally called for 1 egg and 2 egg yolks, cholesterol was also a target. I took out one of the yolks and added 2 tablespoons of egg substitute in its place. I could have taken out all of the yolks, but the texture would have changed dramatically—and not for the better. I also added some lemon zest to enhance the lemon flavor.

Often when you take half the fat out, the other flavors don't come across as well. One way to remedy this is to use more of the flavorful ingredients. I could have doubled the lemon extract in this recipe, but since I had some lemons lying around, I opted for the natural approach—using fresh lemons. And since I now had a skinned lemon in my kitchen (I used the zest for the cookie dough), I decided to frost the cookies with a lemon glaze made with lemon juice and powdered sugar. Just this little bit of glaze adds a nice touch. It looks pretty and tastes even better.

⇌ LEMON POPPY SEED COOKIES ⇌

Original recipe contains 133 calories, 7 grams fat, and 42 milligrams of cholesterol per cookie.

Makes 2 dozen cookies

> 2 cups all-purpose flour
> $\frac{1}{2}$ teaspoon baking soda
> 2 teaspoons freshly grated lemon zest, finely chopped
> $\frac{1}{2}$ teaspoon coriander or cardamom
> 2 tablespoons poppy seeds
> 6 tablespoons butter, softened
> 6 tablespoons fat-free cream cheese
> 1 cup white sugar
> 1 egg yolk
> 2 tablespoons egg substitute
> 1 whole egg
> 1 teaspoon lemon extract
> $1\frac{1}{2}$ teaspoons lemon zest, finely chopped
>
> GLAZE:
> about 2 tablespoons lemon juice
> 1 cup powdered sugar

1. Preheat oven to 300 degrees. In medium bowl or 4-cup measure, combine flour, baking soda, lemon zest, coriander, and poppy seeds.
2. In mixing bowl, cream butter, cream cheese, and sugar at medium speed, scraping sides of bowl. Add yolk, egg substitute, egg, lemon extract, and lemon zest and beat at medium speed. Mixture should be light and fluffy. Slowly add flour mixture at low speed just until combined.
3. Coat cookie sheets with canola cooking spray. Use cookie scoop to drop dough two inches apart on prepared cookie sheets. Bake 20 minutes, or just until cookies reach desired doneness. Transfer cookies to wire rack to cool.
4. Blend lemon juice and powdered sugar in a small bowl. Spoon a little glaze onto the top of each cookie.

PER COOKIE: 109 calories, 2 g protein, 17 g carbohydrate, 3.7 g fat, 2 g saturated fat, 26 mg cholesterol, .5 g fiber, 78 mg sodium. Calories from fat: 31 percent.

AN ELAINE ORIGINAL

I really enjoy a good sugar cookie every now and then. And I've been lightening up quite a few sugar cookie recipes over the years. Well, this time I did the unthinkable and cut the fat by only one-third (instead of in half). In the past when I cut the butter in half, I had a cookie that still tasted good, but it didn't have the same texture as a regular rolled sugar cookie. Whereas I think this rolled sugar cookie recipe would be liked by even the pickiest of cookie monsters.

I call it Sugar and Spice Cookies because I spiced it up a little by adding ground cinnamon. It's like having a Snickerdoodle cookie that's all rolled and cut into a cookie cutter shape. I blended $\frac{2}{3}$ cup butter with $\frac{1}{3}$ cup fat-free cream cheese. The amount of sugar stayed the same (after all it is a "sugar" cookie). Because this cookie dough tends to be eaten raw by little helpers in the kitchen, and to cut the cholesterol wherever possible, I replaced the 2 eggs called for with $\frac{1}{2}$ cup of (pasteurized) fat-free egg substitute.

I also doubled the vanilla extract and rolled the dough out with powdered sugar instead of flour (for a nicer finished flavor).

☙ SUGAR AND SPICE ☙
AND EVERYTHING NICE COOKIES

Original recipe contains 135 calories, 6.2 grams fat, and 29 milligrams cholesterol per cookie.

Makes 32 cookies

> 3 cups all-purpose flour
> 2 teaspoons ground cinnamon
> ¾ teaspoon salt
> ⅔ cup butter, softened
> ⅓ cup fat-free cream cheese
> 1½ cups sugar
> ½ cup egg substitute
> 2 teaspoons vanilla
> powdered sugar

1. Combine flour, cinnamon, and salt in bowl. Beat butter, cream cheese, and sugar in another mixing bowl until creamy. Beat in egg substitute and vanilla until fluffy. Beat in flour mixture on lowest speed of mixer.

2. Divide dough in half and wrap each half with plastic. Refrigerate at least 1 hour (preferably overnight).

3. Preheat oven to 350 degrees. Coat cookie sheets with canola cooking spray. Dust dough, rolling pin, cookie cutter, and surface with powdered sugar. Roll out half the dough to ¼-inch thick. Press cutter molds gently into dough. Pull cookies out of molds and place on cookie sheets. Re-roll scraps. Repeat with remaining dough.

4. Bake about 8 minutes or until just golden at the edges. Remove to racks to cool. Store at room temperature or freeze. These cookies can be frosted and decorated like other sugar cookies.

PER SERVING: 117 calories, 2 g protein, 18.5 g carbohydrate, 4 g fat, 2.4 g saturated fat, 10 mg cholesterol, .4 g fiber, 96 mg sodium. Calories from fat: 30 percent.

CAKES, COOKIES, & BROWNIES

BROWNIES

CAKE MIX CARAMEL BROWNIES

PALM BEACH BROWNIES WITH
CHOCOLATE-COVERED MINTS

COFFEE TOFFEE BROWNIES

Q

Dear Recipe Doctor,

Here's my mom's recipe for caramel brownies using a German chocolate cake mix. They are really awesome brownies, but they call for, among other things, 1 ½ sticks of butter. Can you lighten them up?—but only if you keep them equally as awesome.

A

As many veteran Recipe Doctor readers know, I have a weakness for recipes that call for cake mixes. Now don't all you culinary purists get upset—I love lightening up desserts that are really really made from scratch, too (you know, the ones that call for sifting flour, cocoa, sugar, baking powder, etc.), but there is something infallible about the cake mix. I can do all sorts of things to it—add interesting ingredients to boost flavor and add moisture, even totally eliminate the butter or oil called for—and it almost always turns out terrific. You've got to like that.

Anyway, I was intrigued. Within twenty-four hours after receiving this recipe, I found myself in my kitchen at my Kitchen Aid mixer with my box of German chocolate cake mix in tow.

The caramel sauce, made in the microwave with caramels and evaporated milk, stayed the same except I switched to evaporated skimmed milk. For the brownie batter I reduced the butter from ¾ cup to ¼ cup. And since the recipe called for melting the butter, I could easily switch to canola oil. I like to do this whenever I can because canola oil has so many nutritional things going for it. I added some evaporated skimmed milk and chocolate syrup to make up for the lost butter.

I also reduced the nuts to ½ cup (from 1 cup) and the chocolate chips to ⅔ cup (from 1 cup), but honestly, these brownies would still be delicious without the chocolate chips. If you want to trim back the fat and calories even more, you could get by without them.

This reader was right, these brownies are awesome! And I was able to bring the calories down from 180 to 147, the fat from 9.5 grams to 5 grams, the saturated fat from 4.5 to 1.8 grams, and the cholesterol down from 11 to 1 milligram per serving.

⌒ CAKE MIX CARAMEL BROWNIES ⌒

Original recipe contains 180 calories, 9.5 grams fat, 4.5 grams saturated fat, and 11 milligrams cholesterol per serving.

Makes 36 brownies

14-ounce bag caramels, unwrapped
²⁄₃ cup plus ¼ cup evaporated skimmed milk, divided
1 box German chocolate cake mix
¼ cup canola oil
¼ cup chocolate syrup
½ cup chopped nuts
²⁄₃ cup chocolate chips (milk or semi-sweet)

1. Preheat oven to 350 degrees. Coat a 9 x 13-inch baking pan with canola cooking spray.
2. Place caramels and ⅓ cup of evaporated milk in a microwave-safe bowl. Microwave on high for 1 ½ minutes, then stir. Repeat this two to three more times until caramels are melted and a smooth sauce has formed; set aside.
3. Add cake mix, canola, ⅓ cup plus ¼ cup evaporated skimmed milk, and chocolate syrup to mixing bowl and beat on medium-low speed for 1 minute. Stir in nuts. Reserve 1½ cups of the brownie batter for later. Spread the remaining batter evenly in the prepared pan. Bake for about 10 minutes.
4. Remove from oven and pour caramel sauce evenly over the top. Sprinkle with chocolate chips. Then drop heaping teaspoonfuls of reserved batter evenly over the top (not every spot of caramel will be covered). Bake just about 20 minutes longer (don't overcook). Let cool in pan; cut into 36 brownies.

PER SERVING: 147 calories, 2 g protein, 25 g carbohydrate, 5 g fat, 1.8 g saturated fat, 1 mg cholesterol, .5 g fiber, 140 mg sodium. Calories from fat: 30 percent.

Dear Recipe Doctor,

I saw this recipe for Palm Beach brownies with chocolate-covered mints in my local newspaper and my friend told me to send it to you—that you could lighten it up for us.

I could tell from the picture in the paper that this was not your everyday brownie. It was extra tall, rich, and fudgy—jam-packed with nuts and peppermint patties. So I played it a little conservatively when lightening it up. I cut down from 5 eggs to 3 (usually I would have tried to use 2). I still added 5 tablespoons of butter (albeit down from 16 tablespoons). And even though the amount of sugar seemed awfully high, 3 ¾ cups, I only decreased it slightly.

The original recipe called for 8 ounces of unsweetened chocolate. I didn't touch that part of the recipe. I did, however, need to find a replacement for all the butter I was taking out. I noticed the original recipe called for powdered instant espresso. Why not add liquid espresso to replace some of the butter and delete the powder? So I replaced some of the lost butter with chocolate syrup (and I added less sugar to compensate for the extra sweetener) and some with concentrated coffee (I used Victorian House Decaf French Roast concentrated liquid coffee).

I had to shimmy around some of the mixing steps so the coffee and chocolate syrup wouldn't interfere with the important whipping of the eggs with the sugar. I did end up taking these brownies out of the oven 10 minutes sooner than the original recipe in order to get that desirable dense, fudgy brownie texture.

Not only could you not tell that these brownies had been lightened, they were "to die for"—and believe me, I use that phrase sparingly.

PALM BEACH BROWNIES WITH CHOCOLATE-COVERED MINTS

Original recipe (from *Maida Heatter's Brand-New Book of Great Cookies*, Random House, 1995) contains 340 calories, 18.5 grams fat, and 50 milligrams cholesterol per brownie.

Makes 32 jumbo brownies

- 8 ounces unsweetened chocolate
- 5 tablespoons butter
- 3 eggs
- ½ cup egg substitute
- 2 teaspoons vanilla extract
- ½ teaspoon almond extract
- ¼ teaspoon salt
- 3 cups sugar
- ¼ cup concentrated coffee or cooled espresso
- 7 tablespoons (½ cup – 1 tablespoon) chocolate syrup
- 1 ⅔ cups unbleached flour
- 1 generous cup walnut or pecan pieces
- 35 (1½-inch wide) York chocolate-covered peppermint patties, unwrapped

1. Preheat oven to 425 degrees and place an oven rack one-third up from the bottom. Line a 9 x 13-inch baking pan with aluminum foil. Spray the bottom and sides of foil-lined pan with canola cooking spray.
2. Place chocolate and butter in a microwave-safe bowl. Microwave on high 2 minutes, and stir. Microwave another 2 minutes, and stir. If the chocolate is not completely melted, microwave 30 seconds longer or until mixture is smooth and chocolate is melted; set aside.

3. In large bowl of electric mixer, beat eggs with egg substitute, extracts, salt, and sugar at high speed for exactly 10 minutes. While this mixture is mixing, stir coffee and chocolate syrup together in small bowl or glass measure.

4. On low speed, add chocolate-butter mixture to egg mixture and beat only until mixed. Add coffee-chocolate syrup mixture and beat only until mixed. Then add flour and beat on low speed just until mixed.

5. Remove bowl from mixer. Stir in nuts. Pour half mixture (about 3 ½ cups) into prepared pan and smooth top. Place a layer of mints, nearly touching each other and the edges of the pan, all over the brownie batter (do not press down). Pour remaining brownie batter over the mints and smooth the top.

6. Bake about 25 minutes or until a firm, lightly browned crust has formed on top, but a toothpick inserted in center still comes out wet and covered with chocolate. This time will vary with your particular oven. Don't be afraid to dig into the middle of the pan with a spoon just to make sure it is the texture you desire. Let pan cool.

7. Refrigerate the brownies for a few hours or overnight before cutting into bars (although it will still be delicious if you don't wait). Lift foil from pan and place on flat surface. Cut into bars using a long, heavy knife with a sharp straight or serrated blade. Pack in an airtight box or wrap individually in clear cellophane or foil. They can also be frozen.

PER BROWNIE: 255 calories, 4 g protein, 43.5 g carbohydrate, 9.5 g fat, 3.5 g saturated fat, 25 mg cholesterol, 1.5 g fiber, 58 mg sodium. Calories from fat: 33 percent.

AN ELAINE ORIGINAL

We, as Americans, get real serious about our coffee. Let's face it, most of us cannot go one day without it—whether it's the caffeine or simply the coffee flavor fix. My love affair with coffee has nothing to do with caffeine, since I only enjoy decaf. I particularly love using coffee as a flavor enhancer in lower-fat recipes. It helps give the dessert an extra zip when most of the fat in the regular recipe has been zapped.

One night I was inspired to make a pan of brownies—but with a twist. For some reason, I got the idea to make coffee toffee brownies (I think I just liked the way the name sounded). This made sense to me, since I absolutely adore all three major ingredients: coffee, toffee, and brownies.

I reduced the fat in the brownie mix by using only a couple tablespoons of canola oil and replaced the 6 tablespoons I took out with nonfat sour cream. I replaced the water called for with extra strong coffee or espresso. And I used 1 egg and ¼ cup egg substitute instead of 2 whole eggs. Then if you really want to go all out, stir ½ cup of semi-sweet chocolate chips into the batter. I was careful not to overbake the brownies in order to preserve the fudge factor.

Then, as if that wasn't yummy enough, I stirred up a mocha glaze to spread on top of the warm brownies with a small dose of melted semi-sweet chocolate chips (a little chocolate goes a long way), espresso or strong coffee, powdered sugar, cocoa, and a hint of vanilla. The toffee bits can be sprinkled over the glaze or stirred into the batter before baking, it's up to you.

I took the brownies to a party the next day and they evaporated in one minute. Best of all, no one knew they weren't as sinful as they tasted.

⁀ COFFEE TOFFEE BROWNIES ⁀

Makes 18 servings

1 box Betty Crocker Supreme dark chocolate brownie mix
$\frac{1}{3}$ cup espresso or extra strong coffee (triple strength)
3 tablespoons canola oil
$\frac{1}{4}$ cup fat-free or light sour cream
1 large egg
$\frac{1}{4}$ cup egg substitute
$\frac{1}{2}$ cup English toffee bits, such as Skor (I found it in a
    10-ounce bag)
$\frac{1}{2}$ cup semi-sweet chocolate chips (optional)

MOCHA GLAZE:
$\frac{1}{4}$ cup semi-sweet chocolate chips
3 tablespoons espresso or very, very strong coffee
$\frac{1}{2}$ teaspoon vanilla extract
1 cup powdered sugar
2 tablespoons unsweetened cocoa

1. Preheat oven to 350 degrees. Coat a 13 x 9-inch baking pan
    with canola cooking spray. Make $\frac{2}{3}$ cup of espresso or triple
    strength coffee and set aside to cool.
2. Combine brownie mix and pouch of special dark syrup (comes
    with mix), espresso, canola oil, sour cream, egg, and egg sub-
    stitute in medium mixing bowl. Beat briefly until well blended
    with electric mixer or by hand (about 50 strokes).
3. Stir in toffee pieces and chocolate chips if desired. Spread mix-
    ture evenly in prepared pan.

4. Bake about 25 minutes (23 minutes if using dark no-stick metal pan) or until brownies reach your desired doneness. Cool.
5. For glaze, melt chocolate chips in a small saucepan over very low heat. Remove from heat. Stir in espresso and vanilla. Add sugar and cocoa to mixture and stir until smooth. Spread glaze over cooled brownies using the back of a spoon (it hardens somewhat as it dries). Sprinkle toffee bits over the glaze, if you didn't add them into the brownie batter.
6. Store covered. For easier cutting, cool completely before cutting.

PER SERVING: 214 calories, 2 g protein, 37.5 g carbohydrate, 6.5 g fat, 2 g saturated fat, 15 mg cholesterol, 1.5 g fiber, 175 mg sodium. Calories from fat: 28 percent.

Chapter Eight

PIES & MORE

PIES

GRASSHOPPER PIE

SUPER DELUXE KEY LIME PIE

BLENDER FRENCH SILK PIE

1-2-3 MUD PIE

2-LAYER LEMON CREAM CHEESE PIE

WHITE CHOCOLATE FRUIT TART

CARAMEL APPLE PIE

Q

Dear Recipe Doctor,

We're Irish and one of our favorite St. Patrick's Day treats is grasshopper pie. I would make it more often if you could bring down the fat and calories for us.

A

I got this letter in December, and I couldn't wait to try my hand at lightening it up, so I figured it's green, it's minty, it'll work for Christmas! So I confidently lightened it up to take to a Christmas Eve dinner party. It never occurred to me that it might not work.

I had planned to use half real whipped cream and half Dream Whip but my "Dream" Whip quickly turned into a "nightmare." After waiting many minutes for my Dream Whip to thicken, I opted for 100 percent light whipping cream (any excuse to use real whipped cream). But my head was swimming with questions: Does something like Dream Whip even have an expiration date? (I found out later it doesn't, which may not be a good sign.) Did I add 1 cup of milk instead of the ½ cup called for? Did I whip the Dream Whip at high speed for the 4 minutes called for on the box?

I checked the freezer minutes before leaving for the party and it looked like it had worked perfectly. I even cut a sliver from the pie just to make sure the taste was presentable. Not only was it presentable, it was delicious.

So I proudly carted my pie to the party, a 10-minute drive away, and found a spot for it in a very crowded freezer (you know how freezers can get during the holidays). When it came time to serve, I opened the freezer door only to find grasshopper soup had turned into grasshopper pie. Believe it or not, though, that pie was finished before any of the other desserts at the party.

Lessons learned: Make sure the freezer you use isn't overcrowded. Don't take this pie on a long car drive, especially in the summer months. If you are going to use Dream Whip, follow the directions perfectly and you may need to whip it for 6 minutes instead of 4 (or have a carton of light whipping cream as a backup). But finally, the light version of this pie was still popular!

The filling for grasshopper pie is already pretty light, featuring a little milk, marshmallows, and crème de menthe. The only ingredient worth lightening is the whipping cream. I used light whipping cream, but you can use light Cool Whip or Dream Whip if you are so inclined. (I tried using marshmallow creme instead of melting marshmallows in milk over a double boiler. It did seem to work, but by the end I was one sticky mess from head to toe and the marshmallow creme didn't seem to blend with the other ingredients as well as the milk and marshmallow mixture.)

The chocolate cookie crust is where we can really get to work. Instead of crushed cookie wafers, I used reduced-fat chocolate Nilla Wafers (reduced-fat Oreos could also be used in a pinch). Then I cut the melted butter down from $\frac{1}{3}$ cup to 1 tablespoon and added $\frac{1}{4}$ cup chocolate syrup and 1 tablespoon of crème de cacao. The cookie mixture seemed a little dry so I added another tablespoon of crème de cacao.

GRASSHOPPER PIE

Original recipe contains 250 calories, 15 grams fat, 9 grams saturated fat, and 43 milligrams cholesterol per serving.

Makes 12 servings

> ²/₃ cup whole or 2% low-fat milk
> 24 marshmallows (*not* the miniatures)
> ¼ cup green crème de menthe
> ⅛ cup crème de cacao liqueur
> 1 cup (liquid) light whipping cream
>   (makes about 2 cups whipped)*
>
> CHOCOLATE CRUST:
> 1 ¼ cups crushed reduced-fat chocolate Nilla Wafers (or similar)
> 1 tablespoon butter, melted
> ¼ cup chocolate syrup
> 1 to 2 tablespoons crème de cacao liqueur

1. Set mixing bowl and beaters in refrigerator to chill for whipping cream.
2. To make crust, place chocolate wafers in food processor and pulse until fine crumbs form. Measure to make sure it is 1¼ cups of crumbs. Return to food processor, along with the butter, chocolate syrup, and crème de cacao. Pulse until a moist crumb mixture forms. Pat evenly onto bottom and up sides of 9-inch pie plate that has been coated with canola cooking spray. Chill in refrigerator.

3. Scald milk in top of double boiler over simmering water. Add marshmallows and stir, over simmering water, until marshmallows are melted (a few minutes). Cool to room temperature. Stir in ¼ cup crème de menthe and ⅛ cup crème de cacao.
4. Whip cream in cold bowl until soft peaks form. Fold into marshmallow mixture. Turn into chocolate crust and freeze at least 4 hours.

*If you use Dream Whip, reduce the crème de menthe to 3 tablespoons—it tends to have a stronger flavor with the Dream Whip.

PER SERVING: 183 calories, 2 g protein, 26 g carbohydrate, 8 g fat, 4.5 g saturated fat, 43 mg cholesterol, 0 g fiber, 62 mg sodium. Calories from fat: 39 percent.

Q

Dear Recipe Doctor,

I cut this Key lime pie recipe from a newspaper about 10 years ago and I've made it hundreds of times. Everyone always wants the recipe. It could stand to be lightened, though. I hope you accept the challenge!

A

The original recipe interested me right off the bat because it wasn't your ordinary Key lime pie recipe. The crust called for crushed shortbread cookies and macadamia nuts and the filling called for cream cheese in addition to the usual sweetened condensed milk, Key lime juice, and 4 egg yolks.

This recipe wasn't bashful about loading on the butterfat either. The crust calls for 5 tablespoons butter, while the filling calls for a cup of heavy cream. The fat-laden ingredients don't sound too bad on their own but add them together—the shortbread cookies, macadamia nuts, butter, condensed milk, egg yolks, cream cheese, and heavy cream—and you've got one very rich Key lime pie!

But I've got to tell you, the light version was heavenly, especially the crust. Even though I didn't take out the macadamia nuts, I was still able to bring the fat down from 26 to 9 grams, and saturated fat down from 13 to 2.5 grams per slice. I cut the butter down to 1 tablespoon and added ¼ cup corn syrup instead of the ¼ cup granulated sugar called for. We just added the sweetener in liquid form—this way the crust was moist without needing more butter. And instead of using buttery shortbread cookies as the cookie crumbs, I used SnackWell's vanilla sandwich cookies (although you could use whatever cookies you have on hand—oatmeal and coconut work well, too).

For the filling, I used fat-free sweetened condensed milk and cut the egg yolks from 4 to 0, adding ½ cup egg substitute in its place. I didn't necessarily do this for the whopping cholesterol savings but to eliminate any potential risk of consuming raw egg (the pie isn't cooked in this recipe), and egg substitute is pasteurized (with no danger of salmonella).

I added a packet of unflavored gelatin and ¼ cup water just to make sure the pie would firm up nicely (if you don't use it, it still works out but it is a little on the soft side—but with a very creamy texture).

I switched to light cream cheese and eliminated the heavy cream normally added as garnish. Trust me, this pie is so delicious, it doesn't need it. Save the whipped cream for the pumpkin pie.

⇔ SUPER DELUXE KEY LIME PIE ⇐

Original recipe contains 429 calories, 26 grams fat, 13 grams saturated fat, 141 milligrams cholesterol per slice.

Makes 10 slices

CRUST:
1 tablespoon butter, melted
14 SnackWell's vanilla sandwich cookies, broken by hand into small chunks
¼ cup light corn syrup
½ cup chopped macadamia nuts

FILLING:
1 envelope (scant tablespoon) unflavored gelatin
¼ cup water
14-ounce can fat-free sweetened condensed milk
½ cup egg substitute
4 ounces light cream cheese
½ cup Key lime juice (regular lime juice will work in a pinch)
zest from 1 lime, finely chopped (optional)

1. Combine butter, cookies, corn syrup, and macadamia nuts in food processor; pulse until a moist crumb mixture has formed. Press into a 9-inch pie plate that has been coated with canola cooking spray. Put in freezer while making filling.
2. Blend gelatin with the water in a small nonstick saucepan and let sit for 1 minute. Then cook over low heat, stirring constantly, until the gelatin dissolves and the mixture is clear. Set aside to cool.

3. Place condensed milk, egg substitute, and cream cheese in food processor. Pulse until combined. Slowly add the lime juice while the food processor is running. Blend an additional minute until mixture is nicely thickened. Gently pulse in gelatin mixture and lime zest.

4. Pour into chilled pie crust and refrigerate until set (at least 2 hours). Serve each slice with a dollop of light whipped cream if desired.

PER SERVING: 293 calories, 7 g protein, 47 g carbohydrate, 9 g fat, 2.5 g saturated fat, 7 mg cholesterol, .5 g fiber, 217 mg sodium. Calories from fat: 28 percent.

Q *Dear Recipe Doctor,*

My favorite pie in the whole world is Baker's Square French silk pie. But lately I just can't enjoy it as much knowing it is probably loaded with artery clogging fat and cholesterol. Can you come up with a lower-fat substitute?

A I've only tasted that pie once, and it was memorable. You are right on both counts: it is totally rich and wonderful tasting, and it is loaded with fat and cholesterol. I remember feeling the grease on my lips as I ate the pie. I wondered if there was a way to have the same flavor and creamy texture while eliminating the grease factor.

I looked in my library of cookbooks and found two recipes for French silk pie—one that was fairly simple to prepare but involved raw eggs (and the risk of salmonella), and another that cooked the eggs but required extensive preparation.

As I read the latter recipe—simmering the cream and chocolate for 10 minutes, stirring some of it into the egg yolks, then returning the egg yolks back to the chocolate, cooking until thickened (another 5 minutes)—I was beginning to lose interest. By the time I got to the part where you submerge the saucepan in a bowl of ice water only to stir the mixture until it stiffens (another 20 minutes), I had closed the cookbook. Believe it or not there was still a step or two left after that.

Instead, I went to a blender chocolate mousse recipe I had lightened a while back. This one uses egg substitute (which eliminates not only the fat and cholesterol, but the risk of salmonella because it is pasteurized) and involves throwing all the ingredients in the blender. That I can do!

I cut 10 grams of fat and over 400 milligrams of cholesterol by using egg substitute instead of 2 eggs, and I cut the chocolate back and substituted nonfat cream cheese, cocoa, and marshmallow creme (which helped give me the "mousse" texture). I added scalded low-fat milk instead of scalded whole milk or half-and-half. I know it sounds like a stretch, but it really turns out smooth and creamy and very decadent tasting. One blender's worth fills a single baked pie crust perfectly, turning your reduced-fat chocolate mousse into a French silk pie. Of course, the pie crust will add 7 grams of fat per serving.

☞ BLENDER FRENCH SILK PIE ☜

Original recipe contains 441 calories, 34 grams fat, and 114 milligrams cholesterol per serving.

Makes 8 servings

- ¼ cup nonfat cream cheese
- 1 cup semi-sweet chocolate chips
- ⅓ cup cocoa
- ½ cup marshmallow creme
- 2 tablespoons Wondra quick-mixing flour
- ½ cup egg substitute
- 1 cup low-fat milk
- 1 baked single pie crust

1. Combine all the ingredients except the milk and pie crust in the blender.
2. Heat the milk in a small saucepan over medium heat, without stirring, until bubbles form around the edge of saucepan (this is how to scald milk). Pour the milk into the blender, cover the blender, and immediately blend on high speed for 2 to 3 minutes.
3. Pour into baked pie crust (or individual serving dishes). Refrigerate for at least 4 hours to set. Serve each slice with a dollop of whipped cream or light Cool Whip.

Note: without pie crust, each serving contains 206 calories, 6 g protein, 34 g carbohydrate, 7 g fat, 3 mg cholesterol, 92 mg sodium. Calories from fat: 29 percent.

PER SERVING (WITH PIE CRUST): 326 calories, 7 g protein, 47 g carbohydrate, 14 g fat, 6 g saturated fat, 8 mg cholesterol, 2.5 g fiber, 192 mg sodium. Calories from fat: 38 percent.

Dear Recipe Doctor,

For years I have enjoyed ice cream mud pies from Baskin Robbins or the Chart House restaurants. I would love to make a lower-fat version at home. I look forward to the Recipe Doctor column in the newspaper every week!

Who doesn't love mud pie? Even people who normally don't drink coffee seem to love this dessert. Actually, I often have mud pie flashbacks from my college years. We used to get a serving from the Chart House and split it.

It is a great idea to make this at home because that's the only way you are going to find a lighter version. For as good as they look and taste, they really are a cinch to make, too.

I made a lighter chocolate cookie crust using reduced-fat Oreo cookies and blended in 2 tablespoons canola margarine instead of 4 tablespoons butter. I added 2 tablespoons chocolate syrup to replace the 2 tablespoons of butter I took out. I just dumped all three ingredients into a food processor to save time.

A mud pie is only as good as its ice-cream filling, so choosing a great-tasting light coffee ice cream is important. I used Dreyers Grand light espresso fudge chip (with 4 grams fat per 1/2 cup serving) and it was absolutely yummy. You could use a fat-free hot fudge topping; there are a couple on the market, saving about 2.5 grams fat per serving. But, truthfully, it probably isn't going to taste as good as the others. If you use the brand with 2.5 grams fat per 2 tablespoons instead of one with 4 grams fat per serving, it will only save you .7 gram of fat per serving. I made this pie for Easter dessert and it went over quite well with just about everyone.

≈ 1-2-3 MUD PIE ≈

Original recipe contains 620 calories, 36 grams fat, 16 grams saturated fat, and 170 milligrams cholesterol per serving.

Makes 12 servings

25 reduced-fat Oreo cookies
2 tablespoons canola margarine or butter, melted
2 tablespoons chocolate syrup
½ gallon light coffee ice cream, softened slightly (I used Dreyer's Grand light espresso fudge chip)
⅔ cup hot fudge sauce (e.g., Mrs. Richardson's)
¼ cup toasted sliced almonds (optional)
whipped cream for garnish (optional)

1. Preheat oven to 350 degrees. Place cookies, melted margarine or butter, and chocolate syrup in food processor. Pulse until cookie crumb mixture is made. Press into bottom and up sides of 9-inch pie plate. Bake 5 to 7 minutes, then chill.
2. Pack ice cream into chilled crust, shaping into slight mound. Freeze until firm (freezing before adding fudge sauce is essential to keep fudge from slipping off).
3. Pour fudge sauce evenly over pie and freeze until ready to serve. Sprinkle almonds over the fudge top if desired. Garnish the rim of each serving with a dollop of whipped cream if desired.

PER SERVING: 333 calories, 4.5 g protein, 50 g carbohydrate, 10 g fat, 4 g saturated fat, 20 mg cholesterol, 1 g fiber, 263 mg sodium. Calories from fat: 31 percent.

Dear Recipe Doctor,

I love this recipe for lemon cream cheese pie, but I am sure it is loaded with fat and cholesterol. Please tell me how I can make this a little less sinful.

And loaded with fat, calories, and cholesterol it is! A serving of the original recipe contains 407 calories, 84 milligrams cholesterol, and 23.5 grams of fat per modest slice.

There are a few ways to go here. The fat is coming from a few directions—the pie crust, the cream cheese, and other filling ingredients (namely the egg yolks and butter). The obvious first place to start is the cream cheese. I used light Philadelphia cream cheese and it was yummy. Fat-free cream cheese is always an option, but I don't recommend it—most people would not be happy with the results.

I used egg substitute in the cream cheese layer and tossed in some vanilla extract for added flavor. For the lemon layer, I tried to cut out the tablespoon of butter, to save each serving from 1.5 grams of fat. Although I didn't miss it in terms of the flavor or texture, unfortunately, without it my lemon pie tended to bubble over the edges of the pie plate. In this situation the butter must serve as a defoaming agent. So I had to put the tablespoon of butter back in.

Now, on to the egg yolks. I cut out one of the two egg yolks from the lemon layer and replaced it with 2 tablespoons of egg substitute. And to move the lemon flavor up a notch, I added a bit more lemon peel than is normally called for. I find this never hurts and almost always helps.

The last step I took might be the most drastic. I didn't use the pastry crust called for—I used a ready-made reduced-fat graham cracker crust. To me, this sounded more appealing with a lemon and cream cheese filling than a pastry crust anyway. Besides, it is easier to reduce the fat in a graham cracker crust without noticing a difference in taste and texture than your average pie crust. And I personally welcome the chance to get out of making homemade pie crust.

The only problem is, the filling might bubble over ever so slightly because the prepared graham cracker crust is smaller than a homemade crust. Just make sure to leave the edges up on the disposable pie pan (you have to curl the edges up anyway to remove the plastic top from the crust) and bake the pie on a cookie sheet or jellyroll pan.

The result is a quick and tasty pie that went from 23.5 grams of fat and 407 calories to 8 grams of fat and 281 calories. I like to serve each slice with a dollop of light whipped cream or whipped topping with a thin slice of lemon for garnish.

2-LAYER LEMON CREAM CHEESE PIE

Original recipe contains 407 calories, 84 milligrams cholesterol, and 23.5 grams fat per serving.

Makes 8 servings

> 1 reduced-fat graham cracker crust (or similar)
> 1 cup sugar, divided
> 2 tablespoons cornstarch
> 1 cup cold water
> 1 egg yolk
> 2 tablespoons + ¼ cup egg substitute, divided
> 1 tablespoon butter or margarine
> 3 tablespoons lemon juice
> 1 tablespoon grated and finely chopped lemon peel
> 8 ounces light cream cheese
> ½ teaspoon vanilla extract
> light whipped cream (optional)
> lemon slices (optional)

1. Preheat oven to 375 degrees. Curl pie plate edges up from graham cracker crust to remove plastic top (leave edges up to make pie plate a little higher).
2. In medium saucepan, combine ⅔ cup sugar with cornstarch; mix well. Gradually stir in cold water, stirring constantly until blended.
3. In small bowl, beat egg yolk and 2 tablespoons egg substitute slightly; stir into sugar mixture in saucepan. Cook over medium heat until mixture comes to a boil, stirring constantly. Boil 1 to 2 minutes. Remove from heat and stir in the butter, lemon juice, and peel; blend well.

4. In small mixing bowl, combine remaining ⅓ cup sugar and light cream cheese; beat until smooth. Add ¼ cup egg substitute and vanilla, and blend well. Spread evenly into graham cracker crust.

5. Gently spoon lemon mixture over cream cheese, spreading evenly.

6. Bake pie on cookie sheet or jellyroll pan in center of oven for about 35 minutes (center will not be completely set). Cool 30 minutes, then refrigerate 90 minutes to completely chill.

Each slice can be garnished with a dollop of light whipped cream or light whipped topping and a thin slice of lemon, if desired.

PER SERVING: 281 calories, 5 g protein, 45 g carbohydrate, 8 g fat, 5 g saturated fat, 40 mg cholesterol, .5 g fiber, 48 mg sodium. Calories from fat: 25 percent.

Dear Recipe Doctor,

I read your column religiously and now I need your help. I'm looking for an impressive but light dessert to serve formal company this summer. Any suggestions?

I'm not exactly one to formally entertain. But the other day I did happen to lighten up a white chocolate fruit tart that seriously looked too good to eat. We were having a family barbecue in honor of my daughter's birthday, and I, almost as an afterthought, made this extra dessert for the people who might not care for birthday cake. It ended up stealing the birthday cake's thunder. Everyone was interested in tasting this colorful tart, so I put the birthday candles in the fruit tart instead.

True, this recipe is perfect for spring and summer because it showcases those gorgeous fresh fruits (I used sliced kiwi and fresh strawberries and pineapple), but technically you could use canned pineapple, canned mandarin oranges, and pears come winter.

To cut some of the calories and fat grams, I replaced half of the butter in the crust with light cream cheese and it still made a perfect shortbread-like crust. In the custard filling, I hadn't originally planned on reducing the white chocolate chips, but I accidentally used 1 slightly heaping cup and later discovered it was supposed to be 2 cups. So I'm going to go with it. I also used whole milk (instead of heavy whipping cream) and light cream cheese (instead of regular). All I can tell you is it was gone within minutes and I will definitely make this again.

WHITE CHOCOLATE FRUIT TART

Original recipe contains 455 calories, 29 grams fat, 18 grams saturated fat, and 65 milligrams cholesterol per serving.

Makes 12 servings

CRUST:
1/3 cup butter, softened
1/3 cup light cream cheese
1/2 cup powdered sugar
1 1/3 cups all-purpose flour

FILLING:
1 slightly heaping cup (1 1/4 cups) white chocolate chips
1 cup light cream cheese
1/4 cup whole or low-fat milk

TOPPING:
(You choose which fruits to use, but here is an estimate)
8-ounce can pineapple chunks, canned in juice (reserve juice)
3 kiwifruit, peeled and sliced
1 to 2 cups fresh strawberries, sliced

GLAZE:
3 tablespoons sugar
2 teaspoons cornstarch
1/2 teaspoon lemon juice

1. Preheat oven to 300 degrees. Coat a 9- or 10-inch pie plate with canola cooking spray.

2. In mixing bowl, cream butter, $\frac{1}{3}$ cup cream cheese, and powdered sugar. On low speed, gradually add flour; mix well. Press into bottom and about $1\frac{1}{4}$ inches up the sides of prepared pie plate. Bake until lightly browned (about 25 minutes). Cool.

3. While crust is baking, melt chips in a double boiler (I'm sorry, but this is the only way to melt white chocolate chips without turning them into a big clump). Combine 1 cup cream cheese in mixing bowl along with $\frac{1}{4}$ cup milk and beat on low until smooth. Add melted chips and beat until smooth. Spread over cooled crust. Chill for 30 minutes.

4. Drain pineapple (but reserve $\frac{1}{2}$ cup of juice and set aside) and any other canned fruit you might be using. Peel and slice any fresh fruit you will be using. Starting from the outside edge and moving toward the center, arrange kiwi slices, then pineapple and strawberries (or other fruit) over filling.

5. In a saucepan, combine sugar, cornstarch, lemon juice, and reserved pineapple juice; bring to boil over medium heat. Boil for 1 to 2 minutes or until thickened, stirring constantly. Cool; brush generously over the fruit. Chill 1 hour before serving. Store in the refrigerator.

PER SERVING: 295 calories, 6 g protein, 39 g carbohydrate, 13 g fat, 7 g saturated fat, 27 mg cholesterol, 1.5 g fiber, 165 mg sodium. Calories from fat: 40 percent.

AN ELAINE ORIGINAL

Every now and then I come up with a different way of making something "classic"—sometimes it works and sometimes it doesn't. This time it worked—big time. My neighbor brought me a bag of apples from her tree, but somehow making your standard apple pie didn't thrill me. So I decided I would make up a caramel apple pie, which sounded good in theory.

I started with a single prepared pie crust (Pillsbury pie crust). All I did was make a less-sugar apple filling, then drizzled caramel fudge sauce over the apple filling. I topped this with my usual less-fat crumb topping and baked it until golden.

Now all you purists out there who insist on making your own pie crust, more power to you. But admittedly, one of my least favorite things to do in the kitchen is make pie crust. So I personally have no problem using the packaged Pillsbury pie crusts.

Most apple fillings call for anywhere from ⅔ to 1 cup of sugar. I used ⅓ cup since the caramel sauce would be contributing some sugar. They also call for dotting butter over the top of the filling; I make it a habit not to dot, saving the pie from several tablespoons of butter or margarine.

The crumb topping, however, is a different story. Usually ¼ cup of butter or margarine is cut into the flour/sugar mixture with a pastry blender. But if you melt the butter, less butter is required to create a crumblike mixture. You can get by with 2 tablespoons instead of 4.

If you like caramel apples, you will love this pie. True, the caramel sauce adds ½ gram of fat and 48 calories to every serving. But considering the calories and fat in your average 2-crust apple pie (390 calories, 17 grams fat), we are still ahead of the game. If the amount of calories and fat grams per slice of this delectable pie still offends you, lose the crust. You will now be making caramel apple crisp instead, with 120 fewer calories and 7 grams less fat per serving.

⌐ CARAMEL APPLE PIE ⌐

Makes 8 servings

> ½ package Pillsbury pie crust (single crust)
> 6 cups thinly sliced apples
> 1 tablespoon lemon juice
> ⅓ cup sugar
> 2 tablespoons flour
> ¾ teaspoon cinnamon
> ¼ teaspoon salt
> ⅛ teaspoon nutmeg
> 6 tablespoons (¼ cup + 2 tablespoons) caramel fudge sauce
>   (such as Mrs. Richardson's)

> CRUMB CRUST:
> ½ cup flour
> ½ cup sugar
> ½ teaspoon cinnamon
> ¼ teaspoon nutmeg
> 2 tablespoons melted butter or margarine

1. Preheat oven to 375 degrees. Let crust stand at room temperature for 15 minutes. Peel off plastic sheet. Place crust in ungreased 9-inch glass pie pan. Press crust firmly against sides and bottom. Fold excess crust under and press together to form thick crust edge; flute or crimp edges if desired.
2. In large bowl, combine apples, lemon juice, ⅓ cup sugar, 2 tablespoons flour, ¾ teaspoon cinnamon, ¼ teaspoon salt, and ⅛ teaspoon nutmeg; mix lightly. Spoon apple mixture evenly into pie crust.
3. Drizzle caramel sauce over the apple filling.

4.   In medium mixing bowl stir together ½ cup flour, ½ cup sugar, ½ teaspoon cinnamon, and ¼ teaspoon nutmeg. Drizzle melted butter over the top and blend with fork till crumbly. Sprinkle topping evenly over pie filling.
5.   To prevent overbrowning, cover edge of pie with foil. Set pie plate on a cookie sheet or jellyroll pan. Bake for 25 minutes. Remove foil and bake 20 minutes more or till top is golden. Cool on wire rack.

PER SERVING: 375 calories, 2 g protein, 69 g carbohydrate, 10.5 g fat, 3.5 g saturated fat, 2 g fiber, 13 mg cholesterol, 2.5 g fiber, 218 mg sodium. Calories from fat: 25 percent.

PIES & MORE

OTHER DESSERTS

THE FAMOUS HOLLAND AMERICA
BREAD AND BUTTER PUDDING (LIGHTENED)

PEANUT BUTTER BALLS

APPLE CRISP

Dear Recipe Doctor,

Enclosed please find the recipe from a handout received while on board Holland America's Ryndam. *This bread pudding was incredible, but unfortunately, way too fattening. Please see what you can do.*

I couldn't wait to try this recipe. I had to fake it a little, though, because the original recipe left a few things out, like how many slices of bread to use, what size dish to use, and the oven temperature to use.

The original recipe called for equal portions of whole milk and double cream. I used just whole milk and skipped the cream. I cut the eggs down to 1 and substituted 6 tablespoons of egg substitute. I cut the butter down from 3 tablespoons to 1 (I figured I should use *some* butter since the dish is called "Bread and Butter Pudding"). The recipe also calls for 1½ fresh vanilla beans cut open; this can get expensive, so I used 1 bean and added ½ teaspoon pure vanilla just in case. I also added a tablespoon of maple syrup simply for flavor.

Once your bread and butter pudding is golden brown, sprinkle with cinnamon-sugar. I made a mixture of ground cinnamon and powdered sugar and proceeded to heavily dust the top of the bread pudding. This added a little flavor and decadence to the dish. This worked out so well, I hope this reader will send me a recipe from her next Holland America cruise!

THE FAMOUS HOLLAND AMERICA BREAD AND BUTTER PUDDING (LIGHTENED)

Original recipe contains 451 calories, 22 grams fat, 12 grams saturated fat, and 165 milligrams cholesterol.

Makes 5 servings

  2–3 tablespoons raisins
  1⅛ cups whole milk
  1 tablespoon butter
  ¼ teaspoon salt
  1 or ½ fresh vanilla bean (sticks) cut open lengthwise
  ½ teaspoon vanilla extract
  1 egg
  6 tablespoons (¼ cup + 2 tablespoons) egg substitute
  ⅓ cup sugar
  1 tablespoon maple syrup
  8 large but thin slices of bread (carefully trim off the crust)
  ½ teaspoon ground cinnamon
  2 tablespoons powdered sugar

1. Preheat oven to 350 degrees. Place raisins in small bowl, cover with water, and let soak for 10 minutes. Bring the milk, butter, salt, and vanilla bean and extract to a slow boil in a medium-sized very heavy nonstick saucepan. Once it boils, turn the burner off and let the milk cool for a few minutes.
2. Meanwhile beat egg, egg substitute, sugar, and maple syrup together in mixing bowl. Remove the vanilla beans with a fork and slowly add milk mixture.
3. Start to arrange the bread layers in a loaf pan that has been coated with canola cooking spray. Between each layer sprinkle some of the raisins (drained). Pour the milk mixture over the top. Place the loaf pan in a 9 x 13-inch baking dish and fill with

water to about a third of the way up the side of the pan. Bake until golden brown (about 30 to 35 minutes).

4. Combine the cinnamon and powdered sugar in a shaker and dust the top generously with the cinnamon-sugar mixture. Serve warm or cold.

PER SERVING: 305 calories, 10 g protein, 51 g carbohydrate, 6.5 g fat, 3 g saturated fat, 56 mg cholesterol, 2 g fiber, 540 mg sodium. Calories from fat: 20 percent.

Q *Dear Recipe Doctor,*

With the holidays coming, I thought I would send you this recipe for peanut butter balls. It's one of my family's favorites, but I just know it's a nutrition nightmare. Is there anything you can do so it's not quite as bad?

A Lightening up and tasting peanut butter balls is a tough job, but someone's got to do it. I started by switching to reduced-fat Jif peanut butter, which saves you from ¼ of the fat grams. Some of you might be philosophically opposed to using reduced-fat peanut butter, but this peanut butter scored high marks in the taste test we had for my book *Taste vs. Fat: Rating the Low-Fat and Fat-Free Foods*. And when you mix in the sugar and then coat the outside with semi-sweet chocolate—trust me, you'll forget about the low-fat peanut butter.

I added a tablespoon of diet margarine and a tablespoon of light pancake syrup instead of the 3 tablespoons of butter called for. It mixed up well with the peanut butter and powdered sugar, forming the right rolling consistency.

The recipe called for 8 ounces of chocolate! These must be double-coated peanut butter balls. I got by with ½ cup of chocolate chips, just by spreading a thin layer of chocolate on the tops and sides of each ball. How do they taste? Let's just say these lower-fat peanut butter balls give a certain well-known peanut butter cup a run for its money.

☞ PEANUT BUTTER BALLS ☜

The original recipe contains 193 calories, 9 grams fat, and 5 milligrams cholesterol per peanut butter ball.

Makes about 18 peanut butter balls

> ½ cup reduced-fat Jif smooth peanut butter
> 1 tablespoon diet margarine
> 1 tablespoon light pancake syrup
> 1 cup powdered sugar
> ½ cup semi-sweet chocolate chips

1. Line a baking dish with wax paper. Combine peanut butter, margarine, and pancake syrup in small mixer bowl and beat on low speed until combined.
2. Add powdered sugar and beat on low speed until combined. (If you need a little more moisture to make the dough of rolling consistency, add a teaspoon or two more pancake syrup.)
3. Roll dough into balls about 3 centimeters wide and place on wax paper.
4. Melt chocolate chips in a 1-cup glass measure (or similar) in the microwave on defrost for about 2 minutes. Stir, and heat on defrost another 1 or 2 minutes or until the chocolate is smooth and completely melted.
5. Spoon melted chocolate modestly over the peanut butter balls with a small spoon, smoothing the chocolate around the sides (but not the bottom). Refrigerate until needed.

PER SERVING: 92 calories, 2 g protein, 12.3 g carbohydrate, 4 g fat, 1.3 saturated fat, 0 mg cholesterol, .6 g fiber, 61 mg sodium. Calories from fat: 40 percent.

Dear Recipe Doctor,

One of my fondest memories as a child was the smell and taste of mom's homemade apple crisp. I particularly crave it each fall when the apples are plentiful. Can you shave off some of the fat, calories, and sugar, as I have recently become diabetic?

Fruit crisps are by far one of my favorite fall desserts. Fresh out of the oven, all bubbly and browned, served with a small scoop of light vanilla ice cream—mmmm, it doesn't get much better than that. Crisps are quick to make, and they are usually lower in calories and fat than double-crusted fruit pies.

As it happens, I've written a couple of books designed specifically for Type II diabetics, and, as I have come to find out over the years, half of the usual amount of sugar is usually enough in a fruit pie or crisp recipe.

Crisps are usually fruit topped with a mixture of flour, sugar, and oats. Apples and oats may be particularly appropriate for diabetics since they both contain good amounts of soluble fiber, which appears to help diabetics handle carbohydrates better.

I added half the amount of brown sugar called for and added 4 packets of Sweet 'n' Low. If you have an aversion to artificial sweeteners, just leave it out—it is entirely optional. I didn't use a NutraSweet-containing sweetener since they should not be heated. Instead of cutting in butter or margarine, I was able to add half as much just by melting it. Drizzle the melted butter over the flour/oat mixture and stir with a fork. I needed to add a tablespoon or two of buttermilk to reach the desired crumb topping texture.

I tested this light recipe out on a room full of stressed mothers who had just survived week two of back-to-school month. They loved it! I hope you will, too.

☞ APPLE CRISP ☜

Original recipe contains 264 calories, 11 grams fat, and 28 milligrams cholesterol per serving.

Makes 9 servings

> 6–8 cups sliced apples, peeled or unpeeled depending on your preference (or 4 cups boysenberries, frozen or fresh)
> ¾ cup flour
> ¾ cup old-fashioned oats
> ½ cup packed dark brown sugar
> 4 packets Sweet 'n' Low
> ½ teaspoon salt
> ¾ teaspoon cinnamon
> ¼ teaspoon allspice
> 4 tablespoons butter or margarine, melted
> 1 teaspoon vanilla
> 1–2 tablespoons buttermilk (regular milk can also be used)

1. Preheat oven to 375 degrees. Coat 9 x 9-inch baking dish with canola cooking spray. Place apple slices into prepared dish.
2. In medium bowl, blend the dry ingredients. Drizzle butter, vanilla, and 1 tablespoon of buttermilk over the top and blend with fork until the mixture is crumbly. Add one more tablespoon of buttermilk if needed for desired crumbly texture.
3. Sprinkle crumb mixture evenly over the fruit. Bake for 30 to 35 minutes or until apples are tender and top is lightly browned. Serve warm with light vanilla ice cream if desired.

PER SERVING: 190 calories, 3 g protein, 33 g carbohydrate, 6 g fat, 3.3 g saturated fat, 14 mg cholesterol, 2.6 g fiber, 176 mg sodium. Calories from fat: 27 percent.

INDEX